I Remember . . . the North East

Recollections of Yesteryear

I Remember . . . the North East

Recollections of Yesteryear

I Remember . . . the North East

Recollections of Yesteryear

The Pentland Press Limited
Edinburgh • Cambridge • Durham

© The Pentland Press Ltd 1993

First published in 1993 by
The Pentland Press Ltd.
1 Hutton Close
South Church
Bishop Auckland
Durham

ISBN 1 85821 149 2

The spelling of many dialect words varies
considerably throughout the area and, therefore, no
attempt at standardization has been made.

Typeset by CBS, Felixstowe, Suffolk
Printed and bound by Antony Rowe Ltd., Chippenham

CONTENTS

Childhood Tales

Gandhi in a Cloth Cap

I held the reins securely in one hand. My free hand described a throwing arc in slow motion.

'For-waard! Move 'em out! Wagons roll!' I called, eyes narrowed to spot any marauding Apaches skulking behind the telephone box in the early morning mist.

The milkman's horse turned his head, flicked his tail and flooded the road with a prolonged hissing sound.

On Saturday mornings I helped Joe, the Co-op milkman. I collected jugs from doorsteps together with the coloured coupons purchased in perforated sheets at Co-op branches. Joe humped a steel pail with a hinged lid. Using a hook-handled measure he would pour a half-pint for each coupon, periodically refilling his pail from the large churns carried on the cart. The full jugs were returned like Ming vases. I knew that to drop one would mean the end of my unofficial apprenticeship; not to mention the weekly penny or, if we met the baker's van, the warm potato pasty. Midway through the round Joe always disappeared into a neat terraced house for a cup of tea, leaving me in charge of the milk-cart.

'What fettle the day, Al?'

Nick Potts skidded to a halt at the back of the cart. He had a roller skate tied to his right boot with thick string.

'Gizza sup of milk, then!' Before I could reply he dipped the measure into the pail Joe had left and took a long draught.

'I want to see yer when yer finished...Wor backyard. About gettin' a new football...'

At the rattle of a back door lock he hurriedly replaced the measure and assumed the innocent air of one watching pigeons fly.

Joe was smiling to himself as he approached the cart. His face darkened when he saw Nick, noting his moustache of milk.

3

'Whatcheor, Joe!' said Nick cheerfully, 'had yet bit of bait, then?'

'Don't be so lippy, lad! Hadaway now! We've got the round to finish.'

'Aye man, I know. Yer'd better not have far to go, though. Yer horse has just lost aall his petrol!'

He skated off down the street, shirt flapping, his free foot pumping like a piston.

'He's a cheeky little bugger,' said Joe philosophically, 'you want to watch that one, son.'

People were always telling me that.

. . . . . .

I headed towards Nick's backyard wondering what the latest idea would be. Since the shattering news that Norman Cooke was moving and selfishly taking his football with him, we had held dozens of fruitless discussions about raising the money to buy a replacement. I gave our secret knock and was admitted to find most of the gang present. Nick took up a central position.

'Next Sat'day,' he announced, 'it's the Town Carnival.' We all knew that. 'What we've got to do is enter for the Fancy Dress – under 14s. It'll be dead easy, man. Forst prize five bob!'

We digested this easy idea in silence. Tommo was the first to voice an objection.

'Naw – that's no good. Yer'd need a real posh costume.'

I nodded in agreement. Last year's winner had been a fat girl as a bejewelled Queen Victoria in yards of velvet and lace.

'Yer don't!' said Nick. 'Look at this.'

He produced a crumpled sheet of grease-stained newspaper that must have wrapped last night's chips. 'See that!'

He pointed to a large photograph under the headline: 'MAHATMA GANDHI. INDIAN LEADER VISITS LONDON' We peered at a brown, spindly figure wearing wire-framed spectacles and a loin cloth; his pathetic thinness accentuated by the plump, well-fed look of the dignitaries around him.

'This Gandy – he's a famous fella. Like Tom Mix or Hughie Gallagher. I heard me da talkin' about him,' explained Nick. 'He's in aall the papers and on the wireless as well. One of us'll go as Gandy. It'll cost nowt for a costume!'

4

We regarded him with undisguised admiration.

'Only thing is, though...' he sounded a note of caution... 'he won't have to wear 'is cap!'

Our heads turned in unison as we looked at Geordie.

Geordie Skinner was one of life's natural victims. He was tall, skinny and too slow-witted to be other than good-natured; the one we always sent into Brodys' undertakers to ask if they had any empty boxes. He invariably wore a large pitman's cap that had been handed down as a family heirloom. It was wide and deep and weathered with age to the colour of fried mushrooms. With the button on the crown pulled up it formed a narrow pyramid; flattened, it assumed the profile of a dustbin lid. Geordie and his cap were as inseparable as a tortoise and its shell. Even when wearing it was impossible - in school, for instance - he would fold it carefully and stuff it down the front of his trousers. It must have filled the dual roles of talisman and comforter in those deprived days without the benefit of school psychologists.

At Nick's announcement he shrank into the corner of the yard. His eyes watched warily as we discussed the arrangements we would have to make. Tommo could borrow a towel for the loin cloth.

'And aa'll pinch me granda's specs,' volunteered Foxy, 'he's always losin' them.'

Pleased and flattered, in spite of his misgivings, at filling the key role, Geordie was gradually won over to the idea of representing an Indian leader - 'Like Chief Sitting Bull, eh?' - he reluctantly agreed to appear without his cap on condition that he could be the keeper of the new football we would buy with the prize money.

. . . . . .

Carnival Day dawned fine and warm. As the time of the parade drew near an undercurrent of excitement simmered and bubbled. The streets which the parade would follow had been criss-crossed with lines of coloured bunting. Normally drab buildings were gay with flags and streamers. Bandsmen in uniform, carrying instruments, could be seen disappearing into pubs. Groups of chattering children drifted down the backlanes, some in costume, some in uniform, some pushing decorated bicycles; all heading towards the Pit Heap where the parade would assemble.

Our Command Post was Tommo's backyard. His mother was out so we could use the wash-house. Geordie appeared early. He looked nervous and clasped the hand of a small figure wearing an oversized elf's costume.

'It's wor young 'un,' he explained apologetically, 'I've got to look after 'im.'

We sat the elf on an upturned zinc bath with a comic and gobstopper while Geordie modestly withdrew into the wash-house with Tommo's towel. He had insisted on privacy for the first part of the preparations. Meanwhile, in an enamel bowl, we mixed gravy browning and cocoa with water to the consistency of thick soup. When Geordie reappeared it was applied liberally to every part of his fragile frame. Then he was stood in the sunny half of the yard, arms extended, turning slowly while it dried. We examined our handiwork critically, pushing him back and forth like a postcard display stand. By a process of trial and error and frequent touching up with tan boot polish, we reached what we considered was a satisfactory shade of Eastern brown. The spectacles perched halfway down his nose but as they had thick pebble lenses it was just as well. We conceded that he could wear his boots for the parade provided he took them off at the judging. Metal-plated boots were the fashion but Geordie's looked as if they had been studded at Palmers' Shipyard. The final touch was a broom handle he would carry. Nick had nailed on a shoebox lid announcing, in case Geordie was not instantly recognized, 'GANDY FOR HOME ROOL'. Draped in an old blanket, like an arrested suspect, we escorted him and his young brother to the Pit Heap where they were callously abandoned among the chaos of the assembling parade while we hastened to a vantage point on Albert Road.

. . . . . .

From the wall where we sat we had an uninterrupted view over the heads of the spectators lining the pavement. Faintly at first, then more loudly, came the beat of the Police Band. Young children excitedly hopped on and off the pavement, tugging at restraining hands with cries of 'They're coming! They're coming!'

With a clash of cymbals the parade arrived. It was a glorious, traffic-stopping, litter-leaving, heart-lifting parade. There were bands and balloons and banners, clowns with collecting boxes, horse-drawn floats and the Mayor and Mayoress in the municipal motor car. Then, in pride of place in the middle section, came the children in fancy dress. Led by a bespectacled brown skeleton in an off-white loin cloth and hob-nailed boots stepping out with knees high like a demented Pied Piper. A small green elf scampered furiously to keep up with him.

Geordie had obviously found fulfilment in his role. When he spotted us on the wall he beamed. His boots struck sparks as he executed a jubilant war dance, beating the end of the broom handle on the road. We started a cheer. 'Good ol' Geor-or-ar-argh!' His elation suddenly vanished to be replaced by panic-stricken horror when the broom handle disappeared down a manhole cover. His spectacles fell off as he wrestled to retrieve it. For a chaotic few minutes it seemed as if the entire childrens' section would be trampled underfoot to music by the Platers and Boilermakers Silver Prize Band. The big drummer in his leopard skin apron had shunted down three cornets and a trombone before he could be halted. Amid shouted advice and catcalls from the spectators the band untidily marked time while order was restored. A chastened Geordie finally abandoned his broom handle and the parade moved on.

'Stupid flippin' show-off! He's bonkers!' said Tommo disgustedly. Our silence signified assent. The remainder of the parade had somehow lost its sparkle. We climbed down and made our way slowly to the West Park where the procession would end.

In keeping with our mood it started to drizzle as we joined the crowd surging through the park gates. The judging took place at the bandstand end of the park where harassed officials were sorting out the various classes of entrant. It was ten minutes before we found Geordie. He looked close to tears, his brown face a picture of abject misery. Without his boots he had joined the end of a line of damp competitors. Rain dripped from his nose and ears. Tiny rivulets traced white snail-trails across his chest and over his ribs; spiralling round his bony contours in lacy patterns with delicate whorls around the patches of boot polish.

Geordie could stand it no longer. He reached inside his loin cloth, pulled out his folded cap and planted it firmly on his head. His brother huddled closer.

7

'Bloody hell!' groaned Nick, 'yer can forget the flippin' football, lads!'

The judges reached him last. They leaned forward to take a close look; stepped back for a more studied view and conferred with great solemnity.

'Charming! Quite charming. Delightfully different!' said the Vicar.

'Beautifully marked! Such an ingenious idea!' agreed the Mayoress.

She turned to the Carnival Secretary who was hovering, pencil poised.

'First prize to the toadstool with the little elf underneath!'

......

I sometimes wonder whatever happened to Geordie Skinner and whether we will ever meet again. At a future Day of Defrosting, perhaps, when we are stacked, row upon row, in some vast celestial deep-freeze, like souvenir dolls inside plastic cylinders. Among the slowly-reviving white-fleshed puppets I am certain I shall recognize him. Geordie will be the one wearing the cap.

Alan Stewart
Saltburn

Miss Peacock Falls from Grace

V iewed from outside, Knight Street Chapel could have been mistaken for a warehouse. The resemblance was echoed inside by bare, colour-washed walls enlivened at intervals with intimidating texts like *REPENT YE SINNERS AND FLEE THE WRATH TO COME.* On either side of a central aisle stood rows of polished wooden forms on curlicued cast-iron legs. They faced the communion rail and a platform supporting an elaborately carved pulpit. An ancient organ stood in the middle of the wall at the back of the platform, its sheaf of fish-mouthed pipes rising to the rafters. The bellows lever projected from the side with a chair for the organ pumper discreetly concealed behind a red velvet curtain.

For the Anniversary rehearsal we were issued with special hymn sheets. Instead of our usual class formation the infants sat, feet dangling, on the front forms, with the girls behind and the boys at the back. The teachers, forerunners of the modern riot-squads, were seated one at the end of each form adjoining the aisle. I slid along a form beside Nick Potts and Geordie Skinner.

Mr. Grimshaw, the Sunday School Superintendent, strode to the pulpit. He was a small, gingery man with a large voice and bushy eyebrows, much given to 'Hallelujah's' and 'Praise the Lord's'. He began quietly, his voice rising quickly to a crescendo:

'Lord bless our sorvice this afternoon. Lift up our hearts in Thy cause now settle yersells doon. Quiet!'

When the hubbub had subsided he announced:

'The forst hymn is number fower on yer sheets – "Weak and sinful though we be."'

Miss Peacock at the organ nodded to Daft Danny, pulled out the stops and attacked the introduction, her thin back swaying like a metronome.

9

At the Sunday School services, as an act of Christian kindness, Daft Danny was always allowed to pump the organ. He was a cheerful, retarded lad who took obvious pride in this responsibility. He could never accept, though, that he should remain secluded. During most hymns a disembodied head with thick spectacles and a grotesque grin would be thrust through the curtain to bounce up and down in time with his pumping, as if suspended on elastic.

It was a rousing tune. Fifty young voices were raised in approximate harmony:

'We can sing, full though we be...'

When Danny's head stopped bouncing we started on the programme of 'pieces'. Geordie's youngest brother, barely recognisable with a clean face, mounted the platform and gabbled:

> 'I'm only five years owld
> An' very, very smaall.
> I've come up here to tell yers
> That Jesus loves us aall!'

On the return journey he slipped from the platform step, and grace, when he was clearly heard to add: 'Ye bugger!'

The next fifteen minutes saw a motley procession of performers climb to the platform to deliver their pieces with varying degrees of awfulness. Mr. Grimshaw praised each effort profusely. He even commended Abou Ben Adhem who could hardly have been a Methodist. We settled down to make paper gliders from the hymn sheets. Danny sat, elbows on knees, with the red curtain draped over his head and shoulders like a peasant woman, totally absorbed.

'And now,' announced Mr. Grimshaw, 'a recitation by Phoebe Parker.'

Phoebe Parker, with her posh voice and ringlets, was a twelve year old embodiment of feminine refinement. On the rare occasions she deigned to notice us her expression suggested that she had accidentally stepped in dog dirt. She wore a short, yellow dress and matching ankle socks. We hated her.

She walked out confidently, clutching a satin purse, her hips thrust forward like a fashion model. In a deeply dramatic voice she recited a poem of excruciating sentimentality about a girl carrying her crippled young brother to church. When the preacher expressed sympathy about her heavy burden the punch line was, I remember, 'Why, that's no burden, sir, that's my brother!'

There were 'aah's of subdued admiration from the teachers. Pleased with the impression she had created, Phoebe minced back to her place in the row in front of us. Mr. Grimshaw, eyebrows agitated, was clearly moved.

'Well done, Phoebe! I'm sure that pome has helped us aall to see the truth!'

Her self-satisfied smirk as she passed was unbearable.

'We could only see yer yeller knickers!' hissed Nick coarsely.

Geordie and I guffawed and fell about at this witticism.

Phoebe's cheeks turned scarlet. She flapped furiously at his head with her purse.

'Nicholas Potts!' bellowed Mr. Grimshaw, accurately guessing the source of the disturbance, 'Behave yersell! Sit heor where I can see yer!'

Phoebe still simmered, tense with frustration. Then:

'Potty bloody nickel arse!' she spat out.

Something like surprised respect crossed Nick's face before he was hauled out to sit on the front row among the infants.

Peace settled for twenty minutes with no greater distraction than the occasional maiden flight of a paper glider. After the collection had been taken Mr. Grimshaw launched into his pulpit discourse. I suspect, looking back, that he must have suffered from a mild form of religious mania. His remarks gradually took on the shape of a Bible-thumping sermon. His voice rose and eyes rolled as he embarked upon a fierce denunciation of sin. We were harangued on the wrath of the Lord and the eternal damnation that befell all sinners. In the uneasy silence that had fallen on his audience several of the infants could be heard whimpering as they would have done in a thunderstorm. Even the teachers began to exchange alarmed glances. Then, as swiftly as it had blown up, the gale subsided. With a 'Praise the Lord!' he announced the final hymn.

Miss Peacock flexed her bony fingers as she returned to the organ stool. At the prospect of an early release we lifted our voices with more relief than reverence.

'Hushed was the evening hymn, The temple courts were dark...'

In the front row Nick had caught Danny's eye by wrapping his brown scarf round his right hand and forearm, leaving part of two fingers exposed to make a simple hand puppet.

Miss Peacock leaned back, twisting her head to mouth an urgent appeal to Danny for more air.

'The lamp was burning dim, Before the sacred ark...'

This ferret-like creature scuffled around beneath the front of Nick's pullover, popping its head out of the V-neck. Danny was fascinated. His pumping, forgotten, slowed to a halt.

Miss Peacock mimed frantically, arching further back, her arms fully extended. The organ notes took on a strangled, gurgling quality. We sang louder, out of tune and unaccompanied.

'When suddenly a voice divine, Rang through the silence of the shrine...'

A despairing shriek rattled the windows as Miss Peacock fell backwards from the organ stool to lie on the platform, her thin elastic-stockinged legs quivering like antennae. Several girls screeched. Mr. Grimshaw leapt to her aid. Danny, overcome by remorse, began pumping furiously. Sardonic cheers from the boys were quickly stifled as the teachers rose threateningly to their feet. Miss Peacock was assisted to the vestry with nothing seriously damaged but her dignity.

Mr. Grimshaw pronounced the final benediction with a heartfelt: 'Oh! Lord,' his eyes were raised heavenwards, 'Oh! Lord let Thy sorvants depart in peace!'

My mother had an annoying habit of checking on the value of our Sunday School attendances.

'How did the Anniversary practice go?' she asked.

'Alright.'

'What did Mr. Grimshaw talk about?'

'He went on aboot sin.'

She paused for a moment, obviously surprised.

'Sin? What did he have to say?'

I pulled off my tight Sunday boots with relief.

'Aw...he was agin' it.'

Alan Stewart
Saltburn

Reflections in a Jam Jar

'*Maggie*' *was a candle in a jar, probably derived from* '*Snaggie*' *which was a turnip hollowed out and a candle placed inside. These lanterns were carried around on Hallowe'en.*

Jack shine your maggie
candle in a jar,
wind blows the candle out
can't see where you are.

Jack shine your maggie
leaves begin to fall,
blackberries and conkers
winner takes them all.

Jack shine your maggie
it's frosty out tonight,
nips ears, chills hands,
makes feet like ice.

Jack shine your maggie
run about keep warm,
hitchy jumbo, leave-a-go
kicky against the wall.

Jack shine your maggie
it's mischief night tonight,
carbide bangs and howlers
give folk a fright.

Jack shine your maggie
running down the lane,
clip around the ear
won't do that again!

Jack shine your maggie
the time is hallowe'en,
ghosts, ghoulies and witches
round every corner seen.

Jack shine your maggie
penny for the guy,
branches for the fire
rockets to the sky.

Jack shine your maggie
tuppence for the flicks,
Buck Jones, Roy Rogers
Cagney, Bogart or Tom Mix.

Jack shine your maggie
it's poppy time again,
remember our brave soldiers
for our freedom slain.

Jack shine your maggie
have you any swops?
Rover for a Hotspur
Film Fun for Gloops.

Jack shine your maggie
Christmas time draws near,
turkey's at the butcher's
holly in pig's ear.

Jack shine your maggie
toys are on display,
faces pressed to windows
'Bags I that chocolate tray.'

Jack shine your maggie
now it's Christmas Eve,
hang up your stocking
'ere you take your leave.

Jack shine your maggie
time to go to bed,
when we were children
what exciting lives we led.

Lawrence Logan
Burnopfield

The Day Fear was Lost

Emily Jones stood stirring porridge in a big, black pan on the open fire. Her face was flushed with the heat. Although it was a bitter November morning the house was warm. She had banked up the fire before she went to bed and it had burned steadily through the night. After the two little ones got off to school she would blacklead the stove and give the house a thorough 'going over'. She liked everything clean for the weekend.

'Hurry up, you two,' she called. 'You must have finished getting washed by now.' She had filled an enamel dish with warm water and left a clean towel beside it on the scullery table. There was a sound of giggling from behind the door and then the two little girls came in, both wearing white winceyette petticoats.

She looked at them for a minute as they stood in the doorway. Bron, short for Bronwen, and named for Davy, her Welsh sailor husband, would be nine and was very tall and straight. Bridie, short for Bridget, and named to please her Irish father, was almost six and small for her age. They both had mops of fair, curly hair, but there the resemblance ended.

She had met Davy when he was at the Marine School studying for his first Mate's ticket. How upset she had been before she was married in case Davy would want her to live in Wales but there had been no need to worry. He said he loved the old Tyne and the Geordies. Some of his best shipmates were Geordies.

'Get your kilts and jumpers on and have your breakfast, else you're going to be late for school,' she said as she ladled the porridge into bowls. 'It's porridge this morning, it's Friday.'

'I like Friday, it's different,' Bridie announced. Everything about Friday's different, she thought, even the porridge. Usually they had bacon and fried bread for breakfast, but you couldn't eat any kind

16

of meat on a Friday. It was a sin and you might go to hell and that would be terrible.

Soon they were ready for school, well wrapped up in navy blue nap cloth coats and woollen hats and scarves. 'Mind how you cross the road!' their Mother shouted as they went out.

Bridie hoped they wouldn't meet 'the Hoodies' this morning. She wished she wasn't frightened, not of things, like ghosts or the dark or climbing the rocks when they went to the beach, but of people. There was the woman across the road who shouted at you if you even went near her house, then the Hoodies and worst of all, Mr. Carson. Of course, everybody in the street was terrified of Mr. Carson. Mam said she wasn't, but Bridie wasn't sure about that.

Mr. Carson, who lived upstairs to them, worked at the pit. He was often drunk and he had a violent temper. From the kitchen you could hear him shouting and yelling upstairs and the children screaming. Sometimes the gas mantles would break as he stamped across the floor. Mam would say, 'Don't take any notice' but they all sat very quiet until it stopped. Once, Mrs. Carson came down into their house and she was crying. Her eye was cut and bruised where he had hit her. Everyone was very sorry for her.

Today wasn't a lucky day after all. They had crossed the main road and set off down the street to the Catholic School when Bridie saw the Hoodies coming up on the other side to go to the Council School. The Hoodies, a family whose surname was Hood, consisted of a big, tough looking boy, a tall, very dark girl and a little boy and girl. Bron and she pretended not to see them, but the Hoodies began to shout 'Catholic pigs! Catholic pigs!' so they mustered up some courage and shouted back 'Proddy dogs! Proddy dogs!' Bridie was glad when they had passed and she could enjoy the street.

Soon they came to the hoardings where lots of adverts were pasted up. Her favourite at the minute was a picture of a woman holding up a green jumper. On a table near her was a packet of soap powder and underneath a verse which read:

'Worn for years and lovely still,
Rosie's jumper goes to Jill.'

She chanted the verse over and over again until Bron said, 'Oh, for heaven's sake, shut up!'

17

As they passed the Depot, they stopped for a while to watch the horses and the carts waiting to be loaded with coal. The massive horses, their brown eyes calm and gentle, stood patiently still while the drivers, in fustian trousers, caps back to front and faces streaked black with coal dust, had gathered in a little group and were talking and drinking tea from enamel mugs. They stopped every morning to watch the horses and some of the men who recognised them, waved. They waved back, then set off again on their way to school. Bron grabbed Bridie's hand, 'We'll have to run, else we're going to be late,' she said.

The bell was ringing when they got into the school yard and separated to go to their lines.

Friday morning wasn't different, it was just like any other morning, prayers and reading, writing in Cusack's Copy Books and sums on their slates. Bridie had to grit her teeth every time the pencil screeched across the slate. Usually she enjoyed her work but today her mind wasn't on it at all. She was dreaming, dreaming of this afternoon and the concert, which was magic.

At last the time came and she was back in afternoon school clutching the two pennies Mam had given her, in a hand which was hot with excitement. 'I'll collect the school fund and then we'll go to the gallery for the concert,' the teacher said. Bridie felt as though she could scarcely breathe, but soon they were seated in the gallery where the seats went up in rows just like the real theatre Dad had taken them to last time he was home from sea.

The big girls from the Senior School trooped in and then disappeared into a small room opening off the gallery to reappear in minutes dressed as gypsies with bright skirts, tight fitting black tops, huge gold earrings and tambourines from which ribbons of all colours streamed. They danced and sang and beat a rhythm on their tambourines while the little children 'Oohed!' and 'Aahed!' and clapped furiously when they curtsied gracefully and danced out. The concert went on and on: Irish colleens in bright green dresses with red shawls, singing sad songs, then with a change of mood, dancing merry Irish jigs; people reciting poems and at the end, a play about elves and fairies. Bridie wished it would last forever but at four o'clock the school bell rang and it was home time.

Still, Friday wasn't over yet, there was the night to come, when, after Bron had finished her piano practice, Mam would let them play outside because there was no school next day. It would be dark and mysterious and all the children in the street would gather around the gas lamp to play games. Then it was bath night when Bron and she had their hair washed and got bathed in the big tin bath in front of a blazing fire.

Tonight was special because Aunty Jenny was staying with them for the weekend. Bron and Bridie were in their nighties, they had just finished their supper and Aunty Jenny was telling them a story when they heard the knock on the front door. It was a loud banging. Mam looked anxiously at the clock on the mantlepiece. 'It's nearly ten o'clock, whoever can that be?' she said as she went up the passage to open the door. They listened apprehensively and got as close as they could to Aunty Jenny when they heard Mam say politely, 'Oh, come in Mr. Carson.' The dreaded figure walked into the room followed by Mam who said, 'Won't you sit down?' He ignored her and remained standing, glowering with eyes half closed under bushy black eyebrows. He was almost totally bald except for a triangle of black hair on the front of his scalp. For minutes he said nothing, the silence was terrifying. Then he looked directly at Mam, 'That bloody pianna!' he snarled. Mam stepped back, almost as if she were afraid he would hit her. 'I'm sorry Mr. Carson,' she stammered, 'Bron only practises for half an hour.' 'That bloody pianna, I'll smash the bloody thing!' he kept repeating.

Bridie looked at Bron and saw the tears rolling down her cheeks, then she saw Aunty Jenny get up, slip quietly past Mr. Carson, and go out of the room. He was so intent on snarling at Mam that he hadn't even noticed Aunty Jenny. Bridie heard the front door open, then she heard Aunty Jenny shout, 'I'm going for the police, Mr. Carson, I'm going now for the police.'

Mr. Carson lurched, suddenly turned and walked up the passage, followed by Mam with Bron and Bridie trailing after her. He stepped out of the house and was going through his own front door when Aunty Jenny from a vantage point a little way up the street by now, gave a final shout, 'And when Davy comes home he'll punch your face in.' Mr. Carson's door slammed and Bridie heard him lumbering up the stairs.

Mam put the big bolt in the front door and they all went back into the kitchen and sat down. Bron was still weeping quietly. Mam put her arm around her, 'It's all right, Bron, don't cry, he won't

19

come back now.' She turned to Aunty Jenny, 'Well, Jenny, I never thought you had it in you,' she said.

Bridie had been petrified by Mr. Carson but she could scarcely believe it was gentle, quiet Aunty Jenny who had managed to get rid of him.

It was next morning while Bridie was reading her comic that she heard the back door sneck rattle. She looked up and through the window saw Mr. Carson standing. She felt a bit frightened but he seemed different from last night.

When Mam opened the door Bridie heard him say, 'I'm sorry about last night, Mrs. Jones. I've come to apologise, it wouldn't have happened if I'd been sober.'

'It's all right,' Mam said, 'and if you let me know which shift you're on I'll see Bron doesn't practice while you're sleeping.'

'Thank you, I'm really sorry I upset you,' he said and started to walk down the backyard. Suddenly he turned and came back. 'You won't mention it to Davy, will you?' 'No, I won't mention it to Davy,' Mam said.

Bridie felt a warm glow all over. Wasn't she the lucky one, she need never be scared again when she had an Aunt Jenny who could frighten Mr. Carson and a Dad who could, if he wanted to, punch his face in.

'Bron, you know what?' she said.

'What?' said Bron, looking up from the magazine she was reading. 'I'm not frightened of the Hoodies, Bron.'

'Neither am I, not now,' said Bron.

'I'm not frightened of anyone in the whole, wide world,' boasted Bridie.

Bron, who didn't indulge in such extravagances, ignored her and went on reading *The Schoolgirl's Own*.

Kathleen R. Hardy
South Shields

20

The Park Treat

When we asked for the impossible or gave our elders the impression that we expected some nugatory reward in return for a modicum of our service the rebuke would invariably be - 'What do you think it is, a park treat?' and we fully understood the implication.

The joys and expectancy of the annual Sunday School Park Treat gathered momentum from as early a date as Easter and according to our behaviour pattern we were threatened or cajoled with the prospect of it every preceding day.

One final occasion has special significance. To equip the girls in suitable caparison a great deal of white lawn was bought for sixpence a yard and made into dresses edged with lace that for a decade or more had been affixed to, then removed from, a variety of garments and bleached from questionable whiteness to the near acme of purity. When the boys complained their khaki shorts were dull by comparison our dad threatened to make them each a pair of pants from the Union Jack.

At the appointed time on the special day we assembled in the Sunday School hall then paraded to the Jarrow Park. The boys played what they euphemistically termed a 'tune' on a comb and tissue paper; the dogs yapped derisively from the gutter and amid this strange cacophony of sound we triumphantly reached the park. No one passed the edifice of the drinking fountain without a stimulating draught from the iron cup which considerably halted proceedings. Then we raced forward to claim our patch on the crowded green, further establishing our stake by placing oddments of clothing on the spot together with bottles of vintage liquorice water, lemonade crystal beverage and a bottle of fountain produce.

On this, our ten by ten temporary homestead, walled in by

sweltering adults, we would later hand in our dog-eared tickets and receive a generous 'bag' tea.

Once this ritual had been completed it was post-haste to the greasy pole where the boys held contest, battling up and slithering down in an arduous attempt to reach the summit.

I was proud of our eldest brother as he gasped up the pole further than any lad and discounted the fact that he came down minus his voluminous shorts. It was a proud moment in time, even more exhilarating than when he had dangled over a fifty-foot hill escarpment while camping, shouting imperiously – 'Fetch me a ladder.' If it had not been for his knitted jersey on this occasion – a garment tight-fitting through numerous washings – he would never have been dragged to safety.

Since we'd proven from experience that no event is ever perfect, the day accordingly produced a fascicle of dramas. There were the youngsters discovered smoking their halfpenny Woodbines in the confines of the park shed; two youths who had pushed an unattended ice cream cart into the pond; and our four-year-old who was consistently lost, wearily sought for and only recovered after two hours, wearing odd socks and grasping a slice of bread and dripping that had suffered a good munch. She proclaimed on questioning that she had been 'found all the time', a remark suggesting that somewhere she had been in pleasant custody.

We spared a cursory glance for the organised sport but decided the race was definitely for the swift or that exclusive set wearing the most expensive plimsolls, but neither had we any liking for such strenuous contest.

When we returned attention to the labours of the greasy pole our Sunday School teacher was noting down the progress of each contestant and my brother's friend was on his tortuous journey upwards. He was wearing his left boot only because his right one contained his bull frog and had been consigned to the care of the vicar. For years I had envied those black boots from afar. Ostensibly, here was a boy who truly engendered envy, being a recipient of not only free boots but free dinners and free milk. I was unaware then of the catalogue of miseries which were very much a condition of such handouts.

Last up the greasy pole was Ginger, a boy who had appointed himself custodian of a box of rusted nails and a bag of soil. He distributed a handful of each to the lads before they made their ascent, which lessened the effect of the grease. Ginger was last up the pole that day, making the top with the least expenditure of effort since by this time most of the grease was adhering to the other contestants' pants. I have always regarded Ginger as a precursor of organised crime. The dexterity with which he planned his raids on a local turnip patch equalled his scrupulous supervision of the greasy pole.

At the end of the day there were few immaculate oddities who had not been up the pole - in one sense or other - fallen into the pond or been doused when they'd opened their penny bottles of home-brewed ginger beer.

Marching back to the Sunday School hall, a beleaguered few, we were preceded by four small girls with crumpled 'Nora Batty' legs - owing to unattached suspenders. The boys, liberally encrusted with grease-impregnated soil, dragged up at the rear. Our brother's friend was wearing both boots as his bull frog had escaped the vicar.

'Can we sing "Jesus loves me"?' piped a thin reed of a voice from the back as the comb and tissue section limbered up.

'Good idea,' said teacher - 'a fitting end to a perfect day.'

Margaret Phillips
South Shields

The Engine

High o'er the fence leaps Sunny Jim,
"Force" is the stuff that raises him.

T he advertisement was on the back cover of a glossy magazine,
and the pigtailed figure of 'Sunny Jim' intrigued me. What was
'Force', and what sort of taste had it, I wondered. The Attlees had
piles of glossy magazines, and where most folk had 'clippie' mats,
and gas, or even paraffin lighting, the Attlees had carpet squares and
electric lights in elaborate bronze fittings with coloured glass to
diffuse the light.

It was in the early 1920s and Harry Attlee was ten. He was my
friend, and, as it was Harry's birthday, I had been invited to 'come
round for tea.'

How I envied Harry. He had a huge wooden box of bricks, and
he had a bike. A lady's bike, an old one in fact, but with the saddle
at its lowest Harry rode it – it was still a bike.

Above all else, Harry had *The Engine.* There it stood, on top of the
cupboard, gleaming in the soft light, a magnificent model steam
locomotive.

It was heavy. It was beautifully built of brass, copper and steel like
a real locomotive, and deeply stamped in the floor of the tender
were the words 'Made in Germany'.

Mr. Attlee would sometimes steam it on Sunday nights, and I had
been privileged to see it running on several occasions.

After tea Harry and I were building a fort of bricks on the table,
Harry's mother, engrossed in a book, was seated at the fireside,
munching sweets from a bag held on her lap. Harry's dad, at the
other side of the fireplace, suddenly folded up the newspaper he'd
been reading, and stuffed it down the side of the chair.

'Harry,' he said, 'I think we'll give the engine a run.'

The fort was demolished and bricks swept into the box. Harry dived into the bottom of the fireside cupboard and unearthed from a tangle of old shoes, yard long lengths of curved steel rail on wooden sleepers. Chairs were pushed back and in the centre of the floor was laid a wobbly circle of track some six feet in diameter.

Harry had five goods trucks, and these were pushed backwards and forwards round the track to ensure the gauge was consistent, and there would be no derailments at the joints.

A tin tray was put on the floor and the engine was placed on this while it was being made ready for running.

First Mr. Attlee unscrewed the little caps on top of the cylinders and, from a small bottle, put a few drops of red oil in each one, then screwed the caps on firmly. With a small funnel, hot water from the kettle was carefully poured into the boiler. The safety valve was then screwed tightly into the hole through which the boiler had been filled. Then with a tiny brass funnel, Harry's dad slowly filled the burner, with its row of wicks, with methylated spirit, and this done, clipped the burner back under the engine.

He put a match to the burner and the blue flame flickered along under the boiler. Our excitement rose with the steam pressure, and after two or three minutes of sizzling and spluttering, steam started to blow off from the safety valve.

Harry's dad gave the engine a push and it moved forward about eighteen inches, shooting out hot water in all directions. After a pause, another push and it faltered, squirting hot water and steam, then abruptly the spray of hot water ceased, the engine picked up speed and ran sweetly, dragging its five or six pounds load effortlessly behind it.

The speed seemed to increase with every lap, and after four or five laps, the engine with its five truck loads of assorted ironmongery was going much, much too quickly, and with great glee Harry and I anticipated the inevitable crash.

The last truck overturned, and in so doing, brought off the other trucks and the tender, scattering the load of spanners and nuts and bolts all over the floor.

Relieved of its load, the engine shot forward, came off the track, glanced off a table leg, sped under a chair, and careered the length of the room, leaving in its wake, a fiery trail of burning methylated spirit across the carpet. It banged into the skirting board and whilst its forward progress was halted, its wheels spun wildly on the varnished floorboards that bordered the room.

With what vigour Harry and I attacked the little pools of blue flame across the carpet! We thumped them with glossy magazines, we jumped on them till all were gone. And from the depths of her novel, Mrs. Attlee's voice said quietly, 'You'll ruin that carpet,' but her eyes never left the page.

Harry's dad had dived to the floor after the engine, and had managed to blow out the flame under the boiler, gingerly picking up the hot engine with a duster. It was put back on the tin tray, where we all gazed at it until it was cool enough to handle.

The boiler was refilled, and so, too, the burner, and Mr. Attlee, who I regarded as some sort of genius for he had installed electric light in their house himself, said he would shorten the wicks of the burners and so reduce the speed of the engine. He sometimes ran the engine on a Sunday night, but it wasn't Sunday, it was Harry's birthday, so this was something special.

The burner was lit, and after a couple of minutes, the engine was off again with its train of laden trucks. Round and round it went, Harry and I following its subdued progress with fearful anticipation. Would it de-rail, or catch fire? Might the boiler explode? After about ten minutes the lamp flickered and went out, and as steam pressure dropped, so did the speed. Each time the train passed Harry's dad, he leaned over and deftly unhooked a truck, until only the engine was running, slower and slower until it finally stopped.

'Can you make it go a little bit faster next time?' asked Harry. 'No,' said his dad, 'I think we've had enough for tonight.'

So the lines were put back in the cupboard, the engine was dried, cleaned and oiled and put back on top of the cupboard, to gleam, silently till another time.

What modern electronic, remotely controlled digital on-screen gimmickry could ever match the sheer thrills and excitement of a real, live steam engine? The atmosphere, the sight, the sound, and oh, the smell! Even now, over seventy years later I've only to get a whiff of methylated spirit and I'm back in the Attlee's living room with Harry, his dad and the engine, the glossy magazines and 'Sunny Jim'.

How lucky I thought Harry was to have all that; *and* he had a

No3 Meccano; *and* his dad had a Morgan three-wheeler! Lucky! Twenty years later to the day, on his thirtieth birthday in fact, Harry's ship blew up in the icy North Atlantic.

William Davison
Durham

Night of the 'Landmine.'

Y ou must have heard about the Geordie miner who hopped into
the doctor's surgery?

The doctor asked, 'What's wrong with you then, can't you walk?'

'Work!' he exclaimed, 'Ah kin 'ardly wark nivor mind work!'

My problem is that I grew up during the Second World War in
the belief that my old man was that original Geordie miner. We
lived then in a caretaker's flat in Mosley Street four storeys up,
overlooking St. Nicholas' Cathedral. My father now a disabled
miner was Mosley Street's caretaker come fire watchman. A sort of
North East equivalent of Dad's Army.

Now Mosley Street runs across the top of Dene Street which leads
to the famous bridges of the River Tyne. Every Geordie lad knows
that all his hopes and dreams will be fulfilled 'when the ship sails up
Dene Street,' which could be difficult with a one to three gradient.

Massive water hoses had been laid all the way down to the river
and they pumped water all the way up Pilgrim Street to the Manors
Station fire. They were heavily sand bagged around the ramps that
were placed where the horses and carts had to cross. The drivers
always swore when they had to slow down for the ramps because
they had to get off and help push the carts up the cobbled banks,
and the horses' hooves always slipped on the cobbles. The only
motor vehicle was the occasional fire engine and even some of those
were horse drawn on account of the petrol shortage. Even the
tramcars had stopped running.

At the top of Mosley Street straight ahead is Collingwood Street
leading to Scotswood Road. On the right used to be the old Town
Hall with the Cloth market running up one side. Further up the
Cloth Market was the pub called the Bambras, the starting point of
the famous coach trip to the Blaydon Races on the 9th of June 1862,

28

some eighty years earlier.

Turning left past St. Nicholas' were other famous Geordie land marks such as the Dog Leap Steps, and the Black Museum that was full of suits of armour and instruments of torture, but I did not find this out until after the war. Further still, the old castle that was really the New-castle and from which one could observe the largest level railway crossing in the world and the lines running South over the High Level Bridge into Gateshead.

Now all this heritage should have qualified me to be the world's most authentic Geordie except for one thing – my mother had been childrens' nurse in the service of the rich and famous and a Geordie dialect was not allowed, but a good leathering for disobedience was. So I became what was known as a 'Hedificated Geordie' and a right prat in the eyes of my childhood contemporaries. Trust a woman to spoil it!

Getting back to my story, we all slept in the basement which served as an air raid shelter. Outside in the middle of the night it was almost broad daylight. The Germans had dropped incendiary bombs on Manors Railway Station which was stock piled with relief supplies of butter, margarine and lard, and it was to take the fire brigade more than three weeks to put it out.

A fellow caretaker had slipped my old lady a few large tatties and quarter of a pound of lard, so we were all set for a midnight fry up of chip lardies, the wartime equivalent of a chip buttie – a rare treat in food rationed war-torn Britain! Folks were kind in those days.

The only stove was five storeys up in the caretaker's flat so when the all clear sounded we all crept up to the flat and my old lady made the chips while the old man stood guard at the window. Long before chips were ready I had this lard coated heel clutched in two fists and was busy cramming it when we heard the noise of aircraft engines.

'Diven't worry, the's ne siren, it one of wors!'

Wham! The first bomb just missed the High Level Bridge. Wham! The second near Armstrong's factory. They missed that as well, but they didn't miss Manors. Everything shook and a great deal of glass fell out of many windows. My ears hurt.

Darkness fell, an unseen force clamped my upper right arm propelling me through the door and along the corridor toward the stairs. I was flying, but my arm hurt. The siren wailed.

'Diven't use the lift!'

I could not hear all that was being said but later learned that my father had called into question the genealogy of Adolf Hitler and the entire Germanic Nation simply because he had grabbed a hot chip pan and was spilling hot fat and chips over his feet as we ran.

Three storeys further down the most dreadful hammering was taking place on the double front doors. My father, who had by now overtaken us on the stairs, relieved himself of the chip pan and made the near fatal mistake of opening the front door because of the cries of anguish from beyond.

The 'landmine' must have weighed about eighteen stone. By the light from the fire at Manor's station nearly a mile away she had seen a stick of bombs leave an aircraft directly above. Being a woman she did not understand things like vectors and how bombs from a moving aircraft do not fall straight down but continue to travel in the direction the aircraft was heading. She thought she was being bombed and so she promptly fainted into the arms of my Dad who was about half her size.

'Women just do not understand the technicalities like us lads,' so my father said later. I agreed.

'Git hor off us!' yelled the old man.

The clamp on my arm was released at last and the light switched on so that my mother could best work out how to tackle this horrendous problem. She was enormous.

'Git that b— light out,' yelled the local bobby from across the street.

'Git yer own b— light out!' replied my old lady pointing to the fire at Manors. 'Come here and give me a hand to get my — husband out from under this fat —.'

I was totally shocked! Never had I heard such language before and coming from my own parent to a policeman. Why, hadn't we only a few days ago stood watching the black market kegs of beer and goodies being surreptitiously unloaded at the back of the Cathedral and concluded that nobody in the Church could possibly be 'saved', not like us 'Born again' mission folk. They thought nobody could see them but they forgot about us caretakers four storeys up, not to mention God.

A bellyful of cold greasy chips soon resolved all theological issues. The best thing to do when you are feeling queasy is to curl up somewhere warm and that I did in the basement bed next to the boiler.

Our family never ever forgot the 'night of the landmine'. Well we did not have telly in those days and you had to talk about somebody. I never did find out how they got the old man out from under the 'landmine'. I heard it took two women and three men.

G.E. Best
Tweedmouth

Grandmother's Christmas Ritual

It was nearing Christmas and the talk turned to presents, decorations, chicken, turkey and Christmas cake. It was with this thought of the perfect Christmas cake in mind that Gran embarked every year on her Christmas ritual.

The baking of the Christmas cake was a social and family gathering. Grandmother, Mother and Aunt Lizzie were there for the purpose of baking, my sister, my cousin and I were there for the simple reason we could not be left elsewhere. Lunch over, washing up completed and the ritual began.

'Catherine,' (that's mother), 'you clean the fruit and mix it together. Lizzie, mix the flour, spice and ground almonds.' - then as an afterthought, 'Mix 'em well, mind.' Although Grandmother had no military connections, a sergeant major could not have had a more prompt response to his voice of authority.

The whole room was filled with the smell of nutmeg, cinnamon and lemon peel. Somehow these smells were never mixed, nutmeg pervaded the room and suddenly, as if by magic, this smell gave way to cinnamon. This smell, and the room, made rosy by the coal fire, specially built up to heat the one cubic yard oven, behind the ill-fitting black leaded door, belonged to Christmas and existed at no other time.

When the hot oven had cooled slightly, the 'trier' was put in. I never did see the purpose of the 'trier'. The idea of it was that a small sample of the magical mix was placed in the oven to see if it came up to standard. The same recipe was used every year, the trier was always passed as being delicious but the next year in went the 'trier' again.

The big moment came, in went the cake. To compensate for the ill-fitting door a double sheet of newspaper was folded and wedged

32

along the top of it. The door was closed with egg-handling care, the four hour vigil began and the smell of hot paper joined the already existing aroma.

For four hours we sat, with the apprehension of expectant fathers pacing up and down outside the labour ward, except that we weren't allowed to pace lest the vibrations should have some adverse effect on the sacred spicy idol.

'What if it cracks?' says Gran in low whispered tones. Lizzie and Catherine look at each other with horror. What is so terrible about a cracked cake, I often thought, it's easy to eat round the crack, in any case perhaps the crack would taste better.

At the end of the four hours the door was opened with the care of an over indulgent children's nurse, and the cake was pierced with a knitting needle, if the needle came out dry the cake was done. The needle comes out, twelve eyes stare, three experts are huddled in debate. By two votes to one the needle is declared dry. Jubilation!

One point I would like to add. I hated Christmas cake but I loved the ritual. They ate the cake, my appetite was well served with the taste of the nutmeg and cinnamon.

Joseph Conroy
Ferryhill

The Hammonds of Swaledale

Extracts from a book of memories

The 'living in kitchen' was the main room of the house where everything took place. A large table, scrubbed every week, was the focal point. At meal times Adam, Sarah and the four children each sat in their own place at the table. In the room there was also a rocking chair for mother, a solid wooden chair for father and a horse-hair sofa where the children sat, as well as some three legged stools. There was a large cupboard type piece of furniture known as a press, where crockery, linen, indeed most things used in the house were kept.

Sarah Ann kept a much prized silver tea-pot in the press. It was used only on very special occasions. One day Sarah Ann was entertaining the Chapel Minister and his wife to tea. The tea was brewed in the silver tea-pot. Grace was said and the pouring out began. To Sarah Ann's horror, instead of the usual coloured tea, it was bright green! Unknown to her mother, Mattie had put a green hair-ribbon in the tea-pot for safe keeping.

The top shelf of the press was also the place where the family medicines were kept. People only called in the doctor if an illness was severe. In winter, if the snow was very deep, the doctor would not be able to reach the remote farmhouses anyway, so families had their own, home-made remedies and cures. For a chesty cough, rub the chest and back with camphorated oil, then keep the chest warm with a piece of flannel over it. For a tickly throat cough, suck a sugar cube with a few drops of pure eucalyptus oil on it. For burns and scalds, 'Zambuk Ointment' was the best remedy; it was an antiseptic paste in a flat tin. It was also used to soothe the sting of cuts.

At different times of the year, Mattie remembers her mother taking a bottle from the shelf in the press to dose the family with what she deemed necessary. During winter they needed 'building up', so it was the big brown jar of cod liver oil and malt. In spring there was sulphur and treacle to 'purify the blood'. Epsom Salts were for any time of the year that your system needed cleaning! Adam was a great believer in liberal doses of Scot's Emulsion, a horrible white mixture, which he claimed prevented colds and chesty coughs.

Sarah Ann was convinced of the efficacy of rubbing and heat when it came to treating aches and pains. Hot plasters were applied to painful joints and there was a large bottle of 'Embrocation' for massaging rheumaticky backs.

There was one bottle of ointment which no home was without in those days, 'Rankin's Ointment' which was rubbed into the hair then washed out again, in the ceaseless battle against nits. Head lice were rampant among old and young alike no matter how clean most people tried to be. Mattie also remembers that many children, including herself, had warts on their hands. There were many suggested remedies for these, including bathing your hands in the water at the smithy where the blacksmith had cooled his red hot irons. Iodine was the usual ointment, but it didn't have much effect. However, the warts seemed to disappear of their own accord as the children reached the age of eleven or twelve.

A grand cure-all and a pleasant, soothing drink for anyone feeling off colour, was Ginger Tea made from a spoonful of ground ginger and hot water.

Adam kept his cattle medicines in a box in the cowbyre. Mattie remembers him buying 'Osmond's Cattle Remedies', but does not recall that they did any sick animal any good!

* * *

Sleeping accommodation was limited for two adults, one boy and three girls. The smaller room was divided by screens made of linen stretched over frames and covered with a wonderful assortment of pictures. The girls loved looking at them. Adam bought the screens at a house furniture sale. A family in Reeth had sold their possessions and left Swaledale. These screens were quite high, providing Albert with an area of the room for a single bed and a chest of drawers. The three girls slept in a larger bed, two at the top and one at the bottom, in the rest of the room. Adam and Sarah Ann's room was more spacious. In it was an old fashioned dressing table with jug, basin and soap dish for washing, also two rush seated chairs. A tin trunk stood at the top of the stairs. It contained the family Bibles, where records of births, marriages and deaths were kept, hand written on the fly-leaves of the Bibles. There was also a very old clothes box, made by a member of 'Grandma Pedley's' family of Healaugh. It was not valuable, but very useful. In it were kept Adam and Albert's best Sunday clothes and Adam's bowler hat. Albert wore his best clothes on Sundays for several years, because he was organ-blower at the Chapel attended by Sarah Ann and the girls. Adam's clothes seldom came out of the box. He was not a Chapel goer and was happier in his working clothes. His best ones were worn only when he attended a funeral. After many years in the old box, his bowler hat went green. The hat, together with a black suit, celluloid collar, black tie and lace up boots, were known to the family as 'Father's funeral claes' (clothes). The children knew to keep out of the way when father was getting ready to go to a funeral. He did *not* enjoy dressing up!

The stairs - so called - leading up from the living in kitchen, were hewn out of solid blocks of stone. There was a mysterious aperture or hole in the wall of the house, just half way up. No one ever discovered what purpose that box-like hole served in past years. The family kept odds and ends in it. It was almost impossible to keep any kind of covering on the stairs.

The house, with buildings attached, was typical of the houses built in the seventeenth century, true 'Viking Longhouse' style. Hammond's Castle was no exception. Attached to the end of the back kitchen and smaller bedroom was the portion of the outbuildings used as a calf house, where young calves were reared. There was a hay mew above so the hay was easy to reach down and feed the animals in winter time. The buildings continued with a stable for the horse, a cowbyre where the cows were milked and a pig sty. At the very end was the family toilet, an earth closet. A garden, with gooseberry bushes, blackcurrants and vegetables, was nearby.

The single long roof of the house and buildings was covered by stone slabs, used before the time of slates or tiles. Those stone slabs are still doing yeoman service on the roof of Castle house and buildings. Only exceptionally old buildings in the dales are still roofed in stone slabs today and only a few elderly dalesmen know how to lay and fix the slabs in place.

* * *

In the hay field

Farm implements consisted of scythes, single bladed mowing machines pulled by horses, hay sledges, sweeps, forks, rakes etc. all of which were used during the months suitable for haymaking, namely the months of July, August and September. Every member of the family worked in the fields during this time. The men and boys cut the grass with scythes. The grass cutters or mowing machines could only be used in the meadow fields, they were so hilly and stony in parts. Stones of all sizes and shapes were a menace on hill farms. The women and girls 'worked' the drying grass until it was deemed dry enough to be put into the stone built hay mew. The mew was a barn-like building with a square, empty window through which the women forked the dry hay. Inside the mew, the girls levelled and pressed down the hay until the mew became full. A door allowed access to the hay for future use. Any surplus hay was made into stacks by the men.

* * *

Christmas

On Christmas Eve, the children went to bed early, after hanging up their knitted stockings, one each, over the end of the iron bedstead. Christmas morning was sheer joy, as stockings were emptied after 'a visit from Santa Claus'.

Mattie remembers receiving very simple gifts, such as an apple, orange, a handful of nuts, two new pennies, a handkerchief and a picture book or rag doll. Expensive gifts obtainable today were not thought of in those days. Adam and Albert brought in a small tree from the fir plantation and erected it in a bucket of peat. The girls made some decorations out of coloured crepe paper, to hang on the branches. Sarah Ann cooked a chicken and a piece of beef to have with vegetables for dinner. She never aspired to a plum pudding, but a currant dumpling and a rice pudding were eaten heartily.

When dinner was over, it was all hands on deck, to get ready to go to Reeth to Chapel, that is, Sarah Ann, the girls and Albert. Adam stayed at home to see to the stock on the farm and to keep the kitchen fire burning. The walk to Reeth was often difficult if the snow was deep, but country folk were quite used to overcoming difficulties of that sort.

After weeks of rehearsing, the Sunday School children always gave a concert on the evening of Christmas Day. First they were given a good tea, with extra cakes and sweets. There were about forty to fifty children. They talked of that tea for some time afterwards, it was such a treat for so many of them.

After the children had eaten, the inmates of the nearby Workhouse were brought in to have tea. They were mainly little old ladies (widows of late miners) all dressed alike in navy blue uniforms, black straw hats and buttoned boots. The men wore clean and tidy suits and highly polished boots. The Workhouse Master was always on hand to see that all went well. Then followed the players of Reeth Brass or Muker Silver Bands, who had been playing carols on the green in the centre of the village. The tea ladies were kept very busy for a while!

* * *

Working in the shop

Mattie remembers how she eventually got a job at Allinson's bakers, grocery and general store in Reeth. It was a shop which sold a little of most things, but home-made cakes, bread, pastry and other confectionery were greatly in demand. Mattie remembers how much she enjoyed serving behind the counter. All the dry goods stocked by the shop were delivered in bulk. Lard was delivered in blocks of about twelve to twenty pounds and needed a sharp knife to cut it into squares. Although she was nervous of using the knife, after a short time, Mattie found she could cut lard reasonably accurately. Flour came in sacks; dried fruit, currants and raisins came in wooden boxes from Greece; biscuits were in tin boxes, each holding several pounds; salt in sacks; sweets were always in glass jars; sugar came in hundredweight sacks. There were apples from Canada in huge barrels. Beautiful apples they were, juicy and rosy. Tea was the only thing that came to the shop already packaged into quarter or half pound bags. All the rest had to be weighed out into half pounds, pounds, half stones, three quarter stones and stones, which were the weights most in demand. Once weighed, the goods were packed in paper packets. There was a particular way of folding the blue paper packet, so that the contents did not spill out. Mattie eventually became quite adept at it, although she remembers with shame how some of her first attempts resulted in many a shopping basket being full of loose produce!

Mattie (Hammond) Moralee
with *Evelyn A. Moralee*
Billingham

A Life in Teesdale

I keep wondering how my mother managed to keep a small cottage so clean and shiny with a very small income and no mod cons, never mind bringing up three daughters. My childhood days were happy ones - somehow we have lost that quiet rhythm.

My mind goes back and I recall the lovely coal fire - at the back of which you could put a bucketful of coal and use a cowlrake to pull it on the fire as needed. A grid was placed across, on which mother cooked the kippers we loved so much, and on Christmas Eve, as the wind and snow whistled around, we gathered to roast chestnuts on the top bar, and drink Thrumety, which was barley boiled with raisins and currants.

Christmas was a very happy time. Although we didn't receive many gifts we three girls appreciated what we got, which was an orange, an apple, always a new penny, some sweets or chocolates covered with silver paper and one very special inexpensive present for each of us. There were not many years between us. My oldest sister will be 90 in May, the next sister 89 in July and I will be 84 in July. I am still considered to be the baby of the family.

The winter nights were lovely, sitting around the table over which hung a lamp. We all loved reading - then there were the games which our parents shared - draughts, ludo, snakes and ladders, dominoes; and the matting nights, when out came the frame on which was stitched some canvas with a design made with templates or to our own design. We girls helped to cut up the discarded clothes: there was the lighter material cut in strips for the hooky mat, and the thicker material for the clippy mat. These all had to be precise in size - I think the measure was the smallest part around a matchbox so nothing was wasted - even the seams were used and sometimes our fingers ached with the pressure of scissors. Clippy

40

mats were worked the opposite way to hooky. It was a delight to turn a clippy mat over when finished. You could see the hooky as you worked.

The fireplace was blackleaded with steel reckens and fittings on the oven door which positively gleamed, a large steel fender and tidy betty which had brass panels around the top, plus a kettle stand. It was my job to clean them along with the knives and forks, candlesticks and door handles, using a penny bath brick. One day when the vicar called and I was doing these chores, he said to my mother, 'Is this your sister?' I was in my early teens, but never forgot that remark.

The hot water was provided by a boiler at the side of the fire and was always kept filled. On washing days, a large iron pan hung on the reckens and the white clothes were put on to boil. My mother always used penny blue in the rinsing water. On these same reckens she hung the frying pan, and used to make scallops - potatoes sliced and cooked both sides until brown. We got real oatmeal porridge which I still like although it doesn't taste the same. Maybe I was more hungry in those days.

It was lovely coming home from school and being greeted with the smell of baking: bread, teacakes, soda bread and pies - all done in the fire oven. I still like home baked bread and cakes, and still make carroway cakes - I love the flavour.

Sundays was for Church. No games were allowed. We had to walk one and a half miles to morning Sunday School at the Baptist Church and fast down the hill at 1.30 to the Methodists, although my parents were C. of E. We never thought of objecting or questioning it, but I know what that teaching has meant to me along my pilgrimage.

Mondays our Sunday clothes were brushed - I still have the brush Mother used, which was always kept in the bottom drawer of the beautifully polished mahogany press with ornate brass handles - and put away for the next week. On Saturdays we wore what we called our second best and we got our 1d or 2d for pocket money. We always got new rig-outs for Easter, made by a local dressmaker. I remember one special one - a white silk blouse and a tunic (like a gym slip) in blue. I was so proud when I took part in the Sunday School anniversary saying my recitation, which was so sad, I burst into tears. We had to memorize all the poems.

I loved the snow to come and still do. Sledging was great fun. My

41

father was always interested in making things for us and even today, I hear about the sledge on which six children could ride. There was hardly any traffic to stop us riding down the main road, which was quite hilly. He made whatever was appropriate to the season - a top to spin, a kite to fly, a boneshaker for us to learn to ride. He was gentle and kind and would play games around the table in the winter.

We had candles to see us to bed, complete with snuffers - and oil/ paraffin wick lamps which were cleaned daily and the glasses had to be polished.

In those days we mostly walked if we wanted to go to a concert. We were never afraid of the dark and seemed to be able to see our way home. The nearest town was four miles away. How life has changed, now we are afraid of so many things, even in our old age!

My father was an expert in sharpening the razors (cut throats, we called them) for his work pals and he always drew a hair from my long fair locks and made sure that they were sharp enough to cut neatly as he held it in his hand. Those razors were kept on the top of the chiffonier, and we were never allowed to touch them.

My father was a huntsman, until he joined the Chapel. I remember we looked after one of the beagles and mother had bought me some new boots with buttons up the side and left them on the treadle of the sewing machine. We had gone to the local show - quite a famous and popular one it was - and when we got home the puppy had chewed my new boots. It was quite a shock for us.

The show was held late September and I remember we woke up one show morning and all the ground was white with snow. It soon dispersed. My father was a member and contractor and a keen exhibitor at the show. After the judging he used to take the vegetables and distribute them to the travelling gypsies who came for many years. I remember once when the side of the grandstand fell on to my father's head. A cart standing near lessened the blow but it was the gypsies who took him a mile to the doctor to stitch his head.

My father was in the silver band and sometimes played the drums. He also had a good voice and we loved him to sing 'I'll take you home again Kathleen', and the Teesdale songs, 'Down in the Fairy Dell' etc.

Village concerts were a great delight and much talent was discovered or revealed, whether they were at the Chapel or the Village School.

The music and artists were always from the village and surrounding area. I had three uncles who were talented musicians and played the violin and double bass with great pride, accompanying the dances. One of them played on the radio along with the village blacksmith, his daughter and a farming friend who played by ear only. My mother had a lovely voice – I was told once after singing in later life that I couldn't sing as well as she could.

Mother was one of the original members who formed the Romaldkirk and Egglestone Nursing Association, and I remember she was often called out to nurse the sick and dying. She never wanted two of anything. One would be given away. When she passed away at 80 years of age the undertaker said to me, 'She was a *good* woman, your mother, and a marvellous help to me in my work.'

My memories of the First World War still remain with me. Once coming home from the Baptist Chapel I saw a search-light – it was rather eerie. I can still picture a group of prisoners of war marching past our home. They had come from Stanhope – several miles – but I don't know where they were going. I remember the school children collecting items to make soap to send to Russia. I don't remember the ingredients, although I think caustic soda was one.

When peace was declared we had to make a memento from cardboard. Mine had a cross upon it. I had a serious illness during that period (I was 7 years old) and had to be fed on pepsodised milk, and at one point I became unconscious and they thought I was dying. Incidentally, I'm still here thanks to the careful nursing of my mother and doctors. My sisters had to take me out in a wheelchair – I was so weak.

I knitted myself a silk jumper at school and I would love to make a replica because it is such a vivid memory. Again my favourite powder blue, knit in basket stitch and on the bottom a border was crocheted in the Greek key pattern. We were well taught both at home and school in all the skills of knitting, sewing and darning as well as having to memorise spelling and all tables, etc.

My father was a Conscientious Objector, and had to go to work in a mine 6 miles away from home. We had many anxious moments when he failed to return home on time. That was 12 miles cycling. Once he was injured when they was a fall in the pit. I don't think that he was ever the same after it.

I loved to clean out his carbide lamp, taking out the pieces which hadn't been burned and returning them with the new lot put in. The dusty carbide was thrown away. I loved the smell of the carbide, and we used to borrow it to light our small crackers on Gunpowder Plot night.

During the war a lot of wood was felled and in later years my mother and I used to take our lunch and go wood-gathering. I loved the smell of burning wood and miss it now when I only use gas or electric. We would gather a good load together and my uncle used to bring his horse and cart to collect it and bring it to our home about a quarter of a mile away. We then used a cross cut saw (one at either end). When I took up farming in 1944 with my husband, after 11 years in town, I couldn't resist going around the hedges and fields looking for wood to burn and although I live in a cottage alone now, I still get the urge to gather.

Recently a bishop said: 'Unemployment induces feelings of hopelessness leading to crime.'

In my young days there was unemployment but we never felt hopeless or turned to crime.

I was born in the little village of Eggleston in Teesdale and lived in the same cottage until I was married in 1929. I am now in my 84th year.

Lavinia Thwaites
Cotherstone, Teesdale.

The Great North Road

It was 1918, a beautiful spring morning, all that could be heard were the birds singing and the sounds of cattle in the fields around us. Who would believe now that it was possible to be so close to the Great North Road, now the A1, and experience such peace and tranquillity!

The farm belonged to my grandparents and later that year I came to live there with my parents and we stayed twenty years. It was a busy road even in those days, especially when Catterick or Ripon races were on, and I can remember when buses to London started to run regularly. We saw the Jarrow Marchers on their way to London and one day a company of soldiers from a nearby army camp paraded past, accompanied by a military band. Our horses were terrified at the noise and only the yard gates stopped them stampeding. Another time we saw the R101 Airship over Crow Wood.

'Gentlemen of the road' were a common sight in those days, generally one walking on each side of the road, carefully looking to see if there was anything worth picking up. Cattle and sheep were walked along the road on market days and all gates had to be shut to prevent the animals straying.

Farming in those days was extremely labour intensive. Ploughing was with horses, milking by hand, turnip snagging, even the potatoes were set and lifted by hand. At harvest time the corn was cut with a binder then the sheaves were stacked by hand; when dry it was carted into the yard and stacked until threshing day.

I walked about two miles to school, usually on my own. The classrooms were heated by big stoves at the front of the room and at lunchtime we would crowd round the fireguards to get warm. The older girls were taught cookery in an old Almshouse with a black leaded range and no sink. We had to wear white aprons and caps as

45

uniform.

My greatest achievement at school was when I won a prize for an essay on Rural Science in a competition based on lectures on BBC Schools wireless programmes. We didn't have a wireless then but my grandparents had. I had to go to London to receive my prize at the Savoy Hotel, quite an expedition in those days! My mother and I travelled by bus which we caught just outside the front door.

The last time I saw my old home it was empty. The granary had been knocked down to make way for a million pound flyover to Leeming Airfield. Big heavy guard rails have been erected along the garden wall as there have been so many accidents at that spot. The noise from the traffic is deafening – such a great contrast to that far off day in 1918!

Ivy Knox (née Sadler)
Great Ayton, Cleveland.

Whitby

Captain Cook would have walked past our house in Whitby many times in the eighteenth century. We lived at Pier Road, a straight flight of steps led up the side of the house to the crag area behind. The narrow road at the back was once the main thoroughfare as the frontage used to overhang the harbour. There is a painting in Whitby Museum dated 1770 which shows the house with a wide sweep of steps outside.

I remember going down to the pier extension with my parents in October 1914 to see the wreckage from the hospital ship *Rohilla*. Later that year, in December, the German battle cruisers attacked Whitby and we took shelter in the tunnel on the Khyber Pass. Shells were exploding all over the town and it seemed to go on for ever although in reality it was only eleven minutes.

My brother and I attended private schools in the town. Both these schools were bombed in World War II.

During the holidays I used to go and stay with friends at Wardman's Farm, Ings Lane, Redcar. One day I was walking the dog up Redcar Lane when it slipped the leash and ran off. I saw a young man riding a bike and asked him to catch the dog. He did, we got talking and arranged to meet that night. His name was Matthew Jackson from Loftus. We were married in January 1934 at St. Hilda's Church, Whitby. We set up home in Loftus where I have lived ever since.

Elizabeth Welbury Jackson
Loftus

Old Tom - 1882-1954

Tom sat snug in his comfy chair, watching the firelight flicker and flare,
Outside his window it was bitterly cold, as cold as the charity he'd been forced to behold.
Ah! it takes an old dog for a hard road, he thought with a smile,
As he began to wander down memory lane that stretched back many a mile.

When a boy to the station he would go to watch the trains,
Puffing clouds of steam and smoke, as they sped along the rails.
He remembered very clearly the first journey that he made,
It was to visit his Grandma, who wore black and was staid.
Accompanied by his father they were promptly ushered in
To a house so grand, with so much wealth, he felt they were not kin.
His first glimpse of his Grandma, was of a woman in high backed chair,
She wore a funny flowery cap with ribbons on her hair.
'Well, Edward,' she said, in a very cold voice, 'I'm surprised to see you today,
I never thought you'd ever be back, for the reason you went away.'

'The situation has changed, mother,' he said, hoping for a sign of love,
But all he got was a very cold stare, as she toyed with her fingerless glove.
'Frances left me when Tom was six weeks old.
She went back to the theatre without a care, quite callous and cold.'
'You were told before you married her, she was unsuitable in every way,

48

Singing, dancing, showing her legs, a strumpet who held you in
sway.'

'I've come to ask a favour,' said his father full of contrition.
I need someone to care for Tom, because of my position.'
'You should have considered that before you left of your own
volition.
I told you then, as I am telling you now, it was a final decision.
You may leave the boy, I know where my duty lies.
Frivolity has no place in this house, and I've no time for boys who
cry.'

To the attic he was banished to sleep without a candle,
The cold, the fright without a light, was more than he could handle.
For five long years he lived in that house, treated like a servant.
He cleaned the shoes before he went to school, and felt he didn't
deserve it.
Grandma died when he was ten years old, it was then that drudgery
ended.
The will was read, there was nothing for them, just as she'd always
intended;
Her money she left to her daughters three, who found it hard to
contain their glee.
They became very pious, to their brother they said,
'You shouldn't have upset Mamma, to her you were as dead.'

One Saturday in the Market Place, he saw a lady fair of face,
She was dressed with a bustle, and the silk of it rustled, as she
tripped from place to place.
To his surprise his father moved to intercept this lady,
She stopped and stared, and then she smiled, beneath her hat so
shady,
He moved across to his father's side, his big blue eyes were open
wide.
'Frances, this is our son Tom,' he said with pride.
'Tom this is your mother,' he said, and sighed.
This lovely woman touched his head, she gave him a lovely smile
and said,
'Why Tom, you have grown since last we met,' she pressed money

49

into his hand and left without regret.

The years passed by, his father died, he did his best not to cry,
Because his father had never recovered when his mother's perfidy he
had discovered.
Sometime later he left his home town, it had so many memories he
often felt down.
To a new town he travelled some distance away, looked for and
found a new place to stay.

He first met Polly at his rented abode,
She was as pretty as a picture and he thought she really glowed.
Her mother was the owner of the room that he rented.
She looked rather stern, and the rent he never spent it.
The weeks went by, he wondered why Polly looked so pale and often
sighed.
As he passed by her door one day, he heard her mother clearly say,
'Your life is ruined and that's a fact, I must meet his parents and
evolve a pact.'
The meeting with his parents eventually took place;
Marriage was not possible, they were Jews, and offered money
without grace.
Polly's mother thought it inconceivable that they could be so cold,
After all their son was a medical man, thirty-two and very bold.
The fact that Polly, was just sixteen moved them not a jot,
They made it plain that money was king, it was to be her lot.

He remembered the day he married Polly, it was nineteen hundred
and six.
By the time baby Ethel was born, she looked a little minx.
More years passed, two boys, three girls, their family was complete.
Ah! thought Tom, with a twinkle, we accomplished quite a feat.

The first World War reared its ugly head,
Like many men to enlist he sped.
Life in the trenches was hell on earth,
As the guns roared, he wished he had a safer berth.
One young lad was seventeen, it was his first time down the line.
The captain roared 'Over the top' the boy took fright and began to

pine.
Shoulders shaking, eyes dilated he was screaming for his mother,
Snotty nosed Captain drew his pistol he didn't find it any bother.
The poor boy lay in a pool of blood, half his head was missing,
A soldier further down the line, noticed and he was hissing.
As 'over the top' next time they went, the soldier fired his gun,
The captain dropped down in his tracks, and his life too was done.
Well! he thought as he mused in his chair,
He was a snotty nosed bugger!
War was really a terrible thing, it wasn't a game of rugger.

At last the slaughter ended, the carnage they all hoped to forget,
A land fit for heroes to live in, was what they hoped to get.
The reality was very different, there wasn't any work you see,
It was only pain of a different kind, which none of them had
foreseen.
One day things were desperate, no work meant no food in the house,
Polly, was hungry, so were the children, he felt a very poor spouse.

With his elder son Tom, he pushed his bike to collect sea coal on the
beach.
They had to wait until the tide went down, before the coal could be
reached,
Between them they filled two bags to the top, and carried them up to
the road,
He didn't remember passing out, as this was too heavy a load.
When he returned to consciousness he was very surprised to see,
A milkmaid with her dairy-cart, had stopped right by his knee.
She asked them very gently, if they had eaten that morn,
They shook their heads in sorrow, looking so forlorn.
The ladle she dipped into her churn of milk,
To each of them she gave to drink.
When they got home with their two bags of coal, one was kept for
the fire,
The other was sold to pay for the food, which equally they did
require.

One day with a friend he heard there was work, across the Cumberland
fells,

They left quite early on a cold winter's morn, to the sound of the old church bells.
After two days on foot, in very poor boots, they were wet and bitterly cold,
The trail they had lost, very much to their cost, the path that would lead them to gold.
With snow now falling without any food, exhaustion was taking its toll,
When on the horizon a man and his horse who escorted them in from the cold.
Upon their arrival to Charitycare, a meal and bed was provided,
In return for this service some work was required, stone breaking was what was decided.
At last they arrived at their destination, there wasn't any work at the end,
So they turned and went their homeward way, their egos still to mend.

At last the bad times ended, once more he could provide for his own,
It was a happy man with a spring in his step as he quickly walked back home...
Alas, the sorrow that was waiting, inside his own front door,
Polly, had collapsed and was lying, cold upon the old stone floor,
An ambulance was called for, he accompanied Polly, on the way,
A doctor told him gently, she was much too ill to stay.
He couldn't believe it was happening, she was only forty two,
Surely at their age it was normal to have more living to do.
Slowly he watched her sinking, because she couldn't stay,
The Golden Gates stood open, she softly passed away.
He felt that hardship, sorrow and pain were his beyond belief.
The tears he shed were the only things, that brought him any relief.

Once more it was the same sad story, war once again was declared.
Both his sons joined the Army, while he looked on in despair;
Son Tom, was sent to Burma, his job to rout the Japs,
Young Charlie went to Tobruk, and sadly didn't come back.
Once again he knew deep sorrow, he felt anger along with the pain,
He couldn't understand why he was required, to suffer again and again.

52

Slowly his children left the nest, they married one by one,
Young Elsie was the last to go, and then he was left with none.
He was glad when his daughter Frances, offered him her home to share,
The transition took no time at all, why! he was still living there.
Suddenly he returned to the present, as many old people do,
To wonderful smells from the kitchen, dinner couldn't come too soon.

Old Tom, died on a sunny day in nineteen fifty-four.
He had reached the age of seventy-two and he too had to go.
With rose tinted glasses firmly in place, he went to meet his Polly, hoping for God's grace.
Polly had betrayed him with lovers from time to time in her life,
Her deception he never discovered, he thought her a wonderful wife.

Audrey Frances Casey
Seaburn

From Tweed to Tyne

Holidays at Barrowburn

I was a lucky child, living most of the year with my parents, and later, my little sister, in a row of terraced houses running down to the River Tyne, but spending my summers with Nana, Granda and uncles Bill and Jim at Windyhaugh. Getting me there was quite an expedition. No one had cars then, at least no one we knew, so Mam and I got the red United bus in Newcastle and headed north to Morpeth to catch the Rothbury bus. Once a week, on a Saturday, it made two journeys up the Coquet valley past Rothbury, passing even the tiny village of Alwinton and stopping at the Windyhaugh dance hall, right next to Barrowburn and within half a mile of our final destination. Travelling by Wells Fargo must have been something like that journey. The bus, which delivered parcels and all manner of goods, as well as people, clattered and wheezed its way out of the city and into the rolling green Northumbrian countryside, which became wilder and emptier as we approached the pretty market town of Rothbury on the edge of the Cheviots. Here most of the passengers would disembark, usually leaving only us hardy souls to press on right into the hills.

I used to imagine that Mam and I were explorers, or on a wagon train in the Wild West. I felt sorry for the poor folk who could only go as far as Rothbury and were unaware of the delights of upper Coquetdale a few miles further on, but a world away.

Occasionally, there would be someone going as far as Alwinton. A shepherd maybe, who'd ventured into Rothbury to buy a new pair of tackety boots with turned up toes, like the ones Granda and my uncles always wore. But in all the times we went on the bus there was never anyone else going as far as Windyhaugh, which reinforced my belief that the valley was a secret world, known only to its sparse inhabitants and a few privileged souls like me. We would step off the bus at the dance hall and wave to the driver as he turned for the return journey to civilisation. Then off we would go, with a spring in our step to our first port of call, through the big farm gate to Barrowburn, the hub of upper Coquetdale and home of Liza and Geordie Murray and their daughter, Mary.

Hospitality at Barrowburn was legendary. There was even an article about it once in the *Newcastle Journal*, fame indeed for country folk! Passing through the picturesque farmyard with the burn running through it, we were invariably greeted by the sight of Mary's rear end, as she scrubbed the stone flagged entrance passage on her hands and knees. (Barrowburn's front passage must have been the cleanest in the county, Mary scrubbed it so often.) She would leap up and greet us kindly with a 'Come away in, you must be fair famished' as though we'd travelled from the other end of the country, not the county.

Liza herself, foursquare in her wrap-around pinny, would welcome us into the house, eyes twinkling behind her glasses, and seat us on a form by the table on which tea and scones would be set with a triumphant flourish. Liza's aged mother, Mrs. Barton, would be seated regally by the fire, looking like old Queen Mary. Indeed, she was a very important person hereabouts, having served as the community's midwife for most of her life. She would travel to the widely dispersed hill farms on a pony in all weathers to deliver new generations. Such activity seemed hard to believe of her now, presiding over the household from her straight backed chair beside the most fascinating fire place I have ever seen.

It was a black leaded range, polished assiduously to gleaming magnificence by Liza every morning. The fire itself was flanked on one side by an oven and on the other by a set-pot full of water, kept permanently hot by the peat fire. Swinging overhead, like a metal gallows was the 'yettling-on-a-swee' - a device for suspending the huge black cauldron, in which Liza always had a stew bubbling or blackcurrant jam in the making. Swivelling across the fire from each side were two metal plates on which rested the blackened kettle and a pan, and separating the whole thing from the rest of the room was a gleaming brass fender. The rest of the room was equally remarkable. The low ceiling, slung with beams, resembled nothing so much as a massive magazine rack, as stuffed between beams and ceiling, were huge quantities of *Farmers Weekly*s and bundles of hazel shanks waiting to be turned into dressed sticks – the beautifully carved horn headed walking sticks used by everyone in the hills. Suspended from the beams were well patronised strips of sticky brown fly paper and, as at Windyhaugh, hanging between them, were sides of home cured bacon. The floor was stone flagged and covered by colourful clippie mats, made from strips cut from old clothes. The wooden mat frame with the hessian base stretched across it leaned against one wall. The deep windowsill set in the thickness of the outer wall was crowded with pots of bright geraniums, in my memory, always in bloom. In the far corner squatted a huge brass bedstead with a feather mattress covered by a multicoloured patchwork quilt, and staring glassily down on it from the wall above, was a fox's head mounted on a wooden plaque. Geordie used to tell me that if I went outside, I would see the fox's rear end protruding from the outer wall, but I never could find it. In the middle of the room stood a large well scrubbed table, surrounded by wooden forms.

On one occasion, Jen Brodie, younger daughter of the Blindburn household, further up the valley called in to find the whole family about to eat their dinner – Mrs. Barton, Liza, Geordie, Mary and 'Old Tom of Barrowburn', a man of many years and few words, who had worked there as the hired hand since he was a boy. They made space for Jen around the table with rumbles of welcome and kind inquiries.

'Wad 'ee like some hashy?' asked Liza, in her singsong Northumbrian tones. They wad, so it was dolloped on to their plates, steaming mounds of mutton stew. Everyone, except Jen, polished theirs off quickly. Back came Liza with a large bowl of tinned fruit.

'Wad 'ee like some peaches?'

They wad, so they were spooned on to the same plates, already polished clean with chunks of bread – all except Jen's. Her peaches were dumped unceremoniously on top of the remaining 'hashy'. I still don't know whether she managed to eat them or not!

Having renewed old friendships at Barrowburn, we set off on the short walk up the track to Windyhaugh. I ran ahead as the wooden footbridge came into view and clattered over it, excitement mounting, as I saw the tall figure of Uncle Bill in the front field – a hayfield this year. Other years it would grow turnips, potatoes, barley or oats. With his long strides, Uncle Bill came to meet me and grinning broadly, swept me up whirling me through the air on to his shoulders.

'Hallo there Lorna doon and up again!' This was a little joke about my name of which he never tired. Turning to greet my mother, he took my case from her and the three of us ambled through the hay towards the house. I sighed with contentment at the prospect of another carefree summer.

Lorna Laidler
Killingworth

Pit Toon

The half past four Tanky hooted a warning as the four battered carriages it was pulling came alongside the sleeper shuttered platform.

It needed a stout heart just to look at the crazy heaving rails that carried the small trains, never mind ride on them, but ride you did, or you walked or rode a bike, for work or entertainment, nee late buses, or taxis then, it was the Tanky or nowt.

The line connected the collieries of Linton, Ellington, Lynmouth, and Woodhorn to that great city of entertainment, Ashington, the friendly toon.

Ay, it was a Mecca of delights, over twenty working mens clubs. It was a prized possession, your Affiliated club card, they weren't handed out willy nilly them days. A rang word and yi were oot on your lug.

Twenty clubs, aal warm, cosy and aal with 'singing ends' as they were known then. Nowt fancy, wooden chairs and a piano and a good night's singing from the local singers.

The mair weel ter de had a billiard tcheble, ne wimins liberation there them days, but there wor a few exceptions such as the Comrades Social Club on North Seaton Road.

And what aboot the pictures, five that's what we had, five! Where we left the pits, the poss tub and the scrubby stone a million miles away, stepping oot in your best suit, the only one yi had. Wear'nt yi flash ganning upstairs on a Saturday night, so yi could brag about it all the next week, heaven, that's what it waas.

But what about the cream, the jewels in the toon, the dancing palaces, the Rink and the Arcade. Noo there waas two places the whole toon waas proud of, it didn't matter where yi went they had heard aboot the Rink, or to give it its proper title, the Princess

Ballroom. The only ballroom in the north with a floor that rested upon coiled steel springs. Whey man, yi could dance on that floor all night and nivor get tired! Monday - modern dancing, Tuesday - rollerskating, Wednesday - modern dancing, Thursday - rollerskating, people used to come for miles just ti see the local lads and lasses dancing on the skates, they were great. Then on a Friday night it waas modern dancing again, beautiful Friday with a full weekend in front of yi. Aal day on a Saturday up the street spending your hard earned cash.

There were no fancy suppermarkets them days, but we had a shopping centre again the world, yi could buy owt there, an elephant if yi wanted one.

Then we were back to Saturday night at the Rink, the old fashioned night, with an eight piece band blawing its head off. It was the best night of the week, and yi nivor paid mair than a bob for any night, in that waas the best thing about it, it waas always cheap. It had ti be, cos we were always hard up.

Yi should have seen us dancing ti that band! Hollywood had nowt on the talent that was let loose in the Rink on a Saturday night. A few jugs of beer doon the neck at the Grand Hotel and away to the Rink. Yi had ti be in there before ten or yi didn't get in, and if yi did get in, it was cups of tea, Horlicks or lemonade, ne booze! Ay, the old fashioned night was the one, it was worth ganning doon the hole aal the week for. The Dryden band as ah said wad be blawing its heed off as yi entered the ballroom. What a sight, I've always said there must have been four thousand crammed into that room, or at least it looked like it. If yi lost your pals in there, it was odds on that it was Sunday morning before ye set eyes on them again.

And there was something else about the Rink, ah never ever in my life saw tango dancers to beat the lads and lasses there. Whey they could have took Astaire and Rogers on, ay an beat them, an aal.

But if yi liked to think of yourself as taffy nosed or a bit upmarket, whey there was the vary place for you at the store Arcade. Noo that's where yi used ti see the flashy goons and evening suits by the score as we made our way home from night shift, black as crows. Have yi ivor heard of spats? That's what some of them used to wear. Why, ah ask yi, spats! But mind, I have got ti say this, when the Arcade put a night on such as New Years Night dance, it was a night ti remember, and like the F.A. Cup tickets, yi had to be vary lucky ti get one. Being a Rink fan I hate ti admit it, but they had a beautiful hall, perched high on top of the tallest building in town with a high domed ceiling. I can see it now, the full ballroom, the colours of the dresses swinging around the room to the Glen Miller sound, 'do dil oot too to da did aloot', happy days.

And what about Billiard halls? We had some of the best in the country: the Harmonic with six tables, Dochertys with eighteen, the Priestman with six and some of the best players to go with them. Many's the pay packet that was lost on a Friday night at skittles, snooker, or billiards.

But back ti that Tanky, as the young lads hit the platform at the run in a mad gallop ti be forst. Diving through the steam of the Tanky before it was at a standstill. The older men fetched up the rear as the footpath leading to Station Road became choked with blackened bodies. Pitmen hurrying home to get their legs under the tcheble.

The Ashington Colliery bank men finished at half four along with the back shift underground and by the time the Tanky men hit the top of the stairs leading to Station Bridge, stairs with each step worn to a bow by millions of hobnailed pit boots, we are just in time to see the last of five or six hundred varieties of push bike, and notably they were nearly all rusty, but for all that, trustworthy.

The clatter of our hundreds of pit boots joins the Ashington men tramping home sweeping along in a black tide, down Station Road. Eyes and teeth shining through the black pit muck, sweated and sticking to every face.

I stand on the bridge as the noise fades from the memory and look back to the pit heaps and the Tanky and I see green fields, new roads, a new way of life.

No more pitmen hurrying to and fro as I look up the street beside St. Aidens and see the grass growing there, where once stood the proud Regal picturehouse and across the road the harmonic of dancing hall and billiard fame filled with glittering cars.

Ah gan doon Woodhorn Road, past the old Wallaw picture house, now a games emporium. Another love that died. I look up at the Arcade as I pass and through the mucky windows high above I hear, in memory, the Arcadians band softly playing 'Who's taking you home tonight?'. Turning for home I smile to myself, thinking about those spats.

H. J. Speight, Bedlington

A Northumbrian Childhood

I made my entrance to the North East three quarters of the way through the Great War - the day after Josef Locke and two days before Vera Lynn, both destined to be singers of note. Me? I can't sing a note, and Vera Lynn is much prettier than I am.

My first conscious memory is of the buzzer blowing early morning at Swinney's Iron Foundry, near where I was born in the small Northumbrian town of Morpeth. Nestling snugly in the valley of the River Wansbeck, the Latin tag on the town's coat of arms describes it in precise terms: *Inter Sylvas et Flumina Habitans* roughly translated 'Dwelling midst woods and waters.'

Another early memory was of a large solid tyred lorry, carrying a load of full petrol cans which took fire going down Newgate Street. Seventy years on I still retain the sight of the driver leaping from the cab as the lorry became a raging inferno within minutes. By then a large crowd had gathered despite the danger. There was a large 'Awwwh' from the spectators, reminiscent of a near miss at St. James Park, as the brake cables snapped with a loud ping, and the lorry slowly rolled down the slope, setting fire as it did to shops flanking the street. A petrol can was found in the Council School yard near the police station half a mile away.

When I was about eight years old our doctor decided I needed to be circumcised.

Shades of the N.H.S. to be - the operation was performed by our doctor on the kitchen table! Anaesthesia was provided by applying a chloroform soaked pad to the mouth till I went under. Sadly the G.P. was a trifle enthusiastic in the amount of chloroform, and my heart stopped during the operation. It was some years later before I learned what all the fuss was about.

In the middle of a smallpox epidemic, shortly after that incident, my whole skin became afflicted with a proliferation of horrible red spots. My entire family were vaccinated, and I was carried off in a horse drawn ambulance to the nearest fever hospital. The only child there, I was spoilt rotten by the nurses. No visitors were allowed in the wards. When my parents and sister came to see me, I was allowed to stand on the window sill and shout to them through the open top window. For one supposedly afflicted with a killer disease I felt very fit, and couldn't understand what all the fuss was about. One memory I still retain was the attention to hygiene and the baths in pink hot water, with a strong smell of carbolic.

The spots vanished of their own accord and after a fortnight I was sent home.

Days after my return home I became afflicted with a different type of spot. These were diagnosed as being those of chickenpox. As the G.P. said at the time, I couldn't possibly have had both diseases within such a short space of time, so it was concluded that I had never had smallpox.

When we moved to the nearby colliery village of Choppington where my paternal grandfather had a pub, I went to school there, but still spent most weekends and all school holidays with my maternal grandparents at Morpeth. My schooldays were perhaps the happiest of my life. There was something about the well ordered discipline about school life that appealed to me in a big way. And then I was eager to learn.

The head was a kindly old gentleman, who on cold days wore a cap in class. Invariably he used to apologise for that. Many years later I met him when sitting in the cricket pavilion at Ashington, and I was flattered to find out that he still remembered me. At the school we didn't have a football pitch, but we were allowed the use of the local cricket ground. On my debut for the school team, at about ten or eleven, we skittled our opponents out for ten runs. Opening the bowling I took four wickets for three runs in four overs, clean bowling each victim. I was thereby hooked on the good old game for life.

A friend and classmate, Arthur Jenkinson, went on to Morpeth Grammar School, and thence to Cambridge University where he had an outstanding scholastic career.

On Mr. Grocock's retirement, his place was taken over by Will Morgan, he came with us to a brand new school at Guide Post. We thought it was marvellous. The classrooms were large and airy, tables and chairs replaced the cramped Victorian desks, and most of all we had Mr. Morgan.

He proved to be all a man should be in his position, administering firmly but with compassion, and with a remarkable ability to communicate to us the things that really mattered in life. His staff were a truly dedicated bunch who followed willingly along the path the head indicated. All of us could add and subtract accurately, could write a decent letter, and understand most of what we read.

I kept in touch with Mr. Morgan till he died at the ripe old age of 101, last year.

I was fortunate enough to live in a council house with inside toilet and a real bath. The rent was seven and sixpence a week, thirty seven and a half pence in present coinage. Most of my fellow pupils lived at Choppington Colliery. Accommodation could be described in one word - basic - and even that would be stretching a point.

There was a large living-room downstairs, well - not quite right. A ladder led up to a hole in the ceiling which gave access to the bedrooms above. I have heard of people dying upstairs and being lowered in their coffin to the ground below. A huge open coal fire in the living-room was flanked by an oven on one side and a set pot on the other. Long before pit head baths were even a dream, miners had to wash in a large tin bath before the open fire. When washing their husband's back most wives left a black line of coal dust down the man's spine. It was thought to bring ill luck if that line was broken. Similarly if a pitman going to work met a woman he would turn around and go home.

An open gulley ran down the unmade road between the rows of colliery houses, with a single water stand pipe at either end. In summer the road was a dust bowl, in winter a quagmire. At the bottom of each garden an earth midden was adjacent to a brick built coal house. Miners received free coal as part of their wage. Each week the council men came to empty the middens. Not a job for the squeamish or the finicky.

Childrens' amusements were as far away as the moon from the present day crop of computers and high tech games. Tops and whips vied with muggies (marbles) as a popular boys' pastime. There was clique and gorn, an iron hoop, with a steel rod having a curved open end to guide the hoop on its way. When one of the locals killed a pig, the bladder was used as a football. We often played football till darkness came, the goals being marked by heaped ganzies (Jerseys). As more boys arrived the sides often increased to twenty a side.

A cricket bat could be fashioned out of a pit prop, three chalk lines on a convenient wall marking the stumps. A reasonable sort of ball could be made out of strips of vulcanised rubber, stripped from lengths of flexible cable used on the coal cutters underground. In winter an adequate skate could be formed with a lump of wood, and a handle sawn from a metal bucket, nailed to the wood to make a blade. Oddly enough I never saw anyone with two skates. Perhaps the effort of making a single one was quite enough.

There was gang warfare too, the Scotland Gate lot from Choppington versus the Guide Post gang. The Scotland Gate boys had the advantage of an ingenuous system of trenches dug in the huge spoil heap. They defended their end with some resolution. Next day pupils turned up at school sporting cuts, bruises, black eyes, the occasional arms in sling, but never anything too serious.

Our sole cinema, the Star, showed silent films of course, with the resident pianist flogging the ivories to suit the mood of the film. I never ceased to wonder at the amazing ability of the player to transfer the action on the screen to the music. He was worth the admission fee alone. When the talkies arrived one wonder succeeded another.

In those days there were no holidays as we know now, apart from New Year, Easter, Whitsun, August Bank Holiday Monday, and Christmas Day. But there were compensations in Feast Week Ends when travelling fairs came to the village, and of course there was the annual Miners Picnic.

Usually held in June, the picnic was a thing of some moment. It was one event sure of a capacity attendance. Apart from the speakers, there was a brass band contest, and the publicans did a roaring trade. When the picnic was held at Morpeth I once heard the local wag say that the inn keepers drew water from the Wansbeck to supplement the almost empty beer barrels.

The Fair Weekends were also times to savour. Apart from the fair, there were side shows, foot handicaps, boxing booths, wrestling, climbing the greasy pole, and as many other diversions as the human brain could conjure. I remember an occasion when the owner of a boxing booth issued a challenge and a prize of five pounds to anyone who could knock out his star boxer. A local boy climbed into the ring and promptly knocked the champion unconscious with a couple of hefty blows whereupon the manager refused to pay the money, saying that the local had won by a foul punch. Without further ado, the spectators wrecked the ring, seized the manager, and dumped him in the Wansbeck, but not before removing five pounds from his pocket. A nearby policeman turned his back on the proceedings as the man was carried to the river.

Those days have been described as grim. So they were. But there was fun and laughter too, compassion, a sense of love-thy-neighbour and a deep abiding regard for law and order.

Sadly most of these attributes have passed into history.

Tommy Wilkinson
Ashington

The Way We Used to Live

Ashington, Northumberland – The year of my birth: 1921. The whole mode of life for people in this area had recently undergone considerable changes: families, originally from an agricultural background in the Northumbrian countryside, were being sucked in by the industrial upheaval created by the rapidly growing mining industry. Consequently housing had to be provided for them in places such as Ashington and this proved to be quite a mathematical problem as families were large, as was the family unit. Frequently the accommodation provided was cramped and inadequate. I can remember rising in the morning darkness from a 'dess bed', an ingenious piece of furniture with the dual purpose of bed at nighttime and cupboard for clothes and bedding during the day. I never actually had a bed all to myself until I joined the RAF at the age of seventeen!

The family bond was the rock around which life evolved. Everyone had a strong sense of belonging. For the first five years of their lives children were a permanent part of the household, playing within the precincts of their own street, secure bases where they followed the seasonal round of games and pursuits: tops and whips, skates (everyone had one skate), bays, hidey, hoops, mount the cuddy, kick the block, Cowboys and Indians and cigarette card games – pitchy on and knocky doon. On winter nights Jack Shine the Miggy filled many an hour if we could not find the pennies to visit the cinema.

In the fields around the houses there were always horses; the Co-operative complex alone had over seventy horses and in the Wansbeck Road and Morven Terrace area where I lived we had the Store Field, where horses rested, as well as the Sortland Field, the People's Park and a large green area where the High School is now situated.

The abattoir was permanently stocked with cattle, sheep and pigs and in the 1920s these animals were walked from the railway yard. Border collies were an essential part of the Co-op Butchering staff as they drove the animals in flocks along the highway to the Store slaughterhouse.

In the 1920s and 30s the country was struggling economically and a good education was valued by everyone. It seemed that every child wanted to be a good scholar but I suppose, in retrospect, this did not apply to absolutely everyone. The standard of teaching was excellent, particularly when one realises the conditions under which the teachers worked: classes were large; classrooms were separated only by curtains; buildings were bleak and Victorian with outside box toilets and middens; heating was rudimentary in the extreme. Discipline was, of necessity, very strict and if you kicked over the traces you were rewarded more often than not with a 'hot bot'! Respect for 'elders and betters' was engrained in us from birth and there were fewer examples of hooliganism or acts against authority.

Community spirit in Ashington was first class and there were ample facilities for recreation. Sport took up a major part of our lives. Handicap sprint training was popular, the tennis courts were always occupied and then there was football – the League started with 14 year olds, then the 16-18 year old group and finally the 'big league'. Ashington were in the 3rd Division until the 1929-30 season and then were accommodated into the Northern League. In 1932 we acquired swimming baths and an Institute with bowling green, and tennis courts; indoors were billiard tables, table tennis and handicrafts, also a lovely reading room where one could sit in peace and quiet.

Allotments are part of the pitman's heritage, and on them were raised leeks and vegetables and flowers for annual showing, the spirit of competition was strong. Racing pigeons were also reared on the allotments and very often hens or bantams to supplement the family diet with their produce.

There were twenty-six social clubs (but only three pubs) in the whole of the Ashington area. Miners worked hard and played hard.

These are but a few of my memories of times gone by. In conclusion I will leave you with the image of a stream of men, morning noon and night, following a three shift rota, walking to the pit.

Robert Taylor, Ashington

Gulls' Eggs, Rhubarb and Mushrooms!

When I arrived at Bamburgh Church of England School in September 1923 at the age of five, I must have been preceded by eight Nutmans. For me the school was only 100 yards away. There were three classrooms - huge by modern standards. The Infants' teacher was Miss Mary Marshall. I think she had taught all our family and my sisters declared that she had worn the same thick, grey coat for 20 years! She was a sound teacher. We had slates and pencils and I remember Dougie Mather getting his pencil stuck up a nostril - quite a problem to extricate it. The room was heated by a huge stove and it became hot enough for the country boys to have their tin tea containers warmed for dinner (lunch). Even at the age of five children came from as far afield as Waren Mill (3 miles) - no school transport in those days!

We then moved to the middle room - I think two stoves - we were now Juniors, 8-11, and Standards 1-3. Miss Luke was our teacher. She came from Embleton. She was a good teacher - red hair - long nose - and, I remember, Russian Boots - a first for Bamburgh!

Then the final move to the biggest room of all - this time two fires with guards. Ages were 11-14/15 Standards 4-7. I only had Mr. T.W. Little, the Headmaster for a brief period before he retired. We thought T.W. stood for Tobacco Waster. We lived opposite the School House and T.W. seemed, when filling his pipe, to allow more tobacco to fall to the ground than enter the bowl of his pipe! More of T.W. later. At that time there were about 100 children in the school. A few years ago when the school closed there were only 9. The school is now a substantial house as you can imagine.

When Mr. Little retired, Mr. E. Wood was appointed. He was just over 30 years old and was everything a village schoolmaster should be. He was a delightful man - everyone liked him, except the farmer who used to graze his sheep on the castle green (cricket field). The result was soiled white flannels and I wonder who allowed the sheep to stray on to the road!? Mr. Wood, as Captain and Secretary of the Cricket Club got the backlash of the farmer's tongue. But Mr. Wood was an outstanding sportsman at cricket, soccer, golf, tennis. It was said of him with regard to ball games - show him how it is played and he will beat you at it in no time! In addition he was choirmaster - had a fine tenor voice, and he was a pianist. Who better to model one's life on? He was also a firm disciplinarian as my hands showed - and I deserved everything I got.

Furthermore, I became his first Scholarship boy at eleven and proceeded to Alnwick Duke's School in 1930. Sister Nora already attended the Duchess' School. I must digress and say a word about Nora's first years at the Duchess' School. Daily she cycled to Seahouses to catch the 7.30 a.m. train, changing trains at Chathill and Alnmouth before walking a mile from Alnwick Station to school. The return journey was similar. The train journeys each day would be enough for most pupils but the 3 miles from Bamburgh to Seahouses with a north-east gale blowing would nowadays be a case for the N.S.P.C.C.! When the weather was too bad my older brothers would accompany her.

Our humble home where I was born on 7 August 1918 was 5 Grove Cottages. It is now a thriving business as a café and fancy goods shop, called The Copper Kettle. Basically there were four huge rooms, a wash house, an outside lavatory, coal house and shed. In case you wonder how a family of nine could possibly be housed, I hasten to add that my sister Mame was 20 years old when I arrived. She and others had flown the nest by then. We were comfortably bedded, largely due to a super organiser - Mother.

My brother Aidan and I occupied a double bed in the back room which could easily accommodate two or three beds. My side of the bed was next to the wash house and on washing day the heat coming through was like an electric blanket! Father and Mother occupied the living-room with a screen to obscure the bed. The enormous fire also had an oven - our sole means of cooking and source of abundant hot water. The art of balancing two or three pans and a kettle was another of Ma's special abilities. Weekly washing took place when Ma felt there was drying in the air. There was a set-pot in the wash house and we used wood to boil the water. A poss barrel outside the wash house and a poss stick to beat the clothes and we were ready to begin. The clothes were dried on the hedge at the end of the large kitchen garden. Not until I was eleven did we have a cold water tap at the back door, so the water had to be carried 50 yards down the back lane from a tap; alternatively, from a pump 50 yards at the bottom of the grove. If you wanted to avoid getting your legs wet from spillage you used a guard. About 10 yards away with access on the back lane was the ashpit and netty (earth closet) – two seater! Bad enough in daylight but if I was 'taken short' on a winter evening Ma made sister Nora accompany me with a candle (later torch). There was also a coal house and shed where potatoes were stored I think. In the living-room/kitchen on a high mantelpiece stood the alarm clock. Ma always knew the exact time but this was never shown on the clock – it was always 20 or 30 minutes fast! In any case, for verification all you had to do was to go to the front door and look at the castle clock!

The back lane which the tradesmen used was, at various times, a football pitch, a cricket pitch, a boxing ring or a tennis court. The family owned one tennis racquet with some strings missing – the other player used the kitchen shovel, but the person with the racquet was penalised as the shovel player started 30-love!

Our kitchen garden beyond the lane helped to provide good food for a large family, potatoes, cabbage, brussel sprouts, savoys, lettuce, onions, leeks, peas and beans were grown. Willie Graham, the owner of the Middle Pub, once said that the Nutmans, Sintons and Knox's were so poor they lived on gulls' eggs, rhubarb and mushrooms! Other nourishing meals would include vegetable broth, bacon, bread and home-made scones and beef at the weekend. After W.I. meetings there was often a treat of small cakes brought home by Mother. The W.I. meeting was her only leisure hour. At the top of the garden was a pigsty, where oddly enough we kept hens! Beyond the pigsty was a huge haystack and it was great fun jumping from the sty to the stack – providing you didn't get caught.

In the winter we had an Aladdin lamp on the kitchen table. This helped with Nora's homework and later mine. In those days there was no T.V. and the only radio was at McDougle's garage where on Saturday evenings at 6p.m., we would go and hear the football results. One of our occupations on winter evenings was to help make proggy mats. Also we had a golf competition with my brothers.

One had to putt a golf ball from a mat over lino, over another mat and finally another piece of lino and hit the kitchen table leg – quite a feat! Nowadays my friends tell me I'm quite a good putter – I can only say that my apprenticeship started at the age of ten – at the Copper Kettle!

Church played an important part in our lives. Mother was a very devout Christian and Father the Verger. Sunday School was at 10a.m. and my teacher was Miss Thorp. We had to learn the Collect for the day and we looked forward to the Sundays when the Collect was a short one! For Matins the bells (8) were rung from 10.45-10.55a.m. Then my father rang a single bell until 11a.m. He then went behind the organ and his job was to 'pump the organ'. I kept him company. Later, at nine, I joined the choir with other boys. I shall never forget an occasion, after Matins. We used to play a stupid game where we had to race about 50 yards to the church gates. As I hared down the path I tripped and headed a gravestone and the next thing I knew I was having my head bathed in the Vestry. (I had been baptised years before!). I soon recovered. Evensong was at 6.30p.m.

There were also special services. On Armistice Day, after a short service in church, we processed to the War Memorial at the foot of the castle. Ex-Service Men (1914-18 vintage) joined the parade and a comment was made that the Germans must have been a poor bunch if this lot beat them! I suppose the same could be said by the youth of today with regard to us 1939-45 veterans. Many wreaths were laid at the War Memorial – mostly chrysanthemums. To this very day when I smell chrysanthemums I think of Armistice Day at Bamburgh! The church was sometimes full and such an occasion was when the Border Boys Brigade had their annual camp at Budle Bay. It was exciting to hear the pipes coming over Shada Bank and getting closer and closer (little did I think that 10-15 years later I would be marching to the music of the pipes of the Cameron Highlanders).

Weddings at Bamburgh were special too – involving the 'jumping of the petting stool' and then the 'scramble' when the best man threw out coins, mostly coppers – nowadays it would be at least florins (10p).

I had a lot of pals and the special ones were Jack Sinton (Sint), Selby Knox (Selb) and Joe Metcalf (Met).

One of our favourite haunts was to visit the dungeon at the

castle. This was about 50 yards south of the War Memorial. It is now cemented over. We had to open a trap door and climb down an iron ladder and walk about 20 yards 'into' the castle, when we came to the wall of the well. Upwards was a faint light from the Keep. Downwards it was pitch black, but if you threw a stone you could hear it plop. An iron ladder was attached to the well's side. The tale goes that the owners were having a meal one day and a head appeared over the top of the well and so the decision was made to padlock the top.

Another area we frequented was the 'middens' (tip). We went there to try to kill rats but they quickly ran off, so we lined up bottles and had fun breaking them - were we vandals? Near the middens was a steep sand dune and when it was frosty we had fun sliding down on tin trays (of which there were plenty at the middens).

Quite near the middens was the 'wilderness' - a pond created, illegally, by damming a stream. This provided an excellent skating rink. Not many people were aware of the origin of the stream water - fortunately!!

In the summer we often went for a 'dook' (swim). We were all self taught - most in the Half Moon (which was the beginning of a quarry near the 'rock end'). We started swimming at Whit and continued until September. Brother Aidan swam at least once a month throughout the year!

Selb and I often spent time at the blacksmith's shop watching Jack, Selb's father, making shoes and shoeing horses. His assistant was his daughter who 'blew the bellows'. Jack was an excellent shot at spitting on the anvil - it seemed to assist the hammering and bending of the horse shoes!

Just outside the village on the Seahouses road was the 'plantation' - a wood - mostly firs. This was a great playground and we constructed camps and tree houses and were a little scared of the darker areas. The story goes about an infamous character Tom Wake (Don Q) who was walking back from Seahouses rather inebriated and was conscious of the noise of the wind in the trees and the crackling of branches. He was bidden to say, 'God is good, God is good'. Further along there were also trees on the other side of the road and he was further bidden to say, 'Aye and the Devil isn't a bad chap either!' Covered both ways!

Brother Ernie tells the story involving himself and the local squire and P.C. They were determined to catch him for poaching rabbits but were seen through the plantation by Ernie and his dog. The dog was told, 'Hadaway to your mother', and dutifully sloped off, passing the squire and P.C. on the way to Bamburgh. Ernie immediately lay down and covered himself with pine needles – lost to the squire and P.C.!

During the summer holiday we went caddying (before the advent of caddy cars). We would go off before 9a.m. with 'bait' in a bag and walk the mile to the Golf Course. Mostly jobs started 9.30-11a.m. and took about 21/2 hours. Then having scoffed your bait it was off to the pools to fish. I still remember the names of the pools – Aad Laddies, the Aad Mens, Poddler Creek, Poddler Hole, Table Bay, Cat Pool, The Gun and the Egg Pool which was for swimming. If you were lucky you might get a job about 2p.m. and be home by 5p.m. Sometimes you had to wait till 4p.m. and return home at 6.30p.m. By this time you were ravenous and so eager to get home that you ran a telegraph pole and walked a telegraph pole! For all this you were paid the princely sum of 1/6 (7½p) and 6d tip if you were lucky. So on a good day you would come home with 4/- (20p)

What did we do with this wealth? First things first – a new pair of football boots and maybe some clothes – it helped the domestic exchequer at a time when agricultural wages were 23/6d a week – £1.60.

September 1930 saw the end of the carefree days at Bamburgh School. Travelling to Alnwick Duke's School consumed a great deal of the day and homework occupied long hours in the evening. Football, cricket and fives extended school hours even further. Another era had begun and the childhood freedom in the North Northumberland village had ended.

John Nutman
Hexham

Salt and Vinegar – And Clogs!

Once a month myself and my two younger cousins, armed with a clean pop bottle and some sheets of newspaper, would set out on what was to us, in the early 1920s, an exciting journey.

Down Bottle Bank we would go, careful not to break into a run otherwise we would end up in the river, so steep was it! Past the gloomy little shops which supplied the ships on the Tyne with ropes and chains and other necessities, on to the Swing Bridge. We always approached the bridge with anticipation, hoping that we would be lucky enough to see it open then we would watch the ships glide through the narrow passage.

Then up the Castle Garth Stairs to the Quayside on the Newcastle side of the river, mysterious and frightening, the walls black with age and a dank, moist smell pervading the air. The steps were shiny with use and there were gloomy openings and passages on each landing. We were all a little frightened but tried not to show it.

One Saturday, as we climbed the stairs we heard a tapping sound from above and, looking up, saw a strange figure outlined against the bright sky at the top of the steps. Somewhat fearfully we continued on up into the light to see a man straddled across a bench working a piece of wood with a knife. We watched, fascinated as the shapeless piece of wood began to form beneath his gnarled hands until gradually it took on the outline of a perfect footprint, the shape of the sole of a boot. Satisfied with his work he took up a piece of leather and began to manipulate it in his fingers, making it soft and pliable. When he deemed it was right he began to fasten it to the piece of wood – it fitted perfectly and before our eyes a perfect clog began to take shape.

He spoke for the first time. 'Know what these are, then?'

'They're clogs,' we chorused. They were beautiful, shiny black with leather laces and bright brass nails.

Now we understood. Every morning as we lay in bed we would hear the tip-tapping sound of the men going down the street to work. Now we had actually seen the man who made the clogs on the landing of Castle Garth Stairs!

But we hadn't got what we had come for so we continued on our journey up to the next gloomy landing where a man sat in a broken down armchair in front of a dirty looking shop.

I summoned up my courage and said, 'Please, can we have three blocks of salt and three bottles of vinegar?' No matter how often we went this man terrified me.

With a grunt he took our bottle and newspaper and disappeared into the darkness behind him. We could hear the sound of a knife rasping and then the sound of liquid being poured. He came out and placed a newspaper parcel and a bottle in front of each of us. 'Let's see now, that's twopence each for the salt and three ha'pence each for the vinegar.'

I handed him tenpence ha'penny - it was always the same amount.

Nothing more was said and we picked up our parcels and set off down the steps, past the clog man, down to the bridge and up the steep bank on the other side. It wasn't easy, carrying a large bottle of vinegar and a block of salt but we somehow managed it. When we reached home the salt was put into a cold place in the pantry and we all heaved a sigh of relief that the ordeal was over for another four weeks.

Tom Clark
Sunderland

Tulips from Tyneside

'We live in deeds, not years, in thoughts, not breaths,
in feelings, not in figures on a dial.
We should count time by heart throbs, he most lives
Who thinks most, feels the noblest, acts the best.'

Those words attributed to one P.J. Bailey are the preface to my grandmother's diary, *Bible words for Birthdays*, printed by Morrison and Gibb Ltd., Edinburgh. Each day provides a scripture reading and a quotation or verse of moral value. Its entries span this century and the latter half of the previous century, recording births, marriages and deaths of four generations of Tulips on the Tyneside, written in my grandmother's and later my father's handwriting. Unfortunately it is not complete.

I never knew my grandparents, they died before I was born, but my grandmother's diary lifts the curtain on the life of Tulips, their friends and relations whom I have come to know only through the briefest of reference made to them in her diary. She was born Elizabeth Swann on 17 June 1843, and my grandfather was John Tulip born 15 March 1838, and they were married at St. Anne's Church, Newcastle on 8 January 1866. She died at 63 years of age on 16 March 1906 having produced five girls and three boys of the Tulip line. She must have been a very devout and precise person for she records in neat, now faded, writing that my great grandfather died at precisely 12 p.m. on January 11th 1871, and that my father was born at precisely 12.05 a.m. on 15 January 1881, at 9 Johnson Hill in the Parish of Westoe, South Shields.

My grandfather is described as a waterman. I am not so sure what a waterman is, but I do have recollections of my father describing him as a wherry-man working cross Tyne in the area of Felling and Wallsend, and I have visions of him handling drag lines at launch

79

times, or ferrying lone sailors to mid stream vessels at anchor. The romantic in me leads me think of a young man with a rowing boat from South Shields meeting and marrying his Newcastle sweetheart, and carrying her back to Shields to set up house.

My name is Norman Clarke Tulip, son of Mathew Tulip. If I were to be asked what were my earliest recollections of life, I would have to say 'The German Zeppelins coming up the Tyne to bomb Jarrow.'. But how could that be? I was not born until 21 January 1916, almost seven months after the raid? But – was I not in my mother's womb? Standing out vividly in my mind is a picture of the family dashing out into the back yard of 3 Dean Terrace, Tyne Dock, where I was subsequently born – old Mrs Hanna was the midwife I am told – and my mother frantically bawling at her brood to get inside under cover, whilst the Zeppelin zoomed over. Age of course brings reason, and no doubt the event was so spectacular as to be repeated often and had impinged itself on my memory but–.

My mother was what would be described today as clairvoyant – she 'read the cards' and she had a perception, sometimes a foreboding, of things to come. I am inclined a little that way myself. My mother's two brothers, Norman and Clarke Whitfield, after whom I am named, were both killed during the Great War, and my mother told me that whilst serving tea at grandmother's home, she saw one of her brothers, I have forgotten which, standing behind grandmother's chair. The following day the sad news came of his death – killed in action. I have a much treasured letter from my Uncle Norman to my mother dated 12 December 1916, in which he sends his love to the bairns, especially 'N.C.' I have also his war medal and certificate, Sgt. N.G. Whitfield, Durham Light Infantry. I think it must have been Uncle Clarke who appeared behind my grandmother Whitfield's chair.

My mother was, as many of her generation were, well versed in the art of needlework, knitting and baking. She had in her time, seen service as cook in a 'big' house. Going into service – domestic or nursing – was the natural thing for girls of the family. My four sisters were shunted off at an early age – two to be domestics and two to be nurses. Baking bread was my mother's pride, with tea cakes and hot cross buns in season. The basement of 3 Dean Terrace was kitchen and living room for the family. It was my mother's domain, where she baked, made and mended clothes, darned and knitted socks in the Great War for the soldiers and, as required, she made rag mats.

I set out to tell you about my mother's cooking, her steak and kidney or rabbit pies could not be beaten, her suet dumplings lined the ribs and warmed the cockles of the heart, but her bread was superb. She had this day, in a huge enamel basin, kneaded the dough, and placed it on the brass fender in front of the grated fire with oven alongside. My young brother would be about 18 months then, not yet into boy's shorts, and just toddling around. Down he sat on the bread - bare bottom and all. He rose more quickly than the bread when mother got at him.

My father was really a railwayman - a guard with the LNER - until a railway accident when shunting left him with sight in one eye only, and to compensate for that he was given a job for life as a timber checker in the docks. It was his good fortune in that it happened at the outbreak of war and he was not called up, and it was further to his advantage that the permanency of the alternative job, stood by him during a period of unemployment and starvation on the Tyneside during the 20s.

He was a wizard with the forerunner of the electronic calculator and computer - the slide rule. I could never master it. In her book *Our Kate*, Catherine Cookson refers to a Mr Tulip, who had a kind but cautionary word for her when as teenager she foraged for wood for the fire on the slacks at Tyne Dock and Jarrow. I imagine that man could only have been my father for he was kind at heart. His entries in my grandmother's diary reveal a strict upbringing with an inclination towards religious influence. There is a rather touching entry for the day his mother died in 1906, showing his devotion for her and ending with the opening words of the Lord's Prayer, and in another passage he records how with twelve others they left Shields for Newcastle at 9 in the morning to attend a convention at Newcastle, returning in the evening at 10 p.m. when the last stage of the rail journey between Tyne Dock and High Shields was spent in prayer. He told me too, of walking as far as ten miles to attend missions; yet he never forced religion upon his children.

He was a jack of all trades. I have to this day in my house small articles of utility furniture made from pine or mahogany recovered from the scrapyards of the Tyne. Shortly after moving to Burdon Road, he started to build a bungalow, unfortunately breaking his leg at the stage of laying the foundations, and I at 8-9 years old had to man the pumps to keep the foundations clear of water. We later did finish the bungalow. My brother Matt and I attended Cleadon Village Infant School on the corner of Sunderland road next to the watering pond in the centre of the village. The elementary school, to which we went later, was above it on the Whitburn Road next to the church. I well remember the infant school, a long old stone building, wooden desks, slates, chalk, and ink powder, and the exceptional kindness of the teacher. I have a photograph of the class and Miss Brown (?) the teacher. Despite the fact that I was a disappointment to my teachers, in that I failed the examination which would have opened the doors of Ryhope secondary to me, I cannot speak too highly of the education they gave me.

I was no model scholar but I did get to the top of Standard 7, and had no difficulty when joining the Army at 15 years of age in passing my First Class Certificate of Education. But it was not just the three R's which helped me rise through the ranks.

There were two things. They say pride cometh before a fall. It was this way –

I was at the impressionable age of about 8 years of age, slightly defiant, aware of a distinction between the village lads from posh houses, and those of us from less pretentious homes whose standard dress was a ganzie of the same quality and durability as those worn by children in care housed in Cleadon Cottage Homes, for whom we were often mistaken. The teacher, as I remember a Mr Gardner, stood at his desk across the front of which lay his 'persuader', about 18" long made of cane about ¾" in diameter – a visual and practical aid which teachers of that day would not be without, and those of this day would do well to adopt. The question was, 'What does your father do?' and out trotted the answers, doctor, bus conductor, gardener, farmer, postman etc. etc., and so to me – 'My father is a secretary, sir.'

We were not a rich family, my father had to walk miles across the fields to catch a bus on the route between Boldon Colliery and South Shields, to get him to work at Tyne Dock, he *was* a secretary but not in terms of paid employment. Trade unions in those post war days of grave unemployment in the North East had an important part to play in improving the lot of the working man, and my father was the Honorary Secretary of the Tyne Dock Branch of the

National Union of Railwaymen - and he had a typewriter, an Oliver, which I was occasionally permitted to handle, I can see it today standing high on that roll top desk, and I mentally compare it with the electronic machine I now use. The inquisition which I went through that day as the teacher ferreted out the facts of employment, was akin to the Spanish inquisition - I was mentally garrotted, and looking back one cannot help but think that perhaps there was a lacking in sympathy with the working classes in the run up to the General Strike and the Jarrow March.

[In a lighter vein - some 50 years later my daughter in her middle class kindergarten was asked the same question of her father. Her answer 'My Daddy is a gunman.' We live in Northern Ireland - I was a firearms examiner with the police!!!!]

He that exalteth himself shall be abased was a lesson well learned. The other lesson was one of discipline. To those who preach non-chastisement in school let me record an incident which happened at Cleadon Village School. Three boys from families of good standing broke into the school and stole books. They were detected, and it was a question of who was to deal with them - the school or the police. With parents' consent the school dealt with them. The whole school was paraded in the assembly hall, three chairs were set out in front, and all three boys (I believe their parents were also present) were brought in, each bent over the back of a chair, and given a number of strokes of the cane over the seats of their trousers. They took their punishment like men, the headmaster and parents visibly moved. What it meant to others I cannot say, but to me it was a lesson I have never forgotten. Some 25 years later I went back to Cleadon Village, and on the war memorial were two names that I recognised. They took their punishment like men, and stood up to be counted afterwards. They were true grit.

Throughout life one is required to complete forms relating to one's education, notably when receiving the Queen's commission or honour to be bestowed. It has been my pride to 'record 'that I was educated at Cleadon Village School.

In 1931 I left home on Tyneside. The Great Strike was over, but opportunities to learn a trade did not come easily to school leavers like myself. I joined the Army as an apprentice armourer, sworn in and taking the King's shilling at Newcastle on 30 April, leaving a tearful mother and equally tearful cousin Mabel (Gregory) and a watchful recruiting sergeant on the platform, as I boarded the train for King's Cross, bound for Portsmouth. I wonder if I am the only recruit who on arrival at his unit was put straight into the cell in the guard room? Fenham Barracks, Newcastle was in quarantine due to an outbreak of (I think) typhoid, and they took no chances with me at Hilsea Barracks. The army being what it was in those days, I was turned out with the guard each time the orderly officer called.

The home which I had left was by then not Burdon Road, it was Oak Avenue, Cleadon Estate where in the winter – when winters *were* winters – sledges and sleighs were made and we exercised ourselves on Cleadon Hills and Quarry Lane, much to the annoyance of Corporation bus drivers. Private cars were not so much in evidence in those days.

It is of interest that my rate of pay on joining the army was 11d per day, out of which we as boy soldiers had to make a compulsory allowance home, mine amounted to 4/- per week. One cannot help but wonder if the reason was not so much to help the folks at home, as to inhibit boys in buying trouble for themselves! Lodged as mine was, in the Post Office Savings Bank, it came in handy when we were home on leave.

After my brother had followed me into the Army some 18 months later, also as a boy apprentice tradesman, memories of the Tyneside are as described in letters from home, and visits home on leave. My parents moved to Simonside, my mother becoming more and more an invalid, and Simonside being practically on the dockside enabled my father to be more at hand. Confined to bed as she so often was, my mother alternated between writing poetry to her children and friends – she would correspond in verse rather than in letter form – and working to complete a self-imposed task started many years before. She was adept with crocheting needle, and had set herself to make a tablecloth for each of her children. Mine was of the Tulip pattern, with a depth of border 18" minimum, and a square centre piece of bleached linen, taken from my Grandmother Whitfield's bed sheet. It was said to have been made out of flour bags. It is a precious keepsake, now an heirloom, which has graced my dining table for the important functions of life, marriage, birth of children, their marriage, and their children's birth.

But she gave me something else, not tangible that can be knowingly left behind – the gift of words, of making verse, for I too express my feelings as she did.

When the war clouds were gathering, nations were mobilising, and Government and people were dithering in the months preceding the outbreak of the Second World War, she wrote of South Shields on 25th June 1939:

BE ALWAYS READY.

Wake up Shields men and show your grit,
Come forward now and do your bit,
The ARP are needing you,
Let them see what you can do.

Little children may one day depend,
On the courage of some friend,
Let them not find you to be deficient,
Make it your hobby to be efficient.

They look for help to One on high,
Far above the bright blue sky,
From that same sky may come destruction,
If you delay ARP instruction.

By being calm and unafraid,
Amply will you be repaid,
To work in team with your fellow men,
The ARP tells you how and when.

It is not much they ask you for,
Just to digest a little lore,
To help yourselves in time of need,
By quick response to word and deed.

Do not smirch your town's good name,
Let others see you can play the game,
Let them find you true and steady,
Uphold your motto - ALWAYS READY.

Grace Jackson Tulip

Norman C. Tulip MBE   Dunmurry Belfast

A Fortunate Accident

During the Second World War quite a number of homes were bombed and many people lost their lives. Some districts were hard hit whilst the inhabitants of other places in the north-east grew very complacent as the initial bomb scares faded.

Walkergate, where I lived when I was nine, was relatively quiet on the nights when the air raid warnings were in progress and mother and I grew rather lazy as far as going down to the Anderson Shelter was concerned.

The shelter had been sunk in the back garden of Number 3, Trojan Avenue, and even though my father had sunk a hole to gather and hold the rain water and built bunk beds for us it remained an unattractive proposition in the middle of a chilly night.

Father, at the ripe old age of thirty-nine, was excluded from the forces and therefore went down to London to help with bomb damage. He had always been the one to insist on the use of the shelter and I'm afraid that when he went away mother and I allowed our attention to detail to abate somewhat; the sirens often sounded but we stayed in bed, warm and cosy.

One afternoon, many months later whilst I played in the front garden I heard the click of the gate and beheld my father, overalls, cap and bag of tools coming home. He had strained his back badly, shovelling clay. He would again take charge and that very night the air raid warning sounded so he insisted that we get dressed and go down to the bomb shelter.

The heating and lighting in those dugouts was fairly rudimentary. The light was of course provided by a candle; the heating was another candle inside a plantpot with another pot upside down on top. I can still see the thing, one could spend an hour watching the smoke spiralling up through the hole. Sometimes we played, 'I Spy With My Little Eye', but this particular night was to be different. No sooner had we settled ourselves in the damp gloom of the shelter than there was a swishing noise, a crescendo and a thud – an unexploded anti-aircraft shell had hit our house entering by the front bedroom window and landing on the bed. It exploded inside the house with disastrous results.

The accident that had brought my father home had saved his family from certain death that night in Walkergate.

Alan G. Gowland
Ryton, Tyne and Wear

Ryton on Tyne

I was born in 1912 at Ryton on Tyne. All my forebears, within memory, were associated with coal mining. My father had gone into the pit at High Spen on leaving school at 13. At 16 he suffered a crippling accident resulting in permanent lameness. While convalescing, he studied at night classes and eventually was accepted by Bede College in Durham. When I was born he was Headmaster of the village Church School, Ryton Thorp.

My memories of the First World War are necessarily vague and unfocused. I recall two uncles in uniform and the excitement of greeting them on leave; a grand sports day to celebrate the end of the war; the victory election where we marched round the village singing 'Vote, vote, vote for Major Waring!' to the tune of 'Tramp, tramp, tramp the boys are marching'; a presentation of mugs to the children of the area at Bradley Hall, the home of Sir Frank Simpson, managing director of Stella Coal Company - and little else.

Ryton Thorp, my first school, was a building of three rooms; two large and one small. There were seven classes or standards as they were called in those days, so that each large room held three classes with three teachers 'competing'.

The rooms were heated by a central stove which quite often gave off fumes. On wet days, too, there was a malodour of damp boys and girls - a vivid memory! There was never any shortage of barefooted children and father was constantly concerned to have something done about it. There were children who suffered from rickets, too, where the diet was inadequate, and bow legs were not uncommon as a result, 'Dowpies' we called them.

The desks in school were long enough to accommodate three or, if pushed, four children each. There were ink wells in the corners and ink monitors had to keep these regularly filled.

In those days automatic promotion up the school was not heard of. If you were a dunce you stayed in Standard 2 until you proved you were good enough to move on. If you were a high flier you could be in Standard 7 at the age of 10. I remember when I first started school we had slates to write on using slate pencils, because of the shortage of paper. Slate pencils could set your teeth on edge, but it was easy to wipe the slate clean.

Other memories of the village school: the schoolyard was unpaved, dusty in summer, clarty in winter, we had a marble season, they were muggles to us and there were many fights over them. Other games in the yard were Monty Kitty, Leave a Holla, where you had to spit over an opponent's head to capture him, and Hitchy Dabber, hopscotch in other parts.

Ryton had six collieries within a two mile radius of the village, Emmaville, Crawcrook, Clara Vale, Stargate, Addison and Greenside. It was quite a common sight to see groups of black faced men with leather helmets walking home from the pit. At home the tin bath would be brought out and filled with hot water from the boiler at the side of the fire. There the miner would take his bath, careful not to have his back washed!

One benefit that miners had that ordinary mortals had not was electricity in their houses. Everywhere else was gaslight. The gaslighter with his rod walked the roads morning and evening keeping the lamps in trim. In the houses gas was the principal fuel for lighting and, in some houses, for cooking too, although a cooking range, coal heated, was much more common. Indeed, when later we moved to Chester-le-Street we had to put up with oil lamps for some years – until 1934 in fact.

I remember the wonderful smell of home baking. Loaves of fresh baked bread and 'stotty' cake seemed to be always around. Pint mugs of tea, oilcloth on the table, beds which folded back on to the wall. I remember, too, going 'guising' at Christmas with my cousins; dressing up in odd garments, putting make-up on and going from house to house performing St. George:

Once I was dead but now I'm alive.

God bless the doctor who made me alive.

I was popular because I sang quite musically and, importantly, in tune and I had quite a wide repertoire, thanks to my father who was a very keen amateur musician.

There were no buses immediately after the war. Everywhere were horses and carts. If we wished to travel far we had to do so by train. The station at Ryton was at the bottom of a steep hill. Getting there was easy, coming back a toil. I recall the platform packed with people waiting for the morning train to Newcastle. This was in the early 1920s when I was travelling to the Secondary school at Blaydon. When the buses started up in the mid 20s the railways felt the pinch. Ryton station no longer exists.

With so many horses on the roads, many of the village lads had small 'bogies' with which they collected horse manure off the roads, either for their father's allotments or to sell for pocket money.

Milk was distributed from cans in pint or quart metal containers poured straight into the jug at the door; not at all hygienic. Fish was also brought to the door by Cullercoats fish lassies with their creels on their backs. Lovely fresh fish it was, too. Herrings were literally two a penny in those days.

There were no fridges or freezers then. Mother had a big earthenware jar which she kept in the pantry where it was cool. This was filled with water, and butter, eggs etc. were placed in to keep at a reasonable temperature. Nor were there washing machines. Washing day was a regular ritual - a day that I hated. Steam all over the kitchen, cinders on the hearth; dirty clothes all over the floor; tempers everywhere frayed and cold meat for dinner. And if it was raining - oh 'eck!

I have quite vivid memories of the 1926 strike when, at first all working men came out in sympathy with the miners. It only lasted 3 days before everyone went back, leaving only the miners to brave it out. I was at Blaydon Secondary School at the time (it was only after the war that it was renamed Grammar School) having passed the 'scholarship' as it was called. Everything was at a standstill. The buses to take us to school were not running, so we had to walk - 4½ miles. This we did until the buses started up again, and thought it great fun. The weather was good - it was May I think? - and about a half dozen of us used to meet at 7.30 and set off. We thought nothing of it.

I remember the soup kitchens being set up to help to feed the families of the miners. I remember, too, the lads of my generation who were kicking their heels with nothing to do. I was the fortunate possessor of a set of cricket stumps - so I was very popular. I was quite happy to take my stumps down to the Willows – a wide stretch of public land adjoining the river – and take part in games of cricket with my mining pals.

Radio – or wireless as it was known then – was beginning to be popular. We had a crystal set with headphones and I recall the frustration of 'fiddling' about with the whisker on the crystal to get good contact and the thrill of getting a good sound. 5 N O was the local station in Eldon Square, Newcastle.

Then came the depression. We moved to Chester-le-Street in 1928 when father became Headmaster at Edmondsley school. This was in a colliery village where the colliery had just closed and the whole village was on the dole. These were the years of the Means Test where money was only paid to the unemployed if they were absolutely destitute. True poverty was very evident. One only had to enter some of the houses to see evidence of this. There may be some poverty today but it cannot compare with that of the 20s and 30s.

Many people were so obviously undernourished. I remember when father was conductor of Chester-le-Street Male Voice Choir, most of the men were on the dole. One, Dick Gill, a lovely man, had been out of work for some years. He greeted us one day with a glowing face. He'd got a job, labouring, and he was over the moon. He lasted two days and then collapsed from sheer exhaustion brought on by undernourishment.

The years between 1930 and '39 were strange years. 1930 – no cloud in the sky, 1933 – stirrings on the German horizon, 1938 – Munich. I remember how the sound of Hitler's voice on the radio used to cause tremors of anxiety and how relieved we all were when Chamberlain came back with his scrap of paper in 1938. It may be fashionable to sneer at his naivety and deplore his so-called cowardice, but those who were there know with what relief we greeted the false respite. To some extent the memory and shadow of the First War were all too present.

Denis Weatherley
Darlington.

'SARRADER'

On a Sarrader when Ah was a bairn
Ah had burrerflies in me tum
'Cos Ah knew that Ah wud be gannin
Te the Palladium
Me brother gav us a ha'penny every fortneet
And on the way there Ah would stop for some sweets.
Cinder Taffy, Shorbet Dab, lickris root or Empire Mixture,
Ah took so long they must have thought
Ah was a permanent fixture!

Then into the flix
Ter see Roy Rogers or Tom Mix
Or a serial that gave yer such a scare
Me sister used to go and sit on the stair.
Some wonderful films we saw.

Coming oot with me pals
And running hyem to tea
With a gobstopper clagged te me jaw.

Joy Rushmer
East Boldon

92

When I was a Lad

The sound of 'When I Was a Lad' being played one afternoon on BBC Radio 2, took me back to the 1920's and 1930's when I was a lad in Benwell, Newcastle.

The singer mentioned 'Dolly Mixtures' and this reminded me that, at home, on Friday nights we were given a halfpenny to spend on sweets. We got one ounce of loose sweets wrapped up in a paper cornet, for our halfpenny, at the local corner shop.

On Saturdays, we got a penny to go to the matinée at the Grand Cinema in Condercum Road, to watch silent films. There was a pianist at the cinema who played accompanying music, but this was drowned by the din, especially when an exciting chase or event was being shown on the screen. Monkey-nuts were on sale and lots of them were thrown about during the performance. Cowboy and Indian films were great favourites and cowboys like Tom Mix and Buck Jones our heroes. We eagerly awaited the serial film to see what had happened to the hero and heroine. The week before we had sometimes seen them apparently going over a huge waterfall in their canoe but now it was miraculously diverted to the edge of the river just before plunging over the waterfall.

About twelve weeks before Christmas, we were told to save up our admission tickets and at Christmas we handed the batch in at the cinema and got a Christmas Stocking. As the tickets were the same size as tram tickets, some lads mixed a few of these in the centre of their batch.

On Sunday afternoons, I went with my pals to the Sunday School at Sopwith Street Mission and on Wednesday evenings we attended the 'Band of Hope' in the basement room of the mission, where there was a prayer meeting and we sang rousing hymns.

There were half a dozen non-conformist chapels in Benwell in those days, and on Good Fridays there was a procession accompanied by bands, round the streets of Benwell. Each chapel had its own banner and each congregation wore a different coloured rosette. The procession usually stopped on Buddle Road and on spare ground beside the Majestic Cinema in Condercum Road and we sang hymns.

Looking back, Easter always seemed to be fine and warm in those days, and boys sported new sandshoes and the girls new frocks and white socks.

At the end of the parade, we returned to our own chapels. At our mission we were rewarded with an apple or an orange, which was greatly appreciated.

During the school holidays the mission organised outings to such places as Ryton Willows, Heddon-on-the-Wall and Whitley Bay. I remember walking with the congregation, one year, from Sopwith Street down to Elswick Station and boarding a steam train which took us to Whitley Bay.

Many streets, as well as houses, in Benwell were lit by gas lamps. A lamp-lighter used to pedal a bicycle round the streets, stop at each street lamp, turn on the gas and light the lamp from a lighted taper on the end of his pole. Later, an automatic lighting system was installed in each lamp.

In the houses, the gas lamps were lit by matches or more usually a piece of paper lit from a coal-fire. If the gas mantle was accidentally damaged, one had to put up with a flaring light until a new mantle was bought at the local corner shop.

On Pipetrack Lane, near the top of Violet Street, there was an abattoir and once a week a herd of cattle and sheep were driven there from the Marlborough cattle market on Scotswood Road. When the herd started to go up Violet Street they seemed to sense danger and tried to scatter. One day a sheep bolted, and as our front door was open, it ran into our passage.

Looking down Violet Street to the River Tyne, it was a common sight to see colliers steaming up river to Derwenthaugh Staithes to load up with coal.

During the school holidays we sometimes used to walk to Derwenthaugh, stopping on Scotswood Bridge to watch men fishing for salmon below. A rowing-boat with the net was rowed out in a semi-circle paying it out and when the boat came back to the shore, the fishermen got hold of both ends of the net and hauled it in.

I have also watched salmon being netted, further up the river, near Newburn. I was told that the fish were destined for London.

The first wireless set we had at home was a crystal set which worked without batteries. It had only one set of headphones. We thought it was marvellous listening to music on the headphones! Sometimes the set would go 'dead' and you had to twiddle the tiny piece of coiled wire known as the 'cat's whisker' to find a 'live' spot on the crystal so that you could hear the music again.

Later, we got a battery-operated radio set with a loudspeaker which had valves and an acid accumulator which needed to be charged once a week. I sometimes got the job of taking the accumulator to a gents' hairdresser on Buddle Road who did accumulator-charging as a side line.

How things have changed since I was a lad!

David A. Lowrey
Washington.

Glimpses of Byker

I was born in Byker and until I was 12 years old I was convinced you got gin from a teapot because my Nan and her friends always drank it out of cups.

On dark, misty evenings I remember the lamplighter turning up the gaslamps at the end of the back to back streets. One lamp was right outside the corner shop which was open all hours. There we could buy sarsaparilla by the jugful and bundles of firewood tied together with wire.

Every house had coal fires sending slaty smoke spirals curling up into the sky – there was no thought for the environment then.

Gran used to take me down to Paddy's Market down by the quayside where she sold bundles of rags, the price decided on by the weight of them. Then we would go straight across to the Big Market to buy one rabbit and a pair of pigeons to make pies for next day's dinner.

No one locked their doors.

On hot summer days the children next door to us would go to school barefoot. Entertainment consisted of going to the pictures, playing cards or board games, skippy, tag, two-baller or blind man's buff.

I was lucky to be an only child and we lived in a three roomed house but we didn't have an outside toilet until I was seven years old. Most of the other families in the same type of house had seven or eight children. We washed in cold water except for a bath once a week in a 'tin coffin' in front of the black range where the water was heated up.

Memories of an old lady, you think, born at the beginning of the century? Not really – I'll be forty-seven next year!

Patricia Middlemiss Middlesbrough.

I Remember when I was Young...

I remember when I was young,
When a ha'penny bought milk in a jug.
Teacher scared us at school then,
If you did wrong, she'd grab you by the lug
And drag you along to the Headmaster's den.

I remember on a Friday, we'd get a penny to spend,
We'd go along to Drakesmith's shop and view all the goods:
Liquorice, fruit balls, lollies galore, there was no end,
I'm certain we drove that poor fellow round the bend.

The fun we had playing games in the street,
Marbles, skippy, whips and tops,
No fancy computers or telly to bother us,
No cars when we played hop-scotch.

Sunday would come along, and dressed in our best,
We'd all go to Sunday School, we were smartly dressed.
Afterwards we'd go for a walk
We daren't get dirty, our Mam would give us whatfor.

When we got home, off with the finery
Before we sat down to Sunday tea,
The best china would be out for our use,
Tinned fruit, jelly, and Swiss roll, certainly no booze.

Oh happy days, where have they all gone?
We hadn't much money, but we all had fun;
I remember when everyone seemed so kind,
In the Good Old Days when we were young......

Elizabeth Jeffrey
Ashington

The Unwilling Horse

It was the annual trip to Tynemouth. The women and children went on ahead, the menfolk promised to follow on soon in a horse drawn trap which they had borrowed specifically for the day.

The men duly set off and travelled as far as White Mare Pool before deciding to stop for a little light refreshment. They all went in to the pub for a drink but when they came out and boarded the trap ready to resume their journey the horse refused to move.

The landlord noticed the difficulty they were having and came out to lend a hand.

'Where did you borrow the horse?' he enquired.

'From the local undertaker,' was the reply.

'Well that explains it,' said the landlord. 'There's only one thing to do. Stand in a line and take your caps off.'

Somewhat puzzled the men did as they were bid.

'Now sing a verse of Abide with Me,' he ordered.

This they did – and the horse moved off immediately!

Reflections

My thoughts go back some eighty years
A lad of nine or ten
To a village known as Littletown
And what things were like then.

No council houses formed a street
Such things were then unknown
Just dreary colliery houses built
Of rubble or limestone.

The women tried to make them home
With poverty to fight;
The brasses round a great coal fire
Were polished clean and bright.

No carpets could they then afford
To cover all the floor,
But lovely mats they made themselves
With colours all galore.

As children woods and open fields
Provided endless joys
And though it's eighty years ago
We wish we still were boys.

The schools were cold and draughty,
Coal fires the only heat,
In winter time we sighed for home
Cold hands, cold feet, cold seat.

We left the school at 14 years
A sparse, poor education,
The grimy pit awaiting us
Our only occupation.

Horse transport went, the car came in
The world rolled on its way,
Inventions came with lightning speed
In this our youthful day.

We settled down to a changing world
To unroll the tangled mesh
With hope the anchor of the soul
Facing up to life afresh.

W.L. Makepeace
Dawdon, Seaham

From Tyne to Wear

Fox

I was born and grew up in a small mining village on the great Northumberland and Durham coalfield. It was hardly a pretty place, just long terraces with back yards and outside toilets. One either lived in the 'long' streets, which ran east to west, or the 'short' streets, which ran north to south. It had a Post Office, a Co-op Store, several shops and a policeman. It also had an unusual and locally famous war memorial. Whereas most of the villages in the area had opted for statues of soldiers or sailors, our memorial was a white marble angel. People said it had caused a sensation when it was first erected. We also had a pub that was persistently called after the landlord rather than its more imposing name, and a working men's club. In a little green wooden hut the local barber blew smoke in our eyes while we had our haircuts. What an experience it was to go in there! The walls were lined with old stained photographs of football teams and the conversation in the smoke-filled atmosphere was usually about football or horses. The barber used to put a box on his chair for kids to sit on and then cut their hair with surgical precision, a cigarette permanently in his mouth and continuing a constant flow of conversation with his regulars.

Most of the men in the village worked in the pit – my father, uncles and both grandfathers did, and for good measure both my grandfathers were Methodist local preachers – what a pedigree!

Just after the Second World War, in those brave days of austerity and rationing, few people aspired to home ownership and the number of cars could be counted on one hand. I was lucky, my uncle and aunt had a motorbike and sidecar, which meant occasional trips to the nearby coast, sitting on my aunt's knee.

There were allotments at one end of the village where families grew vegetables including the giant leeks of Tyneside. Livestock was popular too and some people had pigs, fed by collecting potato peelings and other scraps which were boiled upon coal-fired set pots in the piggeries. The day that the family pig was slaughtered was a gala day with handouts of meat to those who had donated scraps to feed the animals. There was a neighbourliness about the village too – the women gossiped, either across the street standing in their doorways or in each other's houses. I can still almost recite the names of most of the people who lived in my street, we knew where they worked and all their business – we even knew who voted Tory!

Apart from attending the small primary school up the road, we played out in the cobbled back lanes as the seasons for the various games and pastimes came and went. Football and cricket generally followed the national timetables but other activities such as marbles, catapults, peashooters, bows and arrows and kites seemed to follow a mysterious timetable of their own. No one gave a signal, one day it would be marbles, the next day something else. We made the kites and bows and arrows ourselves, as there were very few toys for sale in those days. Old tyres came in useful, either hanging in trees for swings or, for the real daredevils, rolling downhill with the small boy curled up inside. Street games were also popular, usually versions of hide and seek, especially on dark winter nights under the glow of gas lamps. We also devised games with the cardboard tops from the wide-necked milk bottles of those days, although some people still had milk delivered by horse and cart out of a churn. Horses and carts also brought groceries and fruit and vegetables. Mr. Lewis came around on his motorbike and sidecar collecting accumulators to take away and recharge so that we could listen to the wireless. We never missed Wilfred Pickles in 'Have a Go' and even now the sound of 'Friday Night is Music Night' brings back memories of my Friday night bath in the tin bath in front of the fire.

The village was surrounded by the industrial scars left by two or three centuries of coal mining. The whole area was dotted with old pit heaps and pit shafts. The shafts were usually surrounded by high round stone walls and we often climbed up to drop stones down the shafts, listening for the splash into the flooded workings far below. There were also many railways, some working, some long disused, for this of course is where the railways started. The old wagonways for horse or rope hauled coal trains had given way about the time of Waterloo to the iron monsters of William Hedley and George

Stevenson steaming down to the Tyne, hauling unheard loads of coal to the waiting colliers ready to sail to London. These days the area is of interest to industrial archaeologists and the remaining railways are now nature trails or cycle tracks but nobody used the world 'environment' then, we just thought it was a paradise put there for us. We roamed the old lines and pit heaps at weekends and holidays, birdnesting, seeking bees in jam jars, blackberrying in the autumn and catching newts in the many marshy ponds that abounded. Our favourite spot was an old pit heap long reclaimed by briar and gorse, scarred and pitted with the dug-outs of previous generations of children. It was our fortress and haven, used for every game and drama and regularly set ablaze from end to end. We loved playing with matches.

Our constant companion during our forays around the area was Fox. Fox was a red dog of the retriever type and seemed to me the bravest, strongest and wisest dog in existence. He was a handsome dog, lively and adventurous, the Errol Flynn of the canine world. He belonged to a particular family who no doubt fed and accommodated him but he seemed to be always with us wherever we went. Whatever we did he would accompany us getting just as excited as ourselves.

Winter was always exciting, especially after dark when we played many variations of hide and seek in the dim pools of light under the lamp posts. We did not have to worry about cars running us over, the streets were ours. We also made a nuisance of ourselves by knocking on doors then running away – a variation was to tie adjacent door knobs together and then knock and run. November of course meant Bonfire Night, prepared for weeks in advance by the chopping down of local hedges and the collection of various amounts of flammable rubbish from all our neighbours. The prepared bonfire would be built up over a period of weeks. Further excitement was provided by raids on the bonfires of nearby villages, the aim being to set them ablaze before Guy Fawkes night. The lads of a neighbouring village had a terrible reputation. It was said that if they caught anyone raiding their bonfire they would make them drink paint! Two of us raided their village one dark night. We planned it like a military operation, lighting prepared torches made of oily rags while hiding in the outside toilets and then racing across to the bonfire and plunging the torch in. We raced back across the colliery railway line back to the safety of our own dark street, avoiding capture and the dreaded drinking of paint. We didn't take the dog on that one, silence wasn't his best feature.

The local farms provided another source of fun and adventure. Horses were still used in the late 1940s and I can just remember haymaking with the horses decorated with coloured ribbons. Piled into stooks in the fields the hay proved irresistible to us and we were chased home many times by the irate farmer who had seen his hay stooks destroyed. Further up the old wagonway that ran past our old pit heap a gambling school met on Sunday morning. Fifty or sixty men would meet and stand playing pitch and toss. I never discovered the esoteric nature of what they did but many years later I discovered Australians gambling in the same way – only they called it 'swy.' Rumour had it that the local Bobby used to ride down to the gathering on his bike and take a commission for keeping quiet about it. On our way home from spying on this glimpse of the strange world of grown-ups we might help ourselves to a turnip out of the farmer's field. Freshly picked and peeled – I can taste them yet. After such a typical day we would work our way home with the red dog, ready to face the music for being late. Often dirty, usually wet, sometimes singed and always breathless, were there every such happy, healthy boys and did the sun really shine all the time?

What a little world it was. Travel was for other people, most of us had hardly been twenty miles away from home. Chapel trips might take us ten miles to the coast and once a year a dozen buses left the village to go to a local beauty spot or place of interest. The poor dog got left behind on those occasions too. One of the old wagonways ran to a colliery village about six miles away. We never quite got that far as on the way the line ran under a roadbridge under which was supposed to live a dreadful man who did unmentionable things to children – a sort of Tyneside Troll. That village remained only in our imaginations – a small boys' Samarkand.

The years passed and I was separated from my chums to some extent by passing the scholarship, as we called the 11+. I went off to a Grammar School leaving my friends to the supposed horrors of a Secondary Modern where, so rumour had it, new pupils were subjected to terrible tortures and some of the teachers ate small boys for breakfast. We also moved out of our privately rented terrace to a new Council Estate up the road where we not only had a garden but a bathroom. The focus of my life moved away from the cobbled streets and old pit heaps to the wider world of learning, hiking trips to Scotland and, courtesy of a chapel youth club, girls. For a few years, until television transformed children into consumers, no doubt children continued to roam the fields and lines and perhaps Fox still went with them.

The happy days I had spent growing up passed into memory to be rarely recalled amid the new pleasures of a wider and older world. About the time I left school I vaguely remember hearing that Fox was dead, killed in a fight with an alsatian. It would be nice to think that some small boys had given him a burial in keeping with his record of freely given companionship over the years.

Today when I use the Tyne Tunnel and head north I drive over the old pit heap, flattened in the late sixties by a four lane highway. The fields, lines and paths are cruelly bisected by the road and its embankment. The pits are closed too and the only tank engines still steaming are maintained as a tourist attraction. The village is still there with bathroom extensions bringing the houses up to date but the children are all watching television or playing with computers.

Sometimes, though, when I drive past the memories of those brave happy post war days come flooding back. I can almost see the short-trousered boys roaming wild and of course the red dog, tongue steaming, coat gleaming, dancing attendance on the ghosts of my childhood.

Hutton Barton
West Monkseaton
Whitley Bay

Philadelphia & Shiney Row

To tell all the things stored up in my memory, of the first years of my life, would take a very long time; they are very vivid and clear:

It all happened in a place which to me was magic - even though it was Yard Row, Philadelphia.

I was born on November 8th 1910. Yard Row comprised seven stone houses, in a kind of hollow, fronted by a gravel path. A green bank of grass rose up to the road. It was upon this bank that we played.

The Philadelphia Engine Works, surrounded by a high wall, was situated at the end of these houses. The 'Works', apart from the pits, was the main source of employment. It consisted of engine shed, sawmills, 'shops' such as, electricians', plumbers', fitters', painters', founders', sadlers' etc., where all the young men served their time. Just inside the main gates was the Time Office where my father worked. The goods railway line ran through this part of the yard.

A number of children lived in the street, and I had a brother a little older than myself. I must have been registering what was happening before I was three years old. A daughter of one of our neighbours used to take me out quite often, to visit her grandfather in the Joicey Homes at Herrington Burn. On one special occasion, she took my brother and me to New Herrington to watch a procession. We carried our small Union Jacks, and saw King George V and Queen Mary, who had been visiting Herrington Hall - I think - and were returning to Lambton Castle, where they were guests. I believe this would have been a Coronation visit to the North.

These early years in the area were idyllic; we seemed to have many friends and relations and were possessed of a lovely garden, where my father grew vegetables and flowers; when the potatoes were big enough, we roasted them on the fire in the garden. The folk in the mining community were mostly good gardeners.

I started school when I was five years old, at Paddock Style School. By this time the First World War – or the Great War as it was then called – had been on for more than a year. We had had air-raid scares, and we all used to hide under the table in the living-room. We had heard quite a lot about Zeppelins. I am not quite sure about the date when we did have an air-raid very close to us. It was either late 1915, or early 1916, because it was before my sister was born in July 1916. On a Saturday night, on returning from a visit to Houghton-le-Spring, our neighbours began telling my parents that the 'Zepps' were out!

Later that night there was a warning, and bombs were dropped in the farmer's field close to Herrington Wood and also near to the Philadelphia power station, which had been their target.

Next morning my father took my brother and me to see the huge craters in the field where the bombs were dropped. Many house and school windows were shattered, but no severe damage was done.

A vivid memory at this time was of visiting the neighbours I mentioned before: their son was on leave from the army – his fiancée was there – it was a family gathering, and they sang war songs, including, 'Keep the home Fires Burning'.

On my sixth birthday we moved from Yard Row, to a new house in South Street, Shiney Row. Some sort of horse-drawn transport was used to convey the furniture, while I, clutching my birthday cards, walked to the new house with my mother. I also had to attend a new school, Shiney Row. Transport at that time was by Sunderland Electric Tramways, which could take us to Sunderland, Roker, and Penshaw Railway Station. I believe only one doctor at Philadelphia owned a car, though pedal cycles were plentiful.

Home life was good: home cooking and baking in a round oven; coal fires, games and knitting, and also music, on whatever instrument we could afford, usually a small organ.

We began to appreciate nature and the things around us; villages, such as Newbottle with its lovely stone houses and picturesque church at the top of the village; also public houses were plentiful and there was an abundance of Churches and Chapels too, and Sundays were mainly used for worship.

On looking back over a lifetime, working first as a dressmaker and secondly, training as a nurse during the war, what a panorama confronts me. Then marriage and a home in Sunderland and a lovely daughter. The years have brought a host of joys: a number of sorrows as well, but wonderful friends and relations have always been there. Life has been rich and good, and it all happened in the North East!

Olive M. Edgoose
Sunderland

Poor Geordie

We all ran home from school that day, to tell our mothers. Geordie Sample had been taken home. He was bad with tummy-ache. We had watched wide-eyed with wonder as the teacher fastened a cushion on to the cross-bar of his bicycle, wrapped him up warmly and set off for Geordie's house. We were sent home as well. I was excited. He was my best friend and lived next door and we were going to get married when we were very old like our Mams. We had all started school just three weeks before because we were all five. Being his best friend I was very important and they all tried to keep up with me as we made our way home. We flew like the wind. We all lived near each other. You did in the collieries. The cottages were all alike. The streets were all in rows. Everyone was poor. Me Da said it was 'cos of the strike but I didn't know what that meant.

We ran as fast as we could but couldn't keep up with the bicycle. As we were running, the teacher came pedalling back as fast as he could. Not back to school. He rode up Front Street and knocked hard on Dr. Ryan's door. We kept on running, only stopping when we reached our house. Me Ma wasn't there. She was next door with Mrs. Sample. I ran into Geordie's house. The others followed but we were all chased out. Geordie was bad, me Ma said. We all had to be quiet. The doctor and the teacher came back and we were told to get out of the yard where we were standing and go into the street. We could hear Geordie screaming. The doctor came out and rode away again very quickly. Me Ma came out with a cup in her hand. She had been giving Geordie ginger tea to ease his pain. She took me into our house, cut me a thick slice of bread and jam and told me 'that would have to do the day' because she was going back to sit with Geordie and his Ma 'till t'ambulance came to take Geordie to hospital'. 'What's hospital Ma?' but she didn't have time to explain.

'Tell all them bairns to keep quiet mind, Geordie's very poorly.' When I went out again, I thought she must have said the same to them. They were all silent. Some mothers were with them and by the time the ambulance came, there was quite a crowd round the yard door.

Everybody was moved away when the driver and the other man got out. They opened the double doors at the back. I thought this must be the hospital. When I asked Olive Nelson who lived next door on the other side of us, and who sat next to me at school, she said no it wasn't because her Ma had gone in that van, and when she got to the hospital she had her tummy cut open to get their Mary. So that was it! Geordie was going to get a baby! They carried him out on a stretcher. He lay very still on the white sheet and was covered with a bright red blanket. I was petrified. To this day, whenever I see a red blanket my mind goes back to when Geordie was carried out. I didn't see him again. He died that night.

It was my first brush with death. I didn't know people died. Where did they go? Nobody had the time or inclination to tell me. Preparations had to be made for the funeral. 'What's a funeral, Ma?' She hadn't the time to explain. The day came. Everybody was crying. As always happens in colliery villages, almost everyone who was able to, attended. We kids just stood in the street and stared.

There were these men with black clothes and high hats with black veils hanging down the back. There was a lovely glass coach, like Cinderella's, with two men sitting up front driving the horses. They wore the same clothes as the two who were walking. They carried Geordie in a white box, put him inside and locked him in. Then all the people walked behind up to the church. When they came back, the glass coach had gone and so had Geordie. There was a big party after, with people eating ham and tongue and men drinking brown lemonade and all the women drinking tea and serving the food. I was frightened when I went to bed that night. I kept thinking of Geordie on the stretcher with the red blanket and then the glass coach with the white box and I told myself that no matter how poorly I felt I would never ever tell, because they might put me on a stretcher, cover me with a red blanket and I would never be seen again. Goodness knows what they did with the baby!

Phil Mitchell, Billingham

Middleton St. George

Middleton St. George near Darlington was my home village for the first 38 years of my life. Of medium size and quite pretty, away from the industrial areas, it had very nice walks through the fields and woods and along by the river at Middleton One Row. In those days, we spent many happy hours rambling all over the area – quite safely with no fear of being molested, mugged, or worse!

My father, Thomas Wall Oates, was painter and decorator; until 1933 he worked for McDermids in Darlington and, as a small girl, I could remember him being out of work and on the dole every year, particularly during the cold, harsh winter months. We were used to feet of snow and long icicles dripping from roofs and gutterings. People never seemed to want their homes upset with decorators at that time and, of course, outside decorating was completely out of the question. So, winter was the time when our house got upset and dad did any decorating the house required – usually starting about Boxing Day! Life could be very hard, but we made the best of what we had, despite freezing temperatures which nipped hands, toes and noses until they were blue! Mother used to call this period 'the time of the painter's ghost'!

Mother did her best to keep us fed and warm; I wore a liberty bodice, cotton interlock bloomers, long black or brown woollen stockings which were held up by suspenders on the liberty bodice and, oh! those gaiters – I had one pair made of leather, and one pair made of a thick grey velour material. They were buttoned down the sides by about a dozen buttons on each gaiter and elastic ran round the instep of my shoes to hold them in position. In the summer I wore cotton dresses which mother made, always a new one for the Sunday School Anniversary.

I was educated at the local Council School in Middleton St.

George. In the winter it could be rather chilly – the heating was from a single hot water pipe running round the classrooms at skirting board level, the water heated by a coke-fire boiler. There was only one coal fire in the whole school, that was in the domestic science room – one of those old-fashioned ranges which you could throw a hundredweight of coal on and lose it! This room also served as the technical science room for the boys, where the headmaster, Mr. Hobson, and his assistant, Mr. Scott, taught science. Discipline was very strict, but mostly fair. If you misbehaved in the junior school you got the strap, and in the senior school you got the cane, on the hands. I had both, just once, and felt very injured as I was not the culprit! It was someone else who had been doing the talking. It was no use my going home to mother and telling her I had been punished, all she said was, 'Go back and get some more stick, you must have deserved it.'! Although I was never very fond of school, they were good days really!

In 1940 I worked for dad as his 'apprentice'. On the first job I helped decorate a bedroom at Eaglescliffe Golf Club. We started by stripping the old wall-paper off – all 15 of them! A Mr. Fletcher had put the first paper on in 1876 and signed his name with the date on one of the walls. What a job! Next I helped to cover windows and glass panels in the Council Schools at Middleton St. George, Sadberge, Long Newton and Neasham. The netting had a gluey substance in it and, soaked in water, it was placed over every piece of glazing in the windows, partitions, and doors; then all of it was coated with a type of varnish. So far as I know, we never lost a window during the war!

Middleton St. George also had a very good thriving Operatic Society which started in the early thirties and carried on until about the mid 1950s – disbanded during the war, of course. Dad also did the scenery for these shows until about 1954 when he had to give up owing to ill health. They had a small orchestra and a good pianist, Nell Adams. The shows I remember were *The Arcadians, Flora Dora, The Mikado, Pirates of Penzance, The Desert Song, Our Miss Gibb*; they also packed the Parochial Hall out for a full week.

In the 1920s and the early thirties our milk was brought daily by Mr. Harrison in his milk cart – good, clean, fresh milk straight from the cow. Mother put a jug or basin on the doorstep and Mr. Harrison brought his milk can with two ladles hanging on the side, one for a pint and one for a gill. He filled the ladle, poured the milk into the jug or basin, and always a little drop extra for good measure! When Mr. Harrison retired, the round was taken over by Mr. Walton from Thorntree farm. Fresh fruit and vegetables came round by horse and cart right to our door. Occasionally a scissor grinder came round with his grindstone and sharpened scissors, knives or shears for coppers.

Once a year, a fete was held for charity in the Friary Gardens and we performed our dances from the Sunday School concerts and also Scottish and folk dances.

In the 1920s and 1930s Mr. Tom Hall had a horse and Hansom cab which he drove to and from Dinsdale Station down to the Ropner Convalescent Home, transporting patients to the home with their luggage. They stayed for a week for convalescence – employees of Ropner's Shipping Company.

As in many villages, our Church was the focal point for most of our social life. St. Lawrence's C. of E. Church was our local Church; we also had the old Church of St. George, an early Saxon Church at Low Middleton. Post-war we had fund raising events such as the Harvest Supper and, in the summer, a garden fete was organised. Mrs. Mellanby kindly loaned her garden in Middleton-one-Row for the day. A variety of stalls were set up, cakes, tombola, ice cream, raffles etc. My friend, Joyce Smith (Mrs. Carter's niece) and I looked after the sweet stall. We spent the night before making peppermint creams and fudge; we also collected sweets from various people who had promised to give – hoping we would be put under the trees out of the sun. Some of the younger children did some dancing, and sometimes there was a Punch and Judy show for the little ones.

During the 1950s the Caryl Jenner mobile theatre company came to the Chapel Hall, Middleton-one-Row. Three of J.B. Priestly's plays spring to mind *Ever since Eve, An Inspector Calls* and *Summer Day's Dream*. The players were very popular and their performances tip-top! The people in Middleton-one-Row put them up overnight after the shows.

We always had a dog at home. One was a little black and white smooth-haired terrier, for obvious reasons, named Splash! During the war we had a Morrison table shelter in the spare front room which dad used as his office. As soon as the air-raid warning sounded, no matter where Splash was, she tore into that room and was first into the shelter bed. As soon as the 'all clear' sounded she howled to be out. Mother said to put her out as she would go mad! 'No, mam,' I said, 'she knows where she is safe, come on we'll be all right in there,' and we were! There was never any room for dad by the time mother, myself, Tony and Edwin and Splash got in - dad was left outside, his only protection from the bombing was his tin hat! He was usually on ARP duty at the Parochial Hall anyway. Splash died in 1942 at the age of 12, and we got Pete, a ginger, Heinz-57 dog; a most faithful dog which lived to be 15. While we were at work, he was good company for mother who was not in the best of health. One Saturday morning dad was going to Darlington to the bank for the wages and did not want Pete with him, so he went round to the workshop and got the car out, drove round to our back door with Pete and said 'Sorry old chap, you can't go this morning, I am going to town.' Out got Pete looking all forlorn and dad got back into the car and drove up Chapel Street and up to Phillips' shop for his cigarettes. He wondered why the people at the bus-stop were laughing; when he came out of the shop he saw why - Pete was sprawled on top of the car, he wasn't going to be left behind; he got his way and dad took him to the bank with him.

Thorntree House is a large house opposite ours in its own grounds at the top of Middleton Lane. At the time Mr. & Mrs. Forster lived there and dad was asked to paint the outside. This job lasted some three weeks. The weather was warm and sunny and Pete joined the men on the job and laid on the lawn or roamed around the gardens exploring. There was a goldfish pond in the middle of the lawn and Pete stood watching those goldfish day after day; until the very last day of the job when he decided he would have himself a fish. He jumped into the pond, waited until a fish swam by, grabbed it and swallowed it whole. Of course, the poor thing lived for a while inside him and Pete was dashing round the lawn as if a pride of lions was after him!

We had a cinema in the village called The Lyric and Pete used to go to the pictures with dad and mam and sit under the seat. Then he'd go down to the square with dad to the pub, while mam walked down home. I was left looking after my young brothers. Pete always had a packet of crisps, which he opened himself and devoured with a great crunching noise under the settle.

One of my picture-going friends, named Kathleen Nolan, knocked on our door one night and said, 'Are you coming to the pictures,

116

Joan?' they had changed the film and a Sonja Henie film was on instead. The film started at 7 o'clock and this was at 10 minutes to seven – we had to run about three-quarters of a mile to the cinema. Arriving breathless, we put our money on the cash desk, pointed heavenwards, and Mrs. Race gave us our tickets. When we got upstairs the house lights were out, but the film had not started. 'Oh dear, Kathleen,' I said, 'I can't see a thing, will you go first?' So in she went and Annie Dunn, the usherette, said, 'Sorry I can't see you to the seats – I have no batteries for my torch – there's a war on you know!' We were standing in the doorway on a small landing, there were two steps to go down and then a turn right into the middle aisle between the rows of seats. A waist-high partition with a banister along the top ran along the back of the first lot of seats, so Kathleen slid her hand along the banister, spotted a knob shining in the gloom and clamped her hand firmly on top of it. Unfortunately, the knob was alive and turned round and swore at her most profusely – it was a man's bald head! We did manage eventually to get to the seats at the front of the balcony, in a fit of the giggles! Mother said we were not fit to let loose!

These were the years of the 1930s 'depression' and a lot of people were thrown out of work; the consequences being that whole families left the village never to return; including my friend Kathleen Nolan and her family, they moved to Newcastle and we lost touch.

Holidays were spent at Wolsingham in Weardale with my grandparents at Kiln House, where I was born; and later with my aunt and uncle and my cousin Joyce who also lived in Wolsingham. We rambled over the moors and fells in some of the most beautiful scenery in Northern England. One can never tire of our Northern Dales, their way of life and their intrinsic beauty, but that is another story.

Catherine Joan Simpson
(née *Oates*)
Dalton-on-Tees

Return to Castle Eden

We turned off the main road and drove past the still-familiar two rows of neat cottages. The well cared for village church, St. James, looked exactly as it had done when I left the area in 1957.

My husband and I had retired and moved back to live in Durham, and were visiting some old haunts. I had to remind myself that it really was 42 years ago when I had walked out in my lunch hour with my friends and colleagues and read the epitaphs on the graves, trying to imagine the people and the lives they had lived. I remember noticing the name of Burdon on many of the gravestones. I was in my twenties then, single, confident with my whole life ahead of me.

We parked the car outside the church and went through the gate into the Dene. It was more overgrown than I had remembered, and the path we had used all those years ago had vanished into the undergrowth, but it was good to see the signs saying that the Dene was now a nature reserve.

As we went up the winding drive to the castle, I felt sad when I saw how overgrown the grounds had become, but when we reached the end of the drive I stood in disbelief. The picture I had carried around in my mind for so many years was shattered. The building in front of me bore no resemblance to the castle where I had worked as a shorthand typist, when it had been the headquarters for the No. 3 Area of the National Coal Board. It was obvious that more than the weather and the years had contributed to the destruction of the buildings, vandals had clearly removed certain parts. The lawns that had once been well cared for were overgrown; the summer-house in front of the castle was almost wrecked and the sun-trap and seats where we used to eat our lunch in the summer months had disappeared. We walked around the side of the castle to find trees and vegetation pushing their way through what was left of the roofs of the adjoining buildings.

The building was called a castle, but it was really a manor house bought in 1757 by Rowland Burdon. He bought the house and lands at Castle Eden from William Bromley. In 1764 he rebuilt the village church, St. James, and in 1765 work started on the castle, the Burdon's family residence.

Feeling quite depressed, I tried to remember the six years of my life I had spent working there. They were mainly happy, hardworking times. I could recall everyone who had worked there, and wondered about them.

Even though the castle had been converted to offices by the National Coal Board, the interior was still elegant. In the ladies' cloakroom was a huge bath and a deep, flower-decorated washbasin. There were tennis courts in the grounds, and these were used by the staff. The cellars were used for table tennis and darts.

I used to love talking to the gardener who had worked for the former owners, the Burdon family. He would describe all the parties there had been, and how they would freeze the lawns for skating parties.

When I started working at the National Coal Board my Dad had been ill for a number of years, too ill to work, so I became the breadwinner in our family, and my £4 a week was very welcome. In my first year working there he became very ill. The day before he died two of my colleagues and myself went into the Dene and picked masses of daffodils, hoping to cheer him up. He managed a weak smile and said, 'I know where you picked those.' Even at twenty years old, I was being scolded for stealing. I had never stolen anything in my life until then, but I remember thinking that nobody could object had they known the reason. I still feel guilty when I think of it now, as he had been a devout Methodist all of is life, - he was choir master for some time at the Trimdon Methodist Church, and occasionally organist. His name was Joseph, but everyone knew him best as Joe Smith, and he *was* strict, yet he was a cheerful man despite his ill-health.

In 1951, just three weeks after Dad died the terrible disaster hit Easington Colliery, when 83 men lost their lives. As I worked for the Industrial Relations Officer and Medical Officer, I had to accompany them to Easington for weeks, as there was an enormous amount of

119

paper work. I was very angry at my Dad's death at 52, and at the time, I remember thinking it was insensitive of my employers taking me along to Easington Colliery and placing me right in the centre of the pit disaster. Looking back, however, I suppose it probably helped me, seeing all those funerals from the office window - one after another, and knowing we were not the only families suffering a loss. I remember thinking at the time - some children would be growing up without fathers and grandfathers. I knew about that as I had never known a grandfather. My Mother's Father, Thomas Orton, was killed in the coal mine at Trimdon at only 49 years of age.

In 1956 I was married and in 1957 I left the castle and we moved to Leicester.

I looked at what was only an empty building, but it held a lot of memories for me. It also made me think of the coal tubs lying empty now because of all the mines closing.

Apparently attempts have been made to refurbish Eden Castle, but vandals have stolen lead from the roof and fittings from the inside.

Perhaps though, as some of the mines have had a small reprieve, so might the castle, in time.

Greta Soady
Lanchester

Washington and Usworth Colliery

I was born in 1930 in Washington, County Durham, son of a miner. My father worked first at Usworth Colliery and later at Washington Glebe Colliery. Both the Methodist Church and mining played a predominant role in my childhood and most of my outstanding memories relate to one or the other.

In the 1930s and 40s there were few 'Red Letter' days but every year there were certain highlights which we looked forward to and which even today stand out in my memory.

The focal point of the Sunday School year was the Anniversary which was held on two consecutive Sundays in May or June. Children were required to learn a passage of Scripture or a piece of poetry to be recited at the afternoon and evening services. Rehearsals were held at the chapel once or twice a week but these were nowhere near as nerve-racking as those which had to be performed at home in front of Mother and other relatives until you were deemed word perfect! Special hymns not in the Methodist Hymn Book also had to be learned and the choir, some church members and the Sunday School scholars would go around the streets on the morning of the service singing to the accompaniment of a mobile organ, accordion or melodeon. Door to door collections brought much needed funds to the chapel. There were special preachers for the services and the chapel was always packed. All the children were decked out in new clothes - dresses for the girls with ribbons in their hair, and suits - with short trousers! - for the boys. The Sunday School trip was another exciting event for the scholars. Special buses were hired to take children and parents away for the day - usually to Roker or Seaburn, although during the war I seem to remember that our outings were restricted to a day in the countryside near Washington with a bag of cakes and a drink for each child. Another mass exodus

121

occurred every year on the day of the Club Trip. Usworth Working Men's Club, affiliated to the CIU, was a very busy place even when money was tight. Most members were miners and miners were renowned for their thirst and their capacity to hold beer. Members' children had an annual treat when a steam train was hired to take them and their families to the coast - Tynemouth or Whitley Bay. Although my brother and I were excluded from this outing as our father was not a club member we never envied our contemporaries but simply accepted the situation. To me The Day in the year was The Durham Miners' Gala - Big Meeting Day! Much has been written about this day and it merits a book on its own. I was first taken by my parents in 1933, when I was only three years old, and I have been going ever since. I have attended over fifty Big Meetings and also a large number of Miners' Picnics, which were held first at Morpeth and then, after the Second World War, at Bedlington and Ashington. For size, colour, atmosphere and excitement the Durham Miners' Gala cannot be beaten!

There were three collieries in Washington: Washington 'F' (closed 1968), Washington Glebe (closed 1972) and Usworth (closed 1974). On the eve of the Centenary Miners' Gala in 1983 I recall a parade headed by the Washington Welfare Band and the banners of the three closed pits starting at Washington Welfare Hall and proceeding to Usworth Club where a large crowd of people were addressed by Neil Kinnock. From the mid 1950s to the late 60s Rogation Sunday Parades were held in Washington. Headed by the Colliery Band, followed by the Pit Deputies' Banner from Durham and the Washington 'F' Pit Miners' Lodge Banner. I recall the friendly spirit which existed between the officials of NACODS and the NUM - when deciding the order of precedence for the two banners Harry Matthews (NUM) would say to George Appleby (NACODS), 'You go first and do the pre-shift inspection for us!' This was a reference to the legal position underground where a Deputy had to make an inspection at the start of each shift before the men were allowed to commence work. It is sad to think that with the demise of mining in County Durham these great parades and traditions have gradually been phased out and will soon only be the subject of history books.

Derrik Scott,
Springwell, Gateshead

Village Life in Burnopfield

My father, mother and I lived in a stone built terraced house in the village of Burnopfield, just after the 1914-18 war and I still remember with affection the neighbours who made up our street. The blessing of wireless and television had not yet reached us and therefore we had time to be interested in each other and have a chat 'over the garden wall'.

There was no colliery actually in Burnopfield but the majority of the men worked in pits near the village - Hobson, Byermoor, Marley Hill and Friarside. Their work was hard and dangerous but they still maintained a cheerful disposition and a robust sense of humour.

At the centre of our village was the Co-op, affectionately known as 'the Store'. It seemed to me that you could buy absolutely anything there - that is, if you had the money - groceries, haberdashery, furniture, hardware - if they didn't have it they could get it! There was the added advantage of everyone having a share number. I can remember my mother's still - 2381. Every time you made a purchase you gave your number and received a 'check' or receipt and at the end of six months or a year you received a percentage of the profits, a dividend. 'Divi day' was always looked forward to, the women would queue up outside the Store Office eagerly discussing what they would purchase with the money they were about to receive. Usually it went on such luxuries as lino, bedding or clothes for the children.

One day of the year that stands out in my mind was the Annual Flower Show, held in August. On the Friday night we would all go up to the showfield to watch the 'Hoppings' arrive; coconut shies, Aunt Sallies, shooting ranges and, of course, roundabouts and 'shuggy boats'. We could stay there until dark and then wander

123

slowly home down the village, looking back at the wonderful glow in the sky reflected from the show lights and hearing the music from the roundabout organ floating out on the soft summer evening air. It seemed to us that there was a kind of magic in the air. We were completely fascinated.

On reflection I am sure that the music was not so very beautiful but it fitted the scene, and the organ was a very decorative affair, profusely ornamented with young cherubs blowing golden horns.

The 'Big Day' dawned bright and fair - I don't remember the wet ones. The gentlemen of our area who were horticulturally inclined were working feverishly to get their simply perfect products safely into the big marquee to be suitably arranged for the presentation to the judges.

Competition was keen, rivalry rampant - I did not envy the job of the judges, much tender loving care had gone into the production of those perfectly formed fruits and vegetables of every variety - tomatoes, cucumbers, leeks, carrots - to say nothing of carnations, roses sweetpeas, dahlias.

The ladies of the district were not to be outdone. They displayed their fruit loaves, rice loaves every other kind of loaf, jams, jellies, and conserves, their knitting, sewing, handicrafts. Even the children competed, on show was their handwriting and drawing. I remember my effort at drawing a cup and saucer was truly pathetic, but at least it was there.

Towards lunchtime, the men guarding the entrance to the field began to take their places and anyone coming in would pay and have the back of their hand stamped, so if they wanted to leave the field and then come back later, they didn't have to pay again.

About two o'clock it seemed that the world and his wife had congregated in the main street to await the arrival of the brass band which would lead us all up to the showfield. As the first strains of martial music assailed our ears the air prickled with excitement and up we went to see the exhibits in all their glory, now judged and ticketed.

The rest of the day was spent in admiring or criticising the products on display, chatting or being refreshed in the marquee provided for this purpose. All this was rounded off with a dance till about midnight - one which somehow I never attended.

But there's more - Sunday afternoon was yet to come!

Again about two o'clock probably the same people as before returned to the showfield. The field was situated on top of a hill and it may be that the men came up to admire the panoramic view which undoubtedly existed and to listen to the band which played at the foot of the hill. I always had the feeling that the ladies came more to see who was there and to admire (or criticise) 'Mrs. Cannybody's' new hat, blouse or costume.

The girls strolled along the field or gathered in little groups all aware of looking their very best. The young men stood around eyeing them speculatively – admiring, criticising, making choices. Many a fine romance began on Flower Show Sunday afternoon!

By now our 'big Weekend' had reached its peak and was gently descending into normal village life again.

Looking back it seems life in the early part of the century was none too bad. I suppose it must have had its bad points but please let me keep on wearing my rose coloured spectacles!

Margaret L. Brunton
Burnopfield

Sweet Remembrances

I was one of eight children and our half pennies had to be carefully spent. We would scurry along with our precious money to Mrs. Shaw's, she was a tall spare woman who ran a shop in a house at the end of Dawson Street in Crook. The shop window was part of her living-room, sweet boxes supported on trestles in the window. A chenille cloth was draped over her wooden dining table and on entering, our nostrils were assailed by the fragrant smell of newly baked teacakes, cooling on trays on the sideboard. She had two framed mirror pictures on the wall which used to fascinate me, they were painted with bulrushes and flowers, I wondered how she could see between them.

What a selection of sweets she had, sea shells, gelatine cherry lips, midget scented gums – these were dearer than the other sweets, but a small quantity lasted a long time – boiled sweet fishes, pear drops, gooseberries and black bullets, everlasting strips of toffee, these were good for lasting a long time at the 1d. matinee on Saturdays. Pink and white buttons with little inscriptions, such as 'I love you' 'remember me' and 'forget-me-not' etc. printed on them. One of our favourites was horseshoes, these were made of hard cachou mixture, a heel shaped shallow box, when opened there was a little mascot, ring, tin bell, elephant or other little toy such as in crackers now. There were tiger nuts, shrivelled looking nuts, sweet when chewed, huge gob stoppers, hard balls these were, we sucked and sucked them through layers of shades of the rainbow. I once had one stuck in my throat for some anxious minutes, so was somewhat wary of them after that.

Liquorice came in every form from roots to chew, pontefract cakes, ribbon strips rolled into circles with a sweet coloured ball in the centre, liquorice spatula shapes and pipes bespattered at the end with pink hundreds and thousands. A tube of liquorice was tucked into triangular packets of sherbet, we drew the sherbet up from the packet bottom through the liquorice tube until an accumulation of sherbet and chewed liquorice gummed up the end, so the liquorice was eaten and the sherbet licked with our fingers or tipped in a fizzy puff down our throats. She had barley sugar sticks individually wrapped in tall jars, poor quality gritty chocolate drops, small coloured cubes of coconut confections, 'japs', and packets of sweet 'cigarettes' in yellow packets.

Sometimes Mrs. Shaw tried new lines; marshmallow sponge balls with elastic attached were short lived, more successful were small slabs of wrapped toffee called football toffee, each had the name of a team inside and when a whole team was collected, a large slab of toffee was given free. At one time we had a fancy to play girl guides and found that some of Mrs. Shaw's lucky bags had whistles in them, so demanded that she felt them all until we had all been supplied with whistles, she must have been a patient woman. The lucky bags contained little things like dolls' tin scales which we liked to play shops with, dolls' tin frying pans, nutmeg graters etc. What a lot the youngsters of today miss, no time to listen to their whims in the busy supermarkets!

Gladys E. Tomlinson
Darlington

Growing up in Crook

My mother was left a widow with three little girls to bring up. My father had contracted appendicitis which developed into peritonitis, he died in the ambulance on the way to the hospital, a tragedy which would never occur with today's medical care.

As you can imagine there was very little money to spare, our lives were simple and there was little to spend on pleasures or entertainment in those days. My mother started work as a telegraph girl delivering telegrams on foot to all the neighbouring villages until eventually she obtained a position at Crook Post Office. My Gran looked after us when she was at work.

I began my schooldays at Helmington Row School, walking the one mile there and back every day. We took sandwiches for lunch and the teachers made cocoa for us. I stayed there until I was eight and then went to Crook Primary School. There they had special classes for the better scholars – the very good ones went on to Grammar School, if they passed the examination. This consisted of two written papers and an interview; on an average four pupils passed each year. There was also an examination for pupils who wished to go to Durham Commercial College. Ten free places were available and some for those who could afford to pay half fees. I won a free place and learned shorthand, typing, book keeping, commerce and English. I began work in an accountant's office.

Although my mother had strict rules as to what time we had to be home and in bed, for the rest of the time we could roam the countryside around in safety. I can remember wandering over Crook Golf Course with my friends at quite an early age; on Saturdays in the summer we would walk to Witton-le-Wear (about three miles), taking sandwiches and a drink. As soon as we got there we were straight into the river, that is where I taught myself to swim. Winter evenings were spent at home, reading, drawing and listening to Mam and her friends gossiping over the fire.

I was still at school when war broke out, we had to carry our gasmasks everywhere with us. We had quite a few evacuee children from Sunderland, Newcastle and other towns on the coast. Although I do not think bombs ever fell on Crook I can recall going down the shelter at the bottom of our street in the middle of the night.

American soldiers came to Crook, much to the delight of the older girls - I was only fourteen at the time. Many romances blossomed and then the soldiers were posted away - there was a lot of crying and quite a few unwanted pregnancies. Two miles out of Crook there was a prisoner of war camp. There are still some Polish families in Crook.

We could not afford to go on holiday as a family but my sisters and I would take turns in going to stay on our uncle's farm near Ripon. We would travel in the back of my uncle's butcher's van. It was quite an ordeal for me as I was always travel sick and the journey seemed to take all day. Our holidays were spent helping out on the farm, going to Ripon market, and milking the cows. The milk was put into large churns on the back of a cart and taken round the houses. People came out with jugs and cans and had them filled from a pint measure. Sometimes we went out in the butcher's vans on the rounds but I never wanted to go into the slaughter house.

Crook has changed a lot since those days. The three cinemas have gone, the big Co-op building in the market place has been replaced by the large modern Civic Centre and no one works in the mines any more. In many ways life is a lot better but I cannot help but think that children today are missing out on something.

Joan Flynn
Crook

Pre-war Houghton-le-Spring

My husband and I are both 73 years old now and when we look back we are amazed at the changes we have lived through in our lifetime. The manner in which we lived in the times before the Second World War seems to us now like something from a different era.

I was six years old and my brother was three when my parents acquired their first council house in 1926. We moved into one of the first council houses in the area and many people were quite dubious about the whole idea but to us it was like moving into a palace. Four rooms, an inside toilet and electric light at the touch of a switch – this was heaven after the two tiny rooms we used to live in.

My dad was a miner at Houghton pit, a good worker when he got the chance, but many's the time we stood at the front door at six o'clock at night listening for the buzzer. If it sounded then we knew there was no work for the men next day.

However, miners did have their perks – a load of coal would be tipped at our gate every so often and my dad would shovel the coal into the coalhouse whilst we children ran to any of our more hard up neighbours to tell them to come and get a few pailfuls for themselves.

My dad used to eke out his wages by taking tickets at the local cinema and we all used to go regularly, my parents to the first house, we younger children to the second house. The streets were still crowded at 10 o'clock at night but there was never any trouble.

My parents had three other children over the years but unfortunately the oldest of my brothers died in 1933, a victim of the diphtheria epidemic which claimed many children that year.

My husband's childhood was a little different from mine. His father was unable to work because of an eye disease he had contracted down the mine. They did not have the luxury of a council house until he was 14 years old, instead they had an outside earth closet and bathed in the tin bath in front of the fire every Friday night. His mother did have a wash house with a large copper which was frequently used for the boiling of hams and tongues for funeral teas!

As we grew older we all had bikes and many a Sunday we biked to Sunderland, paid 2d to leave the bikes at Turvey's Garage and then took the tram to the sea front.

When the war came our lives were changed almost overnight and nothing was ever the same again.

Rose Mary Dodds
Houghton-le-Spring

Railwaymen's Carnival Week. 1937/38

North Road Locomotive Works, Darlington held a Carnival every two years to raise money for the Greenbank Hospital. Usually it was the last week in July which frequently turned out to be wet, but this was the official close-down of the works for the summer holiday.

I was serving my apprenticeship as a Fitter/Erector and in my spare time I was involved with the children's dancing classes run by Mr. & Mrs. Senior.

Their son Billy was a drummer, I was playing a small accordion and Len Miskin was a violinist. The children of the dancing classes used to go on tour in the North East under the name of the Nig-Nog group sponsored by the *Northern Echo*. What more natural then that we three should volunteer to be the 'band' when the Shell shop decided to build a replica (of sorts) of the Mississippi River boat, to represent the Showboat of the film of that name.

Other shops and factories in the area built their floats to make them as colourful and eye-catching as possible. The big parade was to go through the town on the last Saturday from the Loco Works clock to the South Park via Northgate, Feethams and Victoria Embankment. Money was thrown on to the floats as well as being collected en route by volunteers running alongside the parade.

The rest of the week was filled with sporting events of all kinds along with special attractions and side shows.

Saturday dawned, but heavy clouds hung over the town and the threat of rain was very real in the low light conditions.

The organizers of the parade had put us somewhere near the middle so we had a bit of waiting to do before our turn came to move off into the stream.

It wasn't long before the first spots of rain were felt on our burnt-cork blackened faces, and seeped through the thin cotton shirts. We had to accept it philosophically telling ourselves it was all in a good cause!

We managed to get through most of the songs with a fair degree of success although it was a bit off-putting trying to decide which spots on the music had to be played and which were the rain drops loaded with burnt cork from our faces! But, as usual at these times, the noise of the crowds lining the road covered a multitude of technical slip-ups which multiplied with the rain until it became a downpour.

By the time we reached the park entrance the water was cascading from the top level where we were sat as though contributing to the spectacle of a river boat, and nicely matching the bass tones of the singer with his rendering of Ol' Man River accurately timed for our entrance into the Judging area. The Mississippi mud was well represented as the wheels of our float sank further down into it, along with our spirits; we didn't get a prize. Perhaps the colouring didn't match up to the Judge's idea of what a Showboat should look like!

As the song, and our repertoire came to an end I looked round at the others - I could hardly believe what I saw, jazzy shirts and complexions from the coloured water dripping from the flags and bunting.

Some of the floats, including our Showboat moved up to the hospital grounds to let the children see what the Parade had been like, and to present the Carnival King and Queen to the Matron. If I remember rightly, the sun came out about this time!

The railway works did eventually close down after the War and as far as I know there never was another big parade, but it was a known fact that the Railwaymen's Holiday week was invariably a wet one yet in all those years they never got around to changing it!

William (Bill) Otley
Melsonby
Nr. Richmond

A Country Child's War

I was well into my eighth year when war was declared; in fact I was on holiday at Blackpool with my mother and sister. There had been a bomb scare in Woolworths that week, and when the ancient bakelite radio in our lodging house announced the fact of war there was a concerted rush to leave the coast. Already the beaches were being cleared preparatory to the positioning of mines and rolls of wire netting against invasion. I recall vividly that Mother packed all she could in bags and boxes, rushing out to buy string which became, that week, a short commodity, to send all home to Hunwick by train. What a good job she did! We had to stand in our first queues for several hours to board a train back to Bishop Auckland.

Everyone said 'It'll be over by Christmas' and when it wasn't, the prediction was confidently moved on to Summer, or Haymaking in 1940. To us children, then, the war had not yet developed into the facts of death or loss, but these came soon enough, and with them the first evacuees. One girl came from London having survived being bombed out twice and with shrapnel in one leg. Typically, then eight, I basked in the reflected glory of being her friend. Other evacuees were streetwise dockland kids from Newcastle and Middlesbrough who knew little of country life and viewed with suspicion Mam's home-made rabbit pie and seeing, for the first time, that really milk *did* come from a cow!

We were encouraged to help the War Effort. Virtuously we handed over to the Army Depot in Peel Street, Bishop Auckland our doll's tin teaset because metal was short. We made felt brooches threaded on to safety pins and sold them for a penny at the village fête. The stylish acknowledgement for our ten shillings and threepence hung above Mam's mantel for months. Mam made Wooton pie, Dad dug for victory, and we lived off rations along with what Dad could cadge in the way of fishing, catching rabbits with a ferret, and picking brambles or hazel nuts for a cake.

Gas masks came in. There was a competition for the prettiest container to cover the cardboard box. Dad made ours from lino with a strong shoulder strap, and we held it against him that we didn't win! At school we had gas and air raid training. There were even competitions on which class could get into their scheduled air-raid shelter first.

All this excitement faded when the grim reality of war was personally experienced one bright summer day of 1941 when, along with Mother, we girls walked the five fields from Hunwick into Bishop Auckland for the weekly shopping. A German fighter plane, fleeing its pursuing escort had come more inland than it should, and was off-loading its bombs so as to achieve more speed in escape. Walking directly beneath and with the 'dog-fight' as it was called overhead, Mother clutched both us girls to her then threw us face down into the ditch which bordered the field. I have a recollection even now of her heart beat thudding above mine as she contrived to cover us with her own body. It was then I realised that war was very frightening indeed, and that for others, it was far, far worse than we country people could ever imagine.

My brother had worked on munitions at Stockton Mallable and thus was exempt from war duty. However he had volunteered early on, starting out as a gunner in the Royal Artillery. Later, he was transferred to the Durham Light Infantry and in the Autumn of 1942 he left Britain for his first taste of battle with the Fifty Army assault into Italy and the push on Monte Cassino. I was twelve then and school-boards showed troop movements. Each child who had a relative somewhere in the fighting world had the privilege of placing a flag denoting *their* special someone who was 'over there'. My sister and I in our respective classrooms were thrilled at last to put *our* flag on the board for Ron. We learned then of the fierce hand-to-hand fighting as our army, along with the Americans and the Indian Ghurka regiments perilously scaled Cassino's slopes to gain the derelict monastery now a strategic battle emplacement. In time came the dreaded telegram brought by Sergeant Scott, our village 'bobby', who knew everyone in our village. 'Missing Presumed killed in Action'.

Our small village honoured its losses by having names read out each Sunday by the vicar. That black Sunday found my mother, crying throughout, with Dad, grim-faced, at her side, his hand across her shoulders, alongside us girls to hear Ron's name, along with others. But 'presumed' to Mother meant hope, so after Cassino was captured by the allies she begged the War Office for firm news. His identity tag had apparently been found amongst others, without a trace of him, such had been the carnage. It was then that the Church of St. Paul's held a full memorial service in Ron's honour.

What joy it is belonging to a small community! Fate had Sergeant Scott's daughter nursing in a Naples hospital when Ron, shocked, half blind, and with shrapnel lodged in his legs, was brought in among the Indian wounded. By the Autumn of 1944 he was returned to England by the hospital ship *Orangie* to Liverpool Docks, from where he transferred to Fulford Road Military Hospital in York, wearing the blue demob uniform of a wounded fighting soldier. My parents met him there at last, and as a family it was a proud moment, walking with him through the streets, to see his uniform touched reverently by many with a 'Well done, lad!' accompanying the awe.

Everyone who lived through World War Two can tell you exactly where they were when the 'lights came on again.' We were once again in York. It was V.E. night and both of us were a lifetime away from the 8 and 10 year old girls we had been in 1939. It was night, very dark before the clocks chimed out twelve, and in the Minster square the crush was unbelievable. Among them troops of many nationalities: American, Canadian, Free French, Poles. Proud civilians who had survived shortages and loss. The bridges crushed with figures. Waiting ... waiting ... *Then* the chimes, the last stroke of twelve. Bells ringing loud and clear, taken up by other bells in other churches. Lights! Whistles! Hooting from the cabin cruisers decked with people on the river. Dancing and kissing; being whirled off into an impromptu conga and all laughing. Tears running down our faces! The Bridges were the best, when we at last arrived there with the moving throng. In each direction, as far as the eye could see, each bridge ablaze with strings of lights beneath the arches; reflecting in the water the happiness of everyone. Graceful arcs of colour. It was a night that went on for ever; a night to remember, and one I shall never forget.

Gwenyth Batey, Newton Aycliffe

136

'Roses in December'

Memories of Horden

There it was again, that same old deafening boom in the still quietness of the early morning. I buried my head under the bed clothes, trying to shut out this unseen enemy, for it was still dark, daylight had not yet broken. I can't remember how long I lay, but suddenly there came the clatter of heavy boots on the cobbled lane of Eden Street and the voices of men calling out as they passed, 'Watcher Marrer' or 'Keep Her Gannen'. I was to learn later that the boom was the colliery buzzer blasting out at 2a.m.: a way of telling the men that it would soon be time for the foreshift to begin. Each house had a slate set into the wall and on this would be chalked 2.30 or 3a.m. to signify the time that the 'caller' or 'knocker up' would be expected to bang the knocker on the door, to arouse the men from their slumbers. I don't know which I dreaded most, for both were dreadful sounds to a small child at such an early hour. These were the days when Horden was a thriving village. Of course there were times when a seam would be idle, if only for one day. It was then that the buzzer would be blown at 6p.m. and every household would hold its breath, counting, 1 - all off, 2 - the Hutton Seam, 3 - the Low Main and 4 - the Main Coal. Should an accident occur and the Ambulance was not needed, then the 'wheels' would convey the injured person to his place of residence, with a crowd of children in hot pursuit, the crowd increasing as they passed each street corner.

Days of Glory

In these early days local football provided the relief from the hardworking days at the mine. It only took a match between

Horden and Blackhall or Easington, to fill the ground to capacity, and should a goal be scored by Horden the roar of the crowd must have been heard at 'Shotton Road Ends'. I think the name of Nan Cummings will live on. One of Horden's staunchest supporters, her voice could be heard above all others with cries of 'Off-side', 'Foul', 'Corner' etc. In later years we had our moments of glory. I can remember queuing in the football field at 7p.m.; for tickets to the ties between Newport County, Accrington Stanley and Southport, competing for the F.A. Cup.

Cottage Industry

To supplement the low wages received from the mine, women would take up small money-making activities. It wasn't unusual to see the living-room window in colliery houses converted into miniature sweet shops. Who can forget Grandma Reynold's ginger beer and Sarsaparilla bought for 2d a bottle, from her home in Eden Street? Or Mrs. Lincoln's pies and peas, in Fourth Street? Children would call at houses asking for old rags which would be cut into strips and used in the making of clippy mats or, if it could be afforded, wool would be used for hookey mats. I have many happy memories connected with my village. Picture if you can, groups of men struggling up Eden Street, each carrying a gramophone on their way to the Workmen's Club, where a gramophone contest was to be held. Not your fancy stereo system, mind you, but the old horn and handle type. Prizes were awarded for the best record and the gramophone with the best decorated horn. Some were brass and others were hand-painted with flowers.

Entertainment

Saturday night was the highlight of the week. Every shop would be open until 10p.m. In the Winter time I could stand on my doorstep in Fifth Street, gazing at the bright little lights of these, as far as the bottom of Blackhills Road. Both sides of the pavement around the Empress cinema were always crowded with people, waiting for the First House to come out. Entering the cinema for the second house must have been like venturing down the nursery slopes of the Alps! We were slipping and sliding on the orange peel and monkey nut shells which carpeted the concrete floor. Many must recall Mr. and Mrs. Bocca entertaining us during the running of the film *Abie's Irish Rose*, by singing 'My Wild Irish Rose' and of course, who can forget George Cole at the piano before Lights Down. The Deluxe too, often had variety weeks with turns from goodness knows where. This involved frantic searching for accommodation for these people and things were not always favourable. Some would find that their landlady wasn't over generous on the feeding side. My own Mam often made the traditional 'stotty' cakes to be taken to the cinema by my brother, who worked in the projection room. Street entertainment was provided by visiting buskers and Sword Dancers, always on a Friday – Pay Day. We had a Champion Brass Band which often broadcast from the Newcastle Studios under the direction of Mr. Joe Foster and later Mr. Dennis Scoins. The former was also a composer and his composition, 'Castle Eden', was played at his funeral. My husband, a trombone player at that time, was one of the underbearers. During the 1926 strike, singing contests were held in the Miner's Hall, entrance fee 1 penny.

A Mine of Memories

After the 1939-45 War, I was given the opportunity to go underground at the Horden mine. Not for me the shaft-bottom. I went in with the night-shift men and surfaced at about 9p.m.; this was shortly after the visit of Princess Marina, the then Duchess of Kent. I went 'in-bye' at the Low Main seam. I wouldn't have missed that visit for anything, for now this colliery is no more. I have known a village teeming with its simple pleasures, excitement and pathos. I have watched the youth of yesteryears leave my childhood, grow old and finally pass away, but what a wealth of happiness they created! What will now become of this once thriving village? How would you assess old age? Perhaps by remembering ladies' lisle stockings at 6½d a pair, silk at 1½d, shoes at 4/11d, 6/11d and 8/11d. Men's caps from about 1/6d and a really good one at 2/6d. Luvisca shirt fronts worn with the collarless shirt at 6½d and loose collars from 6½d. Tea was 3d per quarter, 2lbs of sugar at 6d, bacon about 11d per lb, 3½lbs of potatoes for 3d, Woodbines 4d for ten. All these prices were in 'old' money, when 3d equalled 1½ new pence today. We had little money then, but even with today's standards, they cannot replace the enjoyment which was mostly self-created. Too many buttons are easily pushed. I enjoyed my childhood and my youth. One more happy thought remains – I was married from the house I was born in, 50 years previously and now, having come full circle, I can gaze from my present home and see the yard in which I played, now grassed over. Perhaps this keeps my thoughts alive – I would like to think so. Is this the final link in the chain of events? I hope your memories have been awakened by these recollections. You may ask why 'Roses in December' – these words were taken from a favourite quotation –

'God Gave Us Memories So That We May Always Have Roses In December'.

Norah Kaye-Lawton
Horden

Shildon in the Fifties

S hildon, the town where I spent a very happy eight years of my childhood.

I lived with my parents and grandparents in South Street, Shildon - near Bishop Auckland. Like most of the streets, South Street consisted of terraced houses, with back yards and small forecourts. At one end were steps leading to the Wagon works where they maintained the equipment which made up the goods trains. My grandfather was a retired manager for the Electricity Board and my father travelled to and from Darlington where he worked as a Boiler Fireman for Patons & Baldwins.

I went to school at Timothy Hackworth in Byerley Road. On my way to and from school I had to pass Aldersons, the bakers. Whatever the time of day, there was always an inviting aroma of freshly baked bread, buns, teacakes, scones and lovely cakes. When my mother and grandmother were not making their own bread, they bought it from Aldersons. On the opposite side of the road was a Cobblers shop. All our boots and shoes were taken there for repair.

The nearest thing to a supermarket in Shildon was Walter Willson's grocer's shop. Unlike the supermarkets and superstores of today which have automatic scanning devices at their check-outs and check-out operators usually too busy to stop and chat to the customers for any length of time, Walter Willsons was a small, friendly shop. Quite often, my grandmother would go there to buy a packet of tea or a pound of sugar and come back empty handed. She had been talking to the shop assistant who knew Mrs. X, who knew Mrs. Y who said that Mrs. Z was expecting her seventh child. There was always time for a gossip in the local shop.

These small town retailers used to buy butter in churns and scoop it out on request from the customer. It always amazed me that the

141

assistant knew exactly how much to scoop for 1 lb. The butter was served and wrapped in greaseproof paper and taken home to store on the cold slab in the pantry.

We had a greengrocer in Shildon too. At least you knew you were not only buying English but, most likely, home-grown produce. No imports with high prices!

June, 1993, was the fortieth anniversary of our Queen Elizabeth's coronation. This fact reminds me of the wonderful coronation parties we held in the streets of Shildon in 1953. Of course the school was closed for lessons but during that morning our parents escorted us to the school to collect our coronation mugs and silver pieces. After lunch – or dinner, as we used to call our midday meal – we had the fancy-dress parades. I became Little Red Riding Hood for the day, someone else dressed as the Big Bad Wolf and my grandmother Newby put on a nightcap, a long nightie and, carried a candle on a saucer; the three of us led the procession down South Street. There was an enormous feast with a huge cake – decorated with red, white and blue icing of course – in the large hall of the Railway Institute. Later that evening we had music playing in our street and everybody danced on the empty road.

I don't think Shildon had its own dance hall, if it did I was too young to go dancing then, but I do remember that we had two cinemas. The Hippodrome was the larger of the two and my mum used to take me there often. I especially remember seeing the film *Peter Pan*, every year, at Christmas time.

I certainly spent a very happy childhood in Shildon and I also have a lot of nice memories of my time in Darlington. When I married a Southern man in 1966 I went to live in Germany for a time then to Wiltshire but I eventually returned to my roots in the North East. This is where I belong.

Margaret S. Browne
Darlington

The R.A. Field

To this day, some sixty years later, I still don't know what the letters R.A. stand for – but the field itself stood for freedom. It was a children's paradise, a wide open space in which we and our imaginations could run wild, far enough away from our homes for us to be freed from the confines of parental disapproval – yet close enough for us to feel safe. Along one side of the field ran a high, thick hedge, a source of the raw materials for bows and arrows, spears or sticks for use against imaginary foes. In autumn it provided us with a plentiful supply of berries, some edible others used as embellishment for mud pies.

What had once been a high solid wooden fence ran along the top of the field but over the years it had developed large holes which peppered the length of it. In the corner where the hedge and fence met stood a wooden hut, derelict, with gaping holes in the walls, obviously the former pay stile left over from the days when the field had been the scene of local football and cricket matches. All the hut contained was a large iron trunk, complete with padlock – the tales woven around the contents of this mysterious object were the basis for many of the scenarios acted out by us on the field – pirate treasure, dead bodies and the like.

Midway along the fence were the remains of what had once been a grandstand, reduced by the passing of time to three plank seats set one above the other on sturdy supports. With the help of a stout stick from the hedge and an old curtain this was transformed into a ship on which the boys sailed the oceans world wide. When the voyage was over the same curtain would be draped over the seat to make a tent. One end of the grandstand was sacrosanct, reigned over by the girls, and woe betide any over energetic young lad who strayed too far over the invisible dividing line and trespassed there

143

into the domain of the housewives with all their 'paraphernalia' gleaned from the Destructor.

To the uninitiated the Destructor was our name for the local refuse tip. In the days of 'netties', ash and cinders were carried from the house to the yard closet; the council men had the unenviable task of emptying the 'netties' each week, under cover of darkness, and transporting the contents to the Destructor to be burned. Other articles of household waste were also disposed of in the same place. Through the many holes in the fence we raided the refuse piles, being careful to avoid detection by Old Stivy, the furnaceman. From this endless source came pots and pans, trays and tins, vases and boxes, ensuring that the grandstand kitchens were always well equipped and decorated.

Along the bottom edge of the field was the colliery site, now closed and deserted, its ruined buildings offering wonderful opportunities for exploration. One of my earliest memories is of the blind pit ponies being brought to the surface for the last time when the pit closed and being let out into the grassy fields. In spite of their blindness, resulting from years spent underground, they were well fed and groomed. To us children, petting and stroking them, they did not seem at all pathetic nor were they abused. We lavished love and titbits on them before they were taken away. The pit was closed and they were no longer needed. With the closure of the pit another dimension was added to our world in the shape of the pit heap which sprawled across the corner of the field. This became the scene of many epic battles for on the other side lived the Bolchow Street Gang, frequently subjected to surprise raids from 'our lot' who scrambled up the pit heap, bombarded them with missiles and then beat a hasty retreat by sliding back to safety on tin trays purloined from the ever useful Destructor.

Perhaps the most memorable event to take place on the R.A. field in my childhood was the Bonfire Night which came mysteriously early one year. Preparations for Bonfire Night began many weeks before November 5th. Cardboard boxes, wood and any other suitable material was collected by the boys together with tree branches cut and dragged from Brusselton Wood some two miles away. Meanwhile the girls collected empty jam jars from neighbouring houses and took them to Taffy Rowland's scrapyard to exchange for a few coppers to be spent on fireworks. Frequent raids were made over the pit heap to despoil the Bolchow Gang's fire; likewise a guard had to be placed on ours to prevent any retaliation. The days were fraught with worry over the acquisition of enough rubbish and despair over any raid which depleted our stock.

This particular year we had excelled ourselves, for not only did we have a huge mound of combustible material but also in the centre was a space lined and roofed with boxes where we could sit in cosy comfort and discuss future strategy. Access to this den was through a very short tunnel also lined with boxes. For days this hideout was our pride and joy until suddenly disaster struck.

'Chicken' Baker, a rather precocious ten year old was experimenting with the great art of smoking. Having obtained two Woodbines from the slot machine for one penny he despatched me to get some matches from the kitchen, our house being the nearest. Being somewhat in awe of the worldly Chicken I duly obtained the matches and delivered them to him where he sat in the bonfire room.

Feeling guilty about stealing the matches I slipped off home to see if my Mam had missed them – I must have imagined her counting the matches in the box and missing the few I had taken! Because of this I missed the start of the fire which prematurely demolished our wonderful bonfire. Although there was no doubt that Chicken Baker's dubious smoking activities had started the conflagration he strenuously denied it.

How fortunate we all were that it was tea time – otherwise there could have been several small charred bodies pulled from our hide away when it went up in smoke!

Delsie Violette Simpson
Shildon

The Electric House

Mam heard of the 'Electric House' on her Friday shopping excursion in Church Street, Shildon. The house was at Cockton Hill, Bishop Auckland. It had no chimneys and no fireplaces – quite unheard of in 1924 - at least in our area!

Saturday morning found Dad, Mam and myself walking the two and a half miles, over the tunnel top, down Adelaide's Bank to South Church and on to Cockton Hill.

When we arrived at the house we found quite a crowd waiting to go in and view the wonder of electricity and we had to stand in the queue for what seemed to be ages – the people already inside were obviously making a most careful scrutiny of all the amazing appliances on show. The grown ups passed away the time chatting to each other, wondering how on earth did electricity reach Bishop Auckland? How was it installed in the houses? What would such an innovation cost? And, most important of all, how much did it cost to run?

At last, after what seemed to me an interminable time, we were allowed over the front step and into the entrance hall which was brilliantly lit by what appeared to be a small glass ball with wiggly lines inside it. It had a pretty shade covering it. All the other lights in the house were of a similar design. We learnt that the electric wires were let into the walls but what impressed me most at the time was the staircase light which you switched on at the foot of the stairs and switched off at the top. To my very young mind this was pure magic! All the way home to Shildon we talked of the wonders we had witnessed at the 'Electric House'.

The following week there were endless discussions between my parents and my Auntie Alice who owned the house. Eventually the great decision was made – we would have electricity installed. The men came and talked and measured and talked again. Our relations were quite sceptical about the whole thing and the neighbours thought we were getting ideas above our station! At last the big day came when the men arrived to begin work and suddenly the house was in chaos. Poor Mam, I think she rued the day she had ever heard of 'the electric'!

Our walls were chipped away near the doorways to let in long metal pipes through which the wires were fed; the staircase proved tricky until someone in higher authority sorted out the magical ways the switches worked; and, because my parents agreed to allow prospective customers to view the house in all its glory, we had another wonderful invention installed in the living-room - an adjustable light! This meant that Mam didn't have to stand on a chair to plug in the electric iron - amazing!

To this day I still have one of the original lovely glass lampshades from the first 'electric house' in Shildon.

Mary Lakeland
Worksop

Brusselton Sundays

The Old Engine House, Brusselton, now featured on the back of the current five pound note, was the home of William and Hannah Chisem and their descendants for four generations. My Da, eldest son of William and Hannah, occupied the railway house after grandpa's death. Da, Ma and eight offspring moved into the large stone built house in 1918, just before the end of the Great War.

The hamlet of Brusselton consisted of two rows of brick built terraced houses, North and South Terrace. The railway track ran between. Four stone built and thirty-nine brick built houses formed the sum total of occupied dwelling places of railway workers. Three industrious wives used their parlours as general stores – very handy for everyday meals.

My happiest memories are those of Sundays when I was aged between four and eleven years. Sunday was the only day when the whole family was at home. It began like this. Ma and Meg arose at 7a.m. went down the creaking stairs, through the front parlour, into the brick floored kitchen. First the hearth would be swept, ashes put into a bucket, newspaper sticks of firewood and coal would be laid in the grate then lit with a match. A metal blazer was then placed in front of the flames which were drawn up the chimney. The 'damper' was pulled out so that the side oven could be heated. Cold water from the back kitchen sink was taken in a bucket to fill the side boiler. It held about three gallons. There was a small brass tap on the side of the boiler to draw off hot water. That was too slow so a 'laving tin' was used to get larger quantities out of the boiler. Breakfast was then prepared and the clothes of the three youngest kids (not counting baby Dinah) would be placed in piles on the steel fender to warm a bit. These were our Sunday best.

On hearing Ma and Meg go downstairs Frank, George and I

would use the chamber pots from under our beds, then quietly go into the main bedroom - only on a Sunday. There in a massive four poster bed lay my Da. There were curtains around the top of the bed. The deep mattress was filled with straw - on top of that was a thick feather bed - covered with a linen sheet. Beds in those days were snug and warm. Covering my Da was a linen sheet, woollen blankets then a huge patchwork quilt which was home made. I, the youngest, would climb over my Da to snuggle in beside him at his left side. George and Frank would get into bed at the right side. Sometimes my Da would pretend to be asleep and invited a tickle to wake him. One of us would say 'Tell us a story Da.' Young Dinah remained in her cot until she was about three and Frank had decided to withdraw from the Sunday morning rituals.

All lying quiet and sung, my Da would start his many stories, how we loved every word of them and would correct him if he got the stories wrong (deliberately, we thought, as we grew older and wiser). We all knew time was almost up when he started his last tale, it was always the last and how we loved every word of them, either laughing or crying as the story developed and moved us. My Da was the best story teller in the world. Now quite happy to let 'the old man' roll over and doze off to sleep again, we kids would rush downstairs trying to be first to sit on the middle of the fender.

Friday night was family bath night, using a portable zinc bath on a large prodded mat by the fire. Hence Sunday morning we just had hands and face to wash - and sometimes rub our teeth with salt. Rushing back to the fireside we donned our Sunday best, then ready for breakfast. My Ma always saw that my hair was tidy and that my hair ribbons were securely fastened. We kept poultry on the top garden so always had a lightly boiled egg for breakfast on Sunday morning. Brother Frank was a dab hand at cleanly removing the tops of our eggs, all I had to do was to dip my buttered bread into the lovely golden yolk then with a teaspoon get at the set white. We sometimes had a drink of tea or milk.

By this time it was 10a.m. so off we went in turn across the yard into our front garden, where the 'netty' was. We did not have an earth closet like everybody else because the farmer responsible could not get his horse and cart anywhere near, to empty it with a shovel. Instead we had a large metal container placed under the netty seat, ours only had one hole, some families had two holes and one family had three, how time was saved there! Toilet paper was unheard of so we used cut squares of old newspapers which were strung up on a nail in the wall. After a short while Ma would say, 'Are you all ready for Sunday School?' If the united answer was 'yes' – 'then off you go and mind you behave yourselves.'

Brusselton Wesleyan Sunday School was always my favourite and doors opened at 10.45a.m. in readiness for 11a.m. prompt start. The place of worship was not an ornate specially built building, it was an empty terraced house converted and consecrated. It was used by all denominations who found the need for it. The Sunday School teachers were all male, some father and son together. The ladies of the families would be like Ma and Meg, preparing the Sunday dinner. The attendance register was strictly kept, a few hymns and prayers were said before the children were separated into classes, the older children were taken upstairs to the large Community multi purpose hall. We all loved our teachers and Sunday School but most of all how we loved the stories of Jesus. We all enjoyed singing and my favourites were 'Tell me the stories of Jesus', 'There's a friend for little children' and one we could raise the roof on – 'We are marching to Zion – beautiful, beautiful Zion'. There was very little disruption, we were taught obedience. On the odd occasion we would giggle if someone 'pumped' rather unwisely. The material incentive of regular attendance was Prize Giving. The best attender got the best Prize – a special book or Holy Bible.

After Sunday School we would return to our own homes for 'Dinner' usually served up about 12.30p.m. We were all together except my 'Da'. He was on the Committee of New Shildon Working Men's Club and was a founder member of The Railway Institute. He walked down to Shildon after his breakfast and returned at 2 to 2.30p.m. for his dinner which was kept hot for him. The dining table was huge and was covered with a patterned oiled cloth, which was waterproof and easily kept clean. It was oblong shaped – the narrow end fitted nicely by the seat in the kitchen window. The three youngest were settled in there out of mischief and danger of hot pots and pans. The three older lads occupied the long side and sat together on a long wooden settle. This left two sides for Ma and Meg to carve and serve up the meals, and space to sit down to join us. We all had good appetites, brother George was a bit 'finicky', he preferred sugar and milk and sliced apple with his Yorkshire pudding instead of thick rich gravy. We had plenty of home grown vegetables and we got a nice portion of meat on Sundays. The older lads naturally had bigger portions. The pudding was either rice or barley, there would be some disagreement as to whose turn it was for the favoured skin of the rice pudding. This may have been the first meal of the day for the working teenagers. They would dress up and go for a long walk meeting their friends both boys and girls.

Now it was time for the three 'young uns' to get back to Sunday School at 2 o'clock. This time The Anglican Church used the Chapel. Young men and women would be sent from All Saints Church to teach in the Sunday School. The teaching was much the same, stories of Jesus, learning new hymns, keeping a register and again Prize giving yearly. Our family soon built up a large library. After Sunday School we would walk and talk together before going home for tea. Tea was set out on the large table and all except Da would sit down. Whilst the rest of the family were out Ma and Meg would pop for a chat with one of the neighbours. Da would be in bed sleeping off what had been consumed earlier. Tea was nice, sandwiches and apple pie, then the Sunday treat, finish off with a good helping of custard and jelly. It was soon time to return to the Chapel for Wesleyan evening service at 6p.m. We needed a penny for the collection, all the young children sat on the three front wooden benches and were usually very attentive. My favourite preacher was Mr. Malvern a big white haired, white bearded missionary. He was lovely, so like Santa Claus and what interesting stories he told of working in Africa, India and South America. Occasionally we were given a special treat, lantern slides were shown in a darkened Chapel, which made the stories all the more interesting. The closing prayer said then home again to stay. Mother would be sitting in the large wooden rocking chair at the fireside. Da and Meg had both gone out. Meg to meet her boy or girl friend. Da back to the Club.

About 8p.m. the lads with their mates would start coming back to the Old Engine House for male voice choir practice. My brother Frank and a friend Wally Robinson had very good singing voices and led the singing until Meg and Da returned about 10.30p.m. We kids were put to bed at 8.30p.m. and were lulled off to sleep by the choir of about seven or eight. Mother was enjoying every minute and joining in. Doors were never locked and after the days gossip lights out – which was an oil lamp. Candles lit and so to bed a little after 11p.m. Good night and thank God for another lovely day.

Nancy Robson
Shildon

I'll Show you where I used to Play

'I'll show you where I used to play,'
I said to my child the other day,
Looking forward eagerly
Reliving with pleasure those halcyon days
Of childhood leisure.

I remembered with joy that lovely scene
The stream tinkling down through the meadow green.
There were games to play and flowers to press
Buttercups, daisies and watercress.

We'd play there all through the long summer days
Not minding the cows which came to graze.
In winter we'd sledge and snowball each other
Until the tea-time call from Mother.

I gazed with dismay at the dismal scene,
The roads and houses where once had been
My lovely meadow.
And I thought with rage,
'When she's my age,
What will be left for her?'

My 'halcyon days' were spent in Kimblesworth, just outside Durham
City, where I was born in 1922. 'My lovely meadow' was just on the
edge of the village where we used to pick daisies and buttercups.

My earliest memory is of the visit of King George V and Queen
Mary to Newcastle to perform the official opening of the Tyne
Bridge. We were all taken down to the Great North Road to wave

and cheer as they drove past on their way to Durham after opening the bridge.

Once a year we had the Rechabite Trip which we paid for by a penny a week throughout the year. We usually went to Roker or Whitley Bay for the day – it was the highlight of our year.

The other big annual event was the Big Meeting or the Durham Miners' Gala. We used to walk into town and follow the banners through the city and then listen to the speeches down by the riverside. One year we were a little late in setting off and as we were walking along the road a car stopped, it was the colliery manager who offered us a lift. That was my first ride in a car.

During the Miners' Strike in the 20s a soup kitchen was set up in the Miners' Hall. As my father was fortunate enough to continue working during this time (he was involved in safety down the mine) I was not entitled to free soup but all my friends were so I went along with them. The woman serving the soup must have noted the expression on my face because she said, 'Oh, let the bairn have some!' so I sat with my pals and enjoyed a free meal.

On fine Saturdays in the summer the whole family would walk to Finchale Abbey for a picnic. We couldn't afford to pay the penny to cross the footbridge over the Wear so we took off our shoes and 'plodged' to the other side.

My father studied in the evenings and eventually became an inspector of mines. When I was 12 years old we moved to Shotton Colliery but I still remember with affection those wonderful early days when the sun always seemed to shine on Kimblesworth.

Lavinia Love
(née *Powney*)
Billingham

The Peacock Inn

I remember the early years of childhood in an English country village just after the Second World War. You can still find that village if you look on a map today but, the Tanfield Village I knew and grew up in almost half a century ago has gone for ever and remains only in memory.

The years of early childhood were spent at the Peacock Inn, where my father was landlord, in the village of Tanfield near Stanley in County Durham. Here I lived with my mother and father, my elder brother and a wide assortment of pets. An Inn had stood on the site, it is believed, since Tudor times and the property was a fascinating mix of old and very old. We had public rooms, a warm cosy kitchen, cool cellars smelling of beer, a ballroom, an Edwardian sitting room, chilly bedrooms, stables, a coach house (for a stage coach naturally) a washhouse, buildings for storage and my own special secret garden. From the front door of the Inn you could see almost the entire village laid out before you. St. Margaret's Church, the village green, a red telephone box (essential for communication), a handsome farmhouse with a neat garden, rows of cottages and houses and the village hall where we celebrated the Coronation of Elizabeth II on a very wet day in June 1953.

This then was my world - the green where I played, the church where I went to Sunday School, the neat terraced house where my piano teacher lived, the farm where I went for the milk and the occasional pet and the Peacock Inn itself - a place of endless fascination.

Photographs capture time and I can look back through my album and see myself as a child smiling and laughing through the carefree days of childhood. One photo shows a small girl holding a much loved ginger Tom called 'Ginger' and wearing a rather smart

155

red outfit which was new – quite an achievement in 1948. It was all due to my mother's ingenuity, because the material was a dyed army blanket which my mother had sewn into an outfit for me using her old Singer hand sewing machine.

My father and mother worked hard to run the Peacock Inn. I don't remember whether business was good or not but they were certainly busy. The Inn was a large property and the main activities took place in our large, warm comfortable kitchen. Here we had meals sitting round a big old table, we listened to the radio and it was to this room that our visitors came. Its most prominent feature was an enormous black leaded kitchen range. It kept us all warm, produced mouth-watering meals, filled the house with the smell of the freshly baked bread which my mother made every week, various animals had been brought back to health and strength lying beside it – but, my mother hated it. She hated cleaning it and did it without fail every Thursday, my father usually kept out of her way as her mood was never very good. On Thursday morning the fire was never lit so that cleaning could take place and in the winter there would be a chill in the air which I did not like. I was always pleased when the range was lit and cheerfully burning. Since I didn't have to clean it or cook with it I didn't appreciate its failings and I was rather sad when in Coronation Year it was torn out to make way for progress. Behind it the builders discovered another even older eighteenth century semi-circular fireplace with spaces for people to sit and keep warm. This fired my imagination and now our home became the stuff of adventures. We moved upstairs to a modern kitchen and things were never the same again.

Outside were the stables and this was my father's domain. Before he became a landlord he had been a professional jockey and his love of horses remained with him throughout his life. He was happy to have a horse to care for, and having an extensive knowledge of veterinary medicine acquired from his years in racing stables meant that there was often a horse staying with us. I used to like going into the stables with its smell of fresh hay, mustiness, the sharp tang of liniments and the sound of my father grooming the horses. The stables couldn't have changed much over the years apart from a rather dusty poster 'how to spot German aeroplanes' and the brown painted wooden swing which my father placed for me in the doorway. I was never afraid of the horses even though they must have seemed hugh powerful animals to such a small child. My especial favourites were the huge cart horses who used to pull the dray with the all important supplies of beer. They would travel all the way from the Vaux Brewery in Sunderland delivering beer and they always stayed overnight with us. They were indeed gentle giants and the fear, and at the same time excitement, when they would take a sugar lump or some apple from my hand defies description. The hugh soft wet tongue and the enormous eyes that looked down at me were something to remember for ever.

Near the kitchen door was a narrow alley which led to a door in a wall. I would lift up the rusty latch and go into my own special secret garden. It covered about half an acre of land and was surrounded by 10 foot high walls. In my father's tenure it was a wilderness but I loved every part of it. In one corner grew a large flourishing lilac and every Spring it would produce drooping mauve flower heads and the air would fill with a heady scent. I had an eccentric Great Aunt who came every year at lilac time to stay with us so that she could admire this bush in bloom. Further into the garden was a peony rose which used to produce every year gigantic beautiful red flower heads. I loved this flower so much that I had all my beloved pets buried beside it – the cats and the rabbits. It seemed to me to be a fitting memorial to my faithful friends.

I remember freedom. There were boundaries, but within reason I went where I wanted without fear. My border terrier, Trixie, was my constant companion of these early years. She was a present from my brother who brought her home from the farm where he was working. He kept it a secret so that it would be a surprise and I remember hearing his footsteps as he walked down the long passage to the kitchen and her head popping out from his working jacket as he told me, 'This is the surprise I promised.'

There comes a time, however, when the pace and rhythm of childhood change and the first day of school looms on the horizon. I looked forward to this with fear and excitement and my first day is etched firmly in my mind. Getting up early in the dark January morning, dressing in front of the cheery kitchen range, father giving my shoes their final polish and the journey on the bus with my mother and the other village children. I went to the Tanfield Lea Infants and on the very first day I fell in love. The object of my affections was my first teacher, Miss Robinson. I can't recall her

157

features after so many years but I remember a soft spoken voice, a pretty flowered overall, the rags she kept in her pocket for wayward noses, a feeling of security when I was with her, and the joy as I took my first steps into the world of learning. When it was time to go home my father came to collect me and he would often tell this story about our journey home. When we arrived in the village we went past the house of my formidable piano teacher who came out to speak to us. 'Have you had a good day at school?' she enquired and followed this with a silly remark that adults often make to small children, 'And what are you going to be when you grow up?'

According to my father my answer was without hesitation, 'Oh,' I said, 'I'm going to be a teacher just like Miss Robinson.'

I like to think that not only my father would be pleased but also Miss Robinson and my piano teacher for when grew up I took after them both and became a music teacher.

There are many other memories to recall, some happy, some sad. The day Ginger went missing and was found a day later stuck in the washhouse chimney, happy Christmases, my 5th birthday party when the entire village were invited, my brother's 21st birthday, filling the feather beds after the Christmas birds had been plucked, the day sweets came off the ration, Ginger being buried under the peony rose and the day my mother almost died. Sometimes it seems as if all these events took place only yesterday and yet it was a long time ago and the world of my short childhood doesn't exist any more.

Margaret Pattinson
Belmont
Durham

Susie

I am 4. My head hurts, it is dark. My head hurts and I can feel the darkness. I am lying on the settee in the sitting-room. I can hear the clash of the oven door from the next room and then my aunty puts something warm on my chest and back. It makes me feel comfortable and the blackness goes and there is nothing.

I have been asleep, my throat hurts and my head still hurts. My mam stands beside me like an angel. I am hot and my head hurts with a terrible pain. Maybe I can't see, because everything is black or is it always night time? Oh my head, my head! The oven door slams again and I feel my aunty comforting me with warmth on my body. The head pain is unbearable – then it is gone.

I am in a warm, quiet, serene place. The sky is blue as though painted and the grass is like a bowling green. I am playing with my friend, Susie Sellars – we are sitting on a blue checked blanket. I recognise it – it is the one my mam puts on the lawn in the back garden for me to play on – she says grass is always damp and I must never sit on it without a blanket. Susie has black hair and is plump and four years old, like me. Where has she gone? I can't see her or the blanket either. I like this place, it is so peaceful – I wonder if it is heaven – I have no pain here. I wish someone would stop saying my name, Mary – Mary – Mary – over and over again. They are making me leave this place and I want to stay here. I don't want to go back to the hurt in my head.

I am back in the sitting-room. It is daylight and my head doesn't hurt now. My mam is saying, 'The doctor says she can have anything she fancies – guess what she's asked for – chips – she's only eaten one but that's a start. She seems to understand and she seems to hear. Thank God.'

Someone gives me nasty medicine – I refuse it. 'We will get it changed for some nice medicine – here is the new medicine.' They can't fool me by walking into the yard and coming straight back with the same medicine, but I will humour them. I have been ill. I laugh and laugh and everybody laughs with me and the room is filled with happiness. The next time I go out to play I am going to call for Susie, but my mam says Susie has gone to heaven. I tell my mam I know because I was with her. Why hasn't she come back? Her mam must not have called her name, Susie – Susie, as my mam had.

Twenty-one years later, after the death of my mother I recalled this event and my aunt and father told me there had been an epidemic of meningitis at that time. I had contracted it and so had my little friend Susie Sellars and she died from it. The clash of the oven door was kaolin poultices being taken from the oven to be used for relieving the pains in my neck and chest. I had at one time appeared to be unconscious and seemed to be slipping and sleeping 'away'.

My mother never told me I had meningitis as in those days if you did not die from it – it left you deaf or simple minded. It left me all right – I think...!

Pit Strike 1984-85

It was 5.30a.m. After a few hours of exhausted sleep I was awake again. The police! Please let them have abandoned the seige. I eased out of bed, crept across the bedroom floor, looked through the net curtained window. They were still there, across the field, beside Station Bridge with their cars and vans. Hundred strong, high helmeted, blue shirted police, intent on stopping the 'flying' pickets bringing help to their 'marras' at Easington pit. Waiting.

Beyond Station Bridge the North Sea was briskly pushing waves to shore in all directions. No uniformity. White horses haphazardly leaping. The August sun already hot sending flashing sparks off the water. The power of nature – watching.

One glance took in this familiar scene. I have lived in this colliery owned house in this colliery owned street for twenty years. My neighbours sea, railway, pit. I know the mood of the sea reflects the mood of the land. I went back to bed.

I lay worrying about the agitation bouncing from the sea. I

listened to it. I was trying to get used to waking without hearing the clang of coal trucks racing across Station Bridge. Noise that I had never noticed till it was not there. The whistle of engines and warning hoots from the pit yard were my background music. Now hollow silence echoed.

The bedroom window was open, a slight breeze from the sea rattled the catch. Alert, alarmed, a muted noise. Strange to me - I couldn't identify it. I might as well get up. The alien sound drew me to the window.

Thunderstruck I gaped. The field was full of marching striking pitmen. Voices silent, their feet making the mystifying drumming sound, muffled by the grass. As they left the field for the road to the pit it did not empty. More men poured after them keeping the field full.

I hurriedly dressed. The gate slammed. My husband, Jim, a bronchitic retired pitman, was already on his way to the pit. As I opened the gate he was shouting from the bottom of the street, 'Hurry up you've never seen things like this except on the tele!' The pulley wheels were there in the background, black steel silhouetted against the sky blue backcloth. Immovable.

The situation was a lone pitman strike breaker trying to get to work in the pit yard. The police had been helping him day after day. Pickets were drafted in from all over the country to keep him out. Hundreds and hundreds of police from all over the country were detailed to get him in. Hence the police blockade on the main road at Station Bridge. The pickets outwitted them by leaving their buses at Horden and walking through the fields to Easington Colliery.

A contingent of police were at the other end of the village too. Today they had got the scab into the pityard.

So I went. About two thousand people were assembled. The noisy buzzing of angry voices hummed through the crowd.

Suddenly there was complete silence. Hundreds of pitmen in casual shirts and jeans crowded at the top of the sloping wasteland that overlooked the pit gates. The police immaculate in their summer uniforms, blue shirts, well pressed trousers and imposing helmets with visors guarding their faces. Holding a shield in one hand and a truncheon in the other in orderly rows like soldiers ready for battle faced them. Power.

'Zulu! Zulu! Zulu!' the pitmen began to chant. The film about a

Zulu war starring Michael Caine had been on tele that week, the scene was reminiscent of a battle in that story. Then the stone throwing began. The miners surged forward. The police advanced to meet them. A police helmet was snatched and thrown in the air.

The situation appeared uncontrollable. Gradually pit lad after pit lad was arrested. The police were in control. The prisoners were bundled into police vans that came from nowhere. Sirens screaming they sped away from Easington to police cells – well organised.

Some of these pitmen were sacked by the N.C.B. and never employed in pits again. They did not think that fighting to keep pits open would end in their being blacklisted.

The words of my father, dead a score of years came into my mind: 'No good ever came from a pit strike'. He had lived through the 1921 and '26 strikes so I knew he talked a lot of sense. Every time there was an election, local or otherwise he quoted Churchill, 'If they don't work, shoot them', referring to the miners. So if I am a bit prejudiced, it is inherent. The strike was about pit closures. My father had worked in many different pits – Black Prince, Hedley Hill, Hedley Hope, Sunniside and a few more that had closed. Eventually he felt settled in Easington. He called it a 'long life' pit. He was sure he would end his working life here but he insinuated some would not. But he was also sure more pits would open as had always been the way when one closed. Coal would always be needed – my dad said.

I have every reason to dread pit closures with no new pits in the offing. My home, food clothes and nearly everything I own has been bought with money earned at the pit.

The crowd dispersed. A few miners lingered in little groups. Angry but now knowing how to cope with the situation.

The summer was hot. I had never seen so many men walking about the place. Drawn to the pit some would stand and look up to the pulley wheels, still and silent. Others dawdled slowly past, eyes downcast as if unable to look the pit 'in the eye'.

Savings were used up. Insurance policies cashed. The sea was unnaturally calm. The horizon invisible behind a moving haze of silvery dazzling mist which could be hiding a mysterious friend, or enemy, or oblivion.

There were many scenes of violence anger and emotion. Men were arrested for shouting at the police and other men were forced back to work through poverty and despair. One day there was a scuffle between a lone miner and the police among a crowd. He fell to the ground as he was being arrested. He lay face down. Some onlooking miners watched as though emotionless, others turned their heads away. The police pinioned his arms. No one helped him. This was the changing trend, caused not by fear of being injured or arrested but by the overhanging threat of being blacklisted by the N.C.B. Me? I took a photograph.

The summer turned to autumn. The weather changed dramatically. The North Wind was so cold it just about 'cut your face off'. Sleety snow gale blown from the North Sea tasted of salt. Fuel became a necessity. Many wood fences disappeared. The denes became bare. The young ones needed to keep their young ones warm. The trees would grow again. Coalmen toured the streets selling coal. Polish coal they said! Some said it was 'Easington coal'. I tried not to think how it was acquired as I bought it. All pitmen received a coal allowance as part of their wages and were unused to having even to think where household fuel came from, now they had no money to buy it.

I was lucky enough to be working. Through my job I met a lot of pregnant girls. One day a young woman arrived at the ante natal clinic. Her baby was overdue. She and her husband carrying a toddler had walked seven miles. They had no money for fares. Desperation made them do it. They did not walk home. From then on we made sure all patients had their fares one way or another. One of my colleagues was adept at arranging lifts and making sure no one 'lost face'.

March 1985, a strange dark cloud had been hanging over the sea for weeks. The water looked as though it was boiling and as though every now and again a huge rock was hurled from the sea dropping back heavily sending spray a mile high in the air. The mood was reflected on the land, the miners were restless; some not wanting to give in, others wanting to get to work for money to settle their debts.

The seemingly endless strike ended in March 1985. I stood on the crowded pavement and with a lump in my throat watched the pitmen of Easington parade down the main street to the waiting pit open gates. The colourful pit banners fluttered and flapped in the spring breeze. Next the colliery brass band, playing a rousing march. Feet moving in tune, a thousand men in harmony, not triumphant but unbowed.

Relief and frustration were on parade, grim expressions. Union officials Billy, Alan, Bob, Dennis, in the lead. Jack father of four, Joe with two, Keith with one, newly married at the beginning of the strike. Dull eyed, worried faces. Marching.

The shopkeepers came to their doorways. Suddenly the mood brightened. Pay notes to come. Bonuses to be earned. A man started to applaud the shopkeepers, then another until the whole parade and the spectators joined in. Shouting their thanks to each shopkeeper by name for their loyal support they proceeded. These traders had regularly given food to the soup kitchen organised by the women. Also two thousand pounds in cash.

Clapping. Marching. Faster tempo. Hop, skip and a jump to the band. Appreciation shouted. The shopkeepers too had suffered. Not a dry eye on the route. Retired pitmen, women and supporters wept – and me. No victory. The procession disappeared through the pit gates. It was over.

If anything was gained from the strike I have not heard of it. The words of my father, a pitman for more than fifty years, echo in my ears.

Mary Bell
Easington Colliery

Easington Colliery in the Thirties

I was born in Easington Colliery, Co. Durham, in 1923, and lived in the main street there, until we moved away, during the very first week of the Second World War.

My family had a greengrocery business, Bunton's Fruit Shop, and I have vivid memories of my life there.

Although the atmosphere of the early thirties was one of depression, Easington was at that time, much more vibrant than it has been in modern times. Miners' work was by no means secure, and often crowds of dismally clothed men would stand around for hours on the main street corners, near the Black Diamond Hotel, Barclays Bank corner, or across the road, near the miners' hall or the old church hall. Many weeks they only managed to work for two or three days. On idle days, 'schools' of men could be seen, gathered in a circle, playing pitch and toss, a gambling game, which I'm sure most of them could ill afford to lose! As a small girl, all I could see, was the coin being tossed up in the air, and the sudden scurried dispersal of the crowd, if the police should come near.

Sometimes, a fist fight would take place 'out our back'. A circle would be round them, friends from each side egging on their respective hero.

Quite busy every day, the main street was a hive of activity on a Saturday night. Tempting, savoury smells would float out of Cavanagh's pork shop, dips and ducks being very popular.

A paper lad would be shouting 'Echo-er,' competing with the Salvation Army band, coming up the street in full blast, to form a circle on our top corner, which was just three doors up. Here, there would be a playing session, interspersed with members of the band stepping into the centre, to proclaim how they were converted.

My playmates and I used to listen, fascinated, and quite often follow, when the band formed marching order again and proceeded up to their 'citadel'. At the ensuing service, we were given a star on our attendance card, and with six of these, we would be qualified to attend a free pie and peas supper, trust me to develop measles when that happy occasion arrived!

A highlight of every year, was the annual carnival, and in those days, there were a lot of adult jazz bands, sailors, pearly kings and queens, busbies, all kinds of uniforms, all with proudly flying banners. Behind them, came a long crocodile of fancy dress entrants, decorated horse drawn carts and of course, the colliery band. All wended their way to the welfare grounds.

I only took part in a parade once, that was for the Silver Jubilee, when all the school children marched up from the Trust Hotel. I amazed myself, by managing to win a relay race as the last leg, and I can remember being called to the headmistress's room, to be presented with a box containing four toilet soaps - one each!

Funerals were the occasion for another kind of parade. Glass hearses and carriages, with glossy black horses, (Jacky Mitchell's) followed by a long crocodile of darkly dressed people, in pairs. Everyone in the street stood still and the men took off their caps, until the hearse had passed.

If the death was a colliery fatality, which sadly happened too often, then there'd be the colliery band, with draped banner, and a rendering of 'The Dead March' - very moving.

I could have a grandstand view of all the parades, as I could stand out, above the shop front, below our upstairs front room window.

Every year, my friends and I would eagerly look forward to the opening of 'Galley's' Christmas bazaar, when magically, their shop would be extended, and we were allowed to go through into an extra room, filled with toys. I could buy lovely little coloured beads for tuppence, which would give hours of pleasure, as we made necklaces for our dolls. Crepe paper, at the same price, would make fancy outfits for the concerts, which we inflicted on our families from time to time.

Each year, I would be awakened one morning, to Boom! Boom! Boom! as the local band set off for Durham Big Meeting. I was terribly travel sick as a child, so I never managed to go to see this happy event, but my heart stirred to the sound, and in the evening, when they returned, I'd watch the band march down our street.

Tramps quite often paid calls, in our back yard, and they usually got something, perhaps a sandwich, or a pair of boots, once, even my Dad's dinner, which he missed, through being at a football match! Boys would knock at the back door, to offer a pail of coal for sale, a penny for duff, tuppence for roundies. They were never refused, and we knew that as soon as they had enough, they would run up to the pictures!

Times were hard then, but there was a wonderful feeling of belonging. Our property was duly swallowed up, in an extension of Barclay's Bank, so I suppose I can now claim that I was born in a bank!

Never mind, it's not everyone who can say they were born in a place where you can be in Canada, Wembley and even 'Paradise', all in the space of a day!

I hope and trust that Easington will survive the present troubled times, and emerge happily, as it deserves to do.

Vera Sykes
(née *Bunton*)
Ashington

Taties in a Pit Stocking

I remember...
When I had a sore throat my Nana would boil potatoes in their skins, mash them on to a clean white cloth, put them into an old pit stocking and wrap it round my neck.

If there was an outbreak of influenza onions were cut up and placed in every room. (I still do this and I am convinced it works!)

My grandparents had six sons and four daughters and we all went to their house for family gatherings and meals.

My Nana and my mother made clippy mats and I had to help by cutting the cloth into strips.

The walls were painted with distemper and then decorated by dipping a sponge in coloured paint and dotting it all over to make a pattern. Sometimes narrow strips of paper border were put round the walls - just as they are today.

Front door steps were scrubbed and painted white or red. Often when you cleaned your step you would do your neighbour's as well.

At school we were taught the 3Rs plus home nursing, child welfare and first aid. If you did wrong you were punished, often with the cane.

I came from a mining family and at meal times the men were always served first and always had their own chair that no one else would sit in.

We had a wireless and I used to have to take the batteries to the local shop to be charged up.

All the washing was done in a poss tub and I was bathed in the same tub.

We were taught to be clean, respect other people, never spend more than we earned, be content with simple things and make the most of what life brought - not a bad set of rules to live by!

E. Stevens Davison, Easington Colliery

The Inkerman Mining Tragedy

History needs practical people as well as scholars.
Butchers, bakers, and candle-stick makers,
And he who toiled by the light of the candle -
The miner.

D ark and bitterly cold was the morning of January 14th 1934, and facing the grim duty of arduous tool and its attendant dangers, the miners of Inkerman wended their way to their customary labours.

The three drift mines, Ballarat, Main Coal, and Mossy Burn Busty, all belonging to the Inkerman Colliery had that morning started up some two hours earlier, to allow the men to attend the funeral of the colliery owner, his wife, and their two children, later in the afternoon at Crook.

The owner of the colliery was Joseph Edward Wailes of Crook, an inveterate gambler whose actions were to lead to death and unhappiness. His pits had always made a steady profit enabling him to maintain a fine house and chauffeur driven car. But as his gambling debts increased he was forced to borrow capital from other coal industrialists. As can be expected he lost every penny. He returned to his home, a broken man, shot his wife and his two children, then turned the gun on himself.

This ruthless action bore heavily on the minds of those workers beginning that early shift on January 14th, the day of the funeral. Work had hardly commenced when word reached us that John Robert Bradwell, known as Rocky, had met his death due to subsidence in the Ballarat seam that lay under the Black Moss. All men were summoned to gather at the Blacksmiths Cabin that stood on the causeway across the Inkerman Pond. We were told that our assistance was not required, we could only wait. The older men

169

clustered around the blacksmith's fire and lit their candles whilst the younger ones stood out in the cold.

I can recall other accidents at the pit, one or two fatal, but nothing like the big explosions that occurred down in the south east of the county, or for that matter the West Stanley disaster of 1909. As far as I can recall there wasn't any gas at the Black Prince or the Inkerman collieries. At these pits men could work at the coal faces by the light of candles stuck into pit props.

Their wages during the 1920s and the early 1930s were always below £2 for a six day week which may account for the nondescript clothing.

All were in pit 'claes' - no pit head baths in those days, no protective helmets; a motley crew, some in cloth caps, some wearing women's felt hats, minus the brims, and some with berets. Some were wearing normal slacks, others cut down old trousers to just below the knee with long blue woollen stockings. Odd ones had donned top-coats, many old macs. All had saddened, black smudged faces.

Then lights appeared at the mouth of the hillside drift. Soon the stretcher bearers, their heads bared, passed between the waiting comrades into the blacksmith's shop. The body was shielded from public view by a great blanket. The poor beggar's dirty boots, covered in pit sludge projected from under the blanket. His pit bottle and bait tin were put aside. His feet were rested on the anvil - Just another sacrifice on the altar of commerce, an experience that saddened all, even to the verge of tears. A magnificent comradeship, the like of which I have never met elsewhere.

Robert Lowes Graham
Billy Row, Crook

The Days of my Childhood in Tow Law

When I look back through the years I realise what remarkable changes have taken place in Tow Law!

I lived my early life down at Thornley Road Ends, later known as Canada – why, I don't know. Alas, the group of houses is no longer in existence. A passing stranger would never suspect that there, in that place, once lived a strong community of neighbourly, friendly people – some eccentrics and a few fly-by-nights and law breakers included, but still good friends and supporters of each other. This, then, is my account of that part of Tow Law.

Going back to the eccentrics, just one example to titillate your imagination! In Thornley Road there lived an old woman and her husband, Mr. and Mrs. Entwhistle. In their 'one up and one down' house they kept a flock of White Wyandotte hens and a big black and white cat.

One morning the front door opened and out scuttled the hens, followed by the cat, all dyed a bright henna red to match the old lady's hair which she regularly coloured! What consternation that caused – but in mitigation it must be said that the old lady's mind was somewhat deranged. It transpired that her only son had been hanged for murder in Leeds Jail.

An early recollection is of Furnace Bank, now Wolsingham Road, I think, when as a child I used to watch the lamplighter lighting the gas lamps on the bank. There were three, one at the top, one in the middle and one at the bottom. It was a ritual that used to fascinate me.

On the bank itself there were three public houses, Donaghy's at the very top, one in the middle and at the bottom, the Belgian House. This had once belonged to the Tow Law 'millionaire', Joss Richardson and during the First World War was occupied by a

171

family of Belgian refugees – hence the only name I ever knew it by. After the war they returned to Belgium and other families lived there. I remember the Pearts whom I used to visit to see my teacher, Louie Peart, later Mrs. Raper. She was very kind to me and encouraged my love of English Literature and poetry. The building had many rooms but I remember the bar and one bedroom with an old iron bedstead bolted to the floor. Sadly the building fell into decay and was demolished in later years. Over the road from the Belgium House was a field at the top of the old ironworks. The British Legion hired the stables in it and converted them into a clubhouse. On the land they built tennis courts, a croquet lawn (I played on it myself) and a bowling green. We oldies still refer to it as the Bowling Green. This was in the early 1920s and every summer there was a tennis tournament and Tow Law people used to sit on the banks above the courts and watch. It aroused great interest and was a well supported rendezvous on summer evenings. Of course there was great unemployment and poverty in those days.

Our 'Angel of Mercy' in those days was my dear late mother, Elizabeth Hindmoor. She was here, there and everywhere in Tow Law, births, deaths and marriages just a few of her accomplishments. She also took in sewing – making new clothes for children out of old garments. From the 1920s to the 1940s she delivered almost all of the Tow Law babies. There was no NHS then and she frequently brought babies into the world without either doctor or nurse in attendance. She had some bad cases but never lost a baby or a mother.

Similarly she attended the dying and saw to the laying out. I well remember one gruesome case where the man had committed suicide. We used to say that she was never in the house – always attending to someone else, but we children all had our household tasks to perform after school such as polishing the fire irons. Mother washed and baked bread for the women who had been confined – she had a heart of gold and a nerve of steel.

Pig killing was always a bloodthirsty scene – I remember one in our backyard. The two entrances were blocked to prevent the pig escaping and a butcher's assistant was chasing it all round the yard trying to kill it. Everyone was shouting and the pig was squealing with terror. We children watched from the gate until we were chased away. We sometimes used to go into houses where we knew there

172

had been a death and view the corpse in the coffin. These scenes never appeared to upset us but I don't know what present day psychologists would say of us! Peculiar times.

In the summers of poverty children would go to the slag heap and riddle for cinders to keep the 'home fires burning'. In 1927 I saw my first total eclipse of the sun - all Tow Law was on the Cutting Bridge at 6.30 in the morning. It was eerie in the darkness and silence of the early morning - not a bird sang. I could recall many other incidents, like the day Mother joined the first Labour Group for women in Tow Law; or a neighbour coming home on leave from France in the Great War - I can still picture his puttees and remember us trying the terrible biscuits he brought with him. They were small and as hard as iron - I believe they were known as 'hard tack'.

I wonder, have all the changes brought with them the Zest for Life we had in those days, despite the hardships we suffered?

Ida McAninly
Tow Law

Wolsingham 'Grammar'

In 1973 Wolsingham Secondary was still a 'Grammar School' which meant that entry was by selection. I can remember how pleased my parents were the morning they received the letter confirming my place.

For many people their first day at secondary school is traumatic. In my case I found the whole experience quite boring. We were ushered into the Assembly Hall and subjected to a long and boring speech from the Headmaster who then proceeded to read out the class lists and we filed out with our allotted form teacher. In the classroom we were seated in alphabetical order, tidy rows of small children in immaculate uniform, even down to the baggy regulation navy knickers which, rumour had it, could be inspected by any teacher at any time by the simple expedient of lifting up our skirts! The truth was that two weeks later these monstrosities had been replaced by fashionable flowery ones.

Uniform was very strict. My mother bought me two red jumpers with black stripes around the neck and I was told they were not acceptable. We couldn't afford to buy new ones so I had to turn the stripe in and hope no one noticed.

In 1975 there was great excitement when it was announced that girls would be allowed to wear trousers in the winter. The local shops were sold out in two days.

Fashion was very important to us in those days but the only time we could indulge in it was at the school parties. When I look back now at some of the outfits I wore then I cringe.

In the first and second years I wore long 'crimplene' skirts - one was peach and one was a purpley colour because Donny Osmond had said that purple was his favourite colour. Both were hand made and worn with pride.

By the time I had reached the fifth year 'punk' was all the rage but we didn't have the nerve to go dressed in black plastic bin liners.

As a sixth former I felt very sophisticated in a dress sold to me by my best friend because it was too tight for her. It was cream with pink and mauve flowers, a flared skirt and quite a revealing low cut bodice with shoulder straps - very daring! So daring in fact that I kept my cardigan on all night!

That same night we had celebrated our new found maturity by going to the Black Bull for drinks first. This obviously gave me the courage to 'head bang' and 'pogo' all over the dance floor - much to the disapproval of the staff.

I was notoriously bad at games, never liking to catch a ball in case it hurt. The only activity I enjoyed was cross country running - not that running played a large part in it, more of a gentle stroll enlivened by a quick jog past the marshalling points.

Domestic Science lessons were always a fiasco. I remember making pancakes and, on being told to use only half the mixture, I promptly poured all of it into the frying pan. The resultant mess was a pancake half an inch thick. We were supposed to eat our concoctions but I threw mine out of the window. Even the birds wouldn't eat it.

English was my favourite subject and I enjoyed working in those lessons. I shall always be grateful to the English teacher who encouraged me to persevere and attain my goal of eventually studying the subject at University.

I still feel privileged that I went to the 'Grammar' although I do feel that the system had its shortcomings. The curriculum was very academic and narrow in many respects but on the whole I enjoyed my time at Wolsingham.

Dorothy Menzies
(née *Donald*)
Livingston, West Lothian

Running Waters

I was born in 1913 at Running Waters as were all my family. My grandfather worked the farm, which is no longer there, and a stream ran right through the farmyard, giving the place its name. Nearby were four houses rebuilt into two, one for my mother when she married. All six of us were born there.

Next door was the public house which was finally enlarged by taking over our house when my parents died and the family left home. The pub, the Three Horseshoes, is now a popular inn on the main Hartlepool-Durham road. My father planted daffodils in front of it. I hope they are still there.

We all have such happy memories of living on the farm, helping with the work through the different seasons. We had to carry water from a well half a mile away and rain water was collected for washing.

I can just remember my grandfather who died when I was 2 years old. My grandmother ran the farm after that and lived until I was 15. She was known as Grandma Gibson, the grand old lady of Running Waters, who worked hard and was loved and respected by all who knew her. I am called Rachel after her.

Rachel Gale
(née *Johnson*)
Redcar

The High Tops School

Neville's Cross High Tops School was so called because Algebra and French were taught and pupils stayed on after the official leaving age which, in the 1920s, was in Standard Four. It was a very popular school and parents tried hard to get their children in.

The form rooms were two rooms above the Co-op shop. We had no playing fields, only a rough asphalt yard. Every week we formed a crocodile and walked along to Neville's Cross College where the students took us for games. We used to love those days.

Each morning we had prayers and a hymn, usually 'Jerusalem the Golden', which still reminds me of school. Then we had Mental Arithmetic when the teacher would dart around the classroom asking all of us questions. For punishment you got black marks and when you had three black marks you were sent to the headmaster, Mr. King. The long walk to his study was more of a punishment than the cane. He would let us off lightly, only tapping the palms of our hands.

It was a happy school and prepared us well for the Scholarship or 11+ examination. We didn't worry too much about this, if we passed we were pleased but if not, we just accepted it. The year I took the exam eleven of us passed, two boys who went to the Johnston Grammar School and nine girls who went to Durham Girls County School. We thought this was great as it had playing fields, a gymnasium and many amenities lacking at the Tops School. We were the lucky ones!

Doris A. Heron
Darlington

Buried Treasure

The morning is still dark and frosty as I pull my brother along in our home made bogie, the pram wheels making a squeaky sound. I hope they won't fall off until we come back again but still, I have a toffee hammer and some nails in my pocket, always be sure, I say.

The road is dark but not very long, so, passing the police training ground we come to the gap between the fenced off fields, down the slippery track, through a small tunnel lined on each side with grimy white tiles, walls dripping water from the overhead rail track. We splash into muddy water which throws up black smelly blobs. We smell the empty mussel shells, even before we see them lying in a massive pile at the bottom of the cliff.

Now comes the tricky part. In front of us, standing a couple of yards off the cliff edge, is a huge piggery. My brother jumps off the bogie and waits while I sit and pull a pair of old socks over my shoes. He already has his boots covered. Taking his hand I lead him along the narrow slippery cliff edge, our backs pressed against the pigs' house. It takes quite a while to make this journey. If he or I stumble, it's on to the rocks we go. We wouldn't be the first. If we went the easy way on the other side it meant the others would get there before us, and we wanted to get to the best pitch first. We make it. I leave him to remove his sodden socks and ease my way back along the cliff to get the bogie. There's never any problem in dry weather but today it's wet and icy and the wind has started. I must hurry before the rain comes. Our wooden friend is still sitting there. Making sure the sacks are still safely on board I guide and push the bogie along the path I have just taken. I have made this same journey so many times it's easy, even though I slip once as a nosy pig charges at the fence. It must want its breakfast. It's not the only one.

178

The path has now widened and I can see the large concrete steps that lead to the beach. The tide's out. Good. The sea is a long way off. This is the time when the sand smells clean. We get the bogie and make our way down the steps, being careful not to cause any hurt to it or ourselves. We are the first. I knew it! Not many will chance the cliff tops in this weather. Looking about we see just what we had come for. We take hold of the bogie's rope and run across the firm sand to the black mound being drained by the sea.

Small crabs race from us as we thunder along, laughing now. Noses running, feet tingling, stopping beside our treasure we pull away the coating of seaweed and see gleaming there, black shiny sea coal. It's all in one heap, we don't have to go raking all over the beach for it, but we have to go carefully. The sky is lighter now, so we can be sure of not mixing pebbles in with the coal as we fill the sacks. I don't want another beating just because a pebble jumped out of the last lot whilst on the fire. It wasn't my fault I ducked and it broke a vase, although it was the only one she had.

AT LAST! It has taken me hours to fill two good sized sacks. My back aches with bending down so long and even more after pushing and shoving them on the bogie. The third sack has been taken nearer to the sea by my brother. He is digging in the sand with a shovel far too long and wide for him. His sack is now filled with whelks that he has dug out of many holes, carefully cleaning the black shells in the sea before putting them in the now soaking wet sack. I call to him, and putting the wet sack on to the shovel, drag both towards the bogie. Muscles straining, we put the sack on top of the coal.

Looking around for the first time we see the others have joined us. There's a rag and bone man with his cart and horse; he and his mate are putting shovels full of sea coal straight on to the cart. The horse just stands there, waiting. Now I see many others, women with prams, sledges and bogies, all filling sacks. Some of the women are the same ones I have worked the fields with at tatie picking time. They wave and shout hello, and a chorus of 'Gawd, it's bloody freezing the day!'

Now we are ready for our journey back. I slip the rope around my waist and begin pulling slowly towards the cobbled slope beside the steps, brother pushing from the back. We get stuck half way up the bumpy slope, and two of the older women help us up the rest. We

179

now roll along, taking the wider, safer path, still having to pass the back of the piggery where the owner now stands, taking off his cart the slops he has collected from the shops and houses along the way. My stomach heaves seeing the greasy mess which slides and slips about the metal cans with potato peelings and cabbage leaves trying to escape. I'm glad I don't eat bacon.

Now, through the mud, then in and out of the tunnel, up the slope, slipping and falling, filthy from head to feet, we come to the main road, stopping to take a few deep breaths. I leave brother and run across the road to the nearest allotment fence, push back a couple of loose boards and pull out the first things I see. One turnip, four rhubarb stalks and two large beetroot. I hide the rhubarb inside my coat after taking off the leaves and flinging them back over the fence, take off my balaclava and put the turnip and beetroot inside and hide them all inside the sack of whelks. Looking around, brother is standing grinning. With a laugh we set off. If we hurry home and get cleaned up we'll make it in time for school.

Lorene Newton
Sunderland.

Glimpses of a Sunderland Childhood

When I was young we lived in a tenement building along with three or four other families, all sharing the one toilet and cold water tap in the back yard. Poverty and hardship seemed to bring us all closer together and the little we had we were willing to share. I can remember my mother making large pans of broth which she would take round to any of our neighbours whom she knew were short of food; when a new baby was born there was always a plentiful supply of secondhand baby clothes delivered to the door; in times of trouble there was always a friend to comfort you and share your problems. The sense of community was very strong.

In the late 1930s money was very tight and my mother used to take in washing to eke out the housekeeping. A large basket of washing would have to be hand washed, blued and starched and then ironed - for this she received the princely sum of 2/6d! And she used to sing at the top of her voice while doing it!

I remember coming home from school to be greeted by the lovely aroma of home baking, very little was bought in those days. After tea we would get out the proggy mat and sometimes the neighbours would come in and help, for them it was an opportunity to get together and have a chat and relax.

I was thirteen when World War II broke out, I can still hear the sound of the sirens and see my mother bursting into tears. We were all terrified and thought that we were going to be bombed there and then. Later on Sunderland was the target for quite heavy raids and we would be woken up three or four times in the night to go down the shelters - but we still had to go to work the next morning.

I got my first job when I was fourteen years old, in a bakery. One of my duties was to deliver bread to the lighthouse keeper down near the sea front. There were barricades of barbed wire and soldiers on sentry duty. I was convinced that we would be the first to be captured in the event of an invasion because there was a sign pointing out to sea reading 'Germany'! Eventually someone took it down.

People of my age lost their youth during the war as there was very little social life although I do recall some happy times at the local dance hall.

When I look back on those days I cannot help but marvel at our resilience and fortitude. My overwhelming memories are of happiness and comradeship.

Irene Hall
Sunderland

Life Begins at Nine

I lived at No. 11 in a street of terraced houses, three up and three down, tenanted by two families in each. Lighting was by gas and cooking by coal fired ovens. The water tap at the bottom of our yard was next to the magic throne (netty). Bordering our street were the church, the pub, and the local Empire Theatre, so we were catered for spiritually, socially and physically. Garden Place was in the centre of town, barren of gardens, but full of life.

Memories of my childhood started for me at nine years old – the beginning of the war, 1939; the underlying expectancy; the excitement we felt as the gas lighter failed to light the street light. The old brown venetian blinds in the windows of the houses were drawn and usually early, this was our first taste of the black out. After games of hide and seek in this lively black velvet night I became bored and went indoors, then a strange wailing noise both excited and frightened me. My mum explained that they were trying out the air raid siren – Oh! what fun! I didn't notice the worried look on mum's face – so started my war years.

My best friend was Pat, plump and jolly, my comrade for most of my wartime adventures.

At home our improvised air raid shelter was the pantry in the passage under the stairs. Mum took me under her wing like a chick and mother hen. We perched on the shelf and mum would drape her coat with the big fur collar around us. Through a tiny window criss-crossed with tape we would peer into the night. Frequent flashes of searchlight and gunfire lit the sky, wonderland. One night, impervious to mum's tense body, I was overawed to see a wondrous firework display, giant fireworks fell and lit up our tiny back yard. I remember my annoyance as mum dragged me out of the cupboard and ran with me to a house across the road. I soon cheered up when I saw the rest of my friends from our side of the street, all sitting down in the passage whilst our mothers congregated in the kitchen for a natter. We kids topped each other's stories of how many fireworks had dropped in our yards. It was later that I learned that the fireworks were incendiary bombs.

Usually our sojourn under the stairs was boring. Mum was deaf and in some respects I was too, with the big fur collar wrapped around my head. We often fell asleep and there we would be, crouching in the cupboard long after the all-clear had sounded. My hero, my 16 year old brother, would come and wake us up when he returned after his stint as messenger boy for the A.R.P. group.

I remember the night when manna dropped from heaven. The noise had been louder than usual, we had felt a tremor through the house, then lo and behold we had a yard full of assorted clothing and odd shoes. I learnt later that the shops around the corner had been bombed and we were now displaying their wares!

When finally the communal shelters were built we used to disburse to the nearest dug out in our school yard, in the shadow of the power station. Years later I learned of the dangerous significance of it being sited there.

Getting ready to go to the shelter was great fun, we were despatched to neighbours with young families, we helped carry the toddlers of the many large families who lived in the street. The lady next door had six children under seven years old. Her husband was in the Air Force.

Once in the shelter in the dim lights, it was boring, it did not offer the excitement of the wondrous views I had out of our twelve inch pantry window.

The women gathered for a gossip at the entrance of the shelter, kids in the middle where they would start us off in a sing song and then it would seem they forgot about us. After a couple of verses of 'Roll Out The Barrel' and listening to the women chattering about when the fruiterers were expecting their delivery of eggs, and then whispering about Mrs Smith being able to set a good table from what she got off the black market and how did she do it? Our interest started to wane. Mind you I looked on Mrs Smith with a new light, she might be a spy, using the monies the Jerries paid her to spend on the black market.

One night Pat and I explored the dark ends of the shelter and discovered a secret hatch (emergency exit). We lifted it up and gazed up at the sky, at the lovely patterns the search lights made. No one seemed to have missed us so we ventured outside, at first we were frightened to stray from the shelter in case we got a good hiding if found out.

Despite the noise and lights in the sky it was mysteriously quiet and dark on the ground. We walked around the school yard to soak in the mysterious night, it was as if we were the only ones alive. When we crept back no one had missed us, we sat next to the other kids and joined in on the second verse of 'There'll be Blue Birds Over the White Cliffs of Dover'.

However, the next time we were in the shelter we decided to go further afield, we slipped out as before, we left the school grounds and made our way in the dark towards the town, a few minutes walk away. We decided to sidle along against the wall in case anyone saw us, at least that's what we told ourselves, if truth be told I guess we were a wee bit frightened. As the guns boomed away little pieces of metal were falling to the ground. We later picked some up. I had my piece of shrapnel for years. We were just feeling safe on our little escapade when an air raid warden snapped:

'What are you kids doing out of the shelter? Get back in.'

With that, he shoved us to the door in Vaux Brewery where by now we had reached. We seemed to go down hundreds of steps, it was magic. Brightly lit, loads of room, barrels to sit on, someone was playing the accordion, two women were dancing. Just as Pat and I were congratulating each other on finding the place the all clear went, panic lit our faces. We flew out, ran panting back to our shelter and mingled with the other kids as they were coming out. We picked up our young charges and trundled home. Like a charabanc trip with blankets and baskets.

One day the grown ups in the street huddled together talking, there seemed to be an air a glee, the usual worried looks had vanished. Apparently a German plane had been shot down. Pat and I decided to find out where it was. We set off for the town centre, there must be a parade, we thought. The High Street was lined with people, there was an air of expectancy. Suddenly a huge lorry appeared and there on the back was the German plane, a huge cross identified it as such. A huge cheer went up

'We must be winning the war, Pat!'

After that we went sight seeing, looking at the bomb damage in the town, broken window frames and goods from the shops strewn across the pavement, piles of rubble where a shop had once stood. The idea that people may have been killed never once entered our heads. The innocence of childhood.

Pat and I had a couple more escapades from the shelter and visited Vaux's shelter again. It was a lovely feeling being in foreign territory albeit a different shelter. It delighted us to see the surprise of some of our school friends who lived in the area when they saw us in their shelter. Our little journeys were to end sooner than we thought. One night when in our own shelter the bombardment appeared heavier than usual. There were cries from the room as a particularly loud explosion shook the foundation of our shelter.

'My God our street must have gone!'

Must have gone where? What did they mean? We were soon to know. We trundled home to find a huge crater where the end two houses once stood. The earth at the top of the crater was level with the upstairs window of the house next to the bombed one. When we got to our house, there was no front door or windows, the back bedroom had caved in. Looking upstairs we could see daylight and a large metal object protruding through a hole in the roof. It was part of the huge water tank that had stood at the bottom of the street to provide emergency water supplies for the centre of the town. There was rubble everywhere. Dad appeared. I learned later that he had had a lucky escape, he had not gone to the shelter, he had been upstairs looking out of the landing window. When the bomb dropped he had been flung down the stairs and out of the front door. Fortunately no one had been killed, only our cat and its kittens that had been in a box in the back room.

The rest of that night and the next day was spent in the emergency shelter for the homeless, a classroom in Green Terrace School. It was great fun, there we all were, the neighbours from Garden Place sharing camp beds and canteen facilities, like one big happy family.

At this time of the war I was 13 years old and used to deliver morning and evening papers. I remember leaving Green Terrace shelter to do my morning paper round. I was feeling very self important, hadn't we been bombed out! I deviated a little from my paper round to call in and tell my auntie, mum's sister that we were homeless. I then went on to deliver my papers, but what devastation

I found! It seemed a whole row of my customers' houses had disappeared in the bombing raid. I later heard that two people had been killed. My older sister had been staying at her boyfriend's house down Hendon. It too had been bombed. She and Tony had arrived back at Garden Place expecting succour only to find that it too had received a hit.

In an amazingly short time (two days) with makeshift patching our house was once again habitable. I remember in the weeks that followed we used one of the badly damaged empty houses as our gang's den. We used to hold meetings there, make toffee cakes and sit around the fire, oblivious that the place was in danger of collapsing. It was our private place.

At one period of time it seemed we spent a lot of time in the shelters, if the siren went as I was going to school I used to be in a dilemma, whether to turn back home or carry on to school. School usually won, not because it was safe, we used to shelter in the cloak room, but because we used to have songs and say prayers for the relatives of class mates who were in the forces. The teachers always mentioned them by name. I used to stand next to Alice, the girl who lived next door to me, even if she was junior to me, because she had a brother in the Navy. You felt better if you actually knew someone abroad when prayers were said.

My dad had been an army reserve and had been called up at the outbreak of war, he served only a year and was demobbed because he was too old. Once the conscription got underway he could have stayed on as a traffic policeman, but he preferred to return home to his family.

Wherever you went outdoors you had to carry your gas mask with you. I remember the square cardboard box with the string around your shoulder. As the war progressed we became more fashionable, we used to have rexine gas mask holders, the shape of the mask and in pretty colours.

Pat and I vowed that as soon as we were old enough we would join the WRAF and go away to war. Unfortunately for us – but fortunately for the world at large – the war had ended before we could join.

I eventually did go on to join the WRAF in peace time – but that's another story!!!

Brenda Bloomfield, Sunderland

Sad Little Boxes

I was born in Harrison Buildings in 1913. I think these were some of the first council houses – at any rate they were viewed as very 'posh' and the tenants had to keep them sparkling clean otherwise they would be evicted. At the beginning of the war we moved in with my grandparents who managed the Kings Head in Warren Street, Barrack Square was our front street.

Father worked shifts on the railway and callers used to knock him up during the night to go to work. For the 14 years we lived there Mother never had a clock, we just went by the one on Pottery Buildings over the road.

After the war all the soldiers left the Barracks and therefore we were able to use this as a short cut to the South Docks where there was a beautiful beach. My Gran and other women used to buy lengths of unbleached calico which they would soak in soda and water, boil and then spread it out on the sands to bleach and dry in the sunshine.

I went to Moor Board School and every year we would celebrate Empire Day by marching in the school yard, saluting the Union Jack and singing patriotic songs. We always wore red, white and blue as far as possible. One year, when I was in the 'Big Girls' class I had a red and white cotton dress and Mother sent me to Joblings opposite the old market to buy ¾ of a yard of white ribbon – not satin because it wouldn't stand up. How grown up and important I felt, sitting on a chair while the assistant put the money and the bill into a container on wires that carried it to the cash desk which was up above the counters!

I desperately wanted white sandshoes as well but they cost about 6d more and would need cleaning so I had to be satisfied with black ones. I decided that I was going to make them white so got some whitening which was used for cleaning the hearth, thickened it and smeared it on to the shoes until the black was covered over. All went well until we began marching round the school yard, the shoes had dried out and at every step I took clouds of white dust showed where I had put my feet!

My Grandmother Harvey was a wonderful person. I only remember being kissed by her at New Year but if we needed help she was there and she was also the person neighbours called on for confinements or deaths. She took her own white sheets for the laying out and funerals were paid for by the Death Policies into which people put a penny a week.

When small babies died (or were stillborn, as frequently happened) the corpse was put into a small box and carried by the family to Sunderland Cemetery where the undertaker would place it into a grave, often one dug for another corpse.

I remember, years later, when we had moved to Southwick and I was working in a sweet shop, the man who lived in the two rooms above the shop came and asked if I had a box to give him as his wife's baby had been born dead. In those days sweets used to come packed in thin wooden boxes. I found one for him and then he asked if, when he had put the body in it, he could bring it back downstairs and leave it in the back shop until the undertaker collected it in the evening. The poor man could not face carrying it down the street with all the neighbours watching. I don't know how I got through the rest of that day, seeing that little box on the shelf every time I went into the back room!

Another time Gran and Aunt Polly were taking a little 'box' to the cemetery from the East End of the town. It was quite a long walk and they never took the tram. On the way they stopped at a pub in Hendon for a gill of bitter in the 'snug', which was the room where women were allowed to sit. They then continued on their journey and had walked a good way when suddenly Polly stopped and said. ' Mary Ann, we've forgotten the bairn!' and they had to go back to the pub and get it.

I am not one to go on about the 'Good Old Days' as I am not so sure they were, but most of my memories are happy ones – but then, most people's are.

Mary Ivory, Sunderland.

Second Hand Rose

My Dad was of Italian origin, small in stature but big in heart. He owned an ice cream parlour, was a pub landlord, fight promoter and gambler. His name was Peter Ciarella and he ruled the house with a rod of iron. Until the day he died my first thought before making any decision was, 'What would Dad think?' Quite often what he did think was completely the opposite to what I wished, as the following incident will show.

All my life I had been taught to make do and mend. Even when I started work in my Dad's café and had money of my own I bought only second hand dresses or hand-me-downs from other girls at work – in fact Second Hand Rose was my nickname. One day I rebelled, with disastrous consequences!

The cause of the furore was a pair of shoes. All my friends had work shoes and another pair for going out dressed, I had only one pair and they were pretty tatty. I set my heart on a pair of black suede cuban heeled shoes in Stead and Simpsons and decided to have them come what may.

That night we ate our tea in silence as usual then, as I was clearing the table, I said casually, 'Dad, can I have a new pair of shoes?'

'Shoes! Shoes! We haven't got money to waste on shoes!'

My name should have been Cinderella – not Ciarella!

I carried on with the washing up and eventually Dad came into the kitchen and said that I could go and buy a pair of shoes provided I took an older person with me – our neighbour, Ada, as it turned out.

On my next half day I duly met Ada and we made a round of the shops until I eventually steered her up to Stead and Simpsons. In we went.

'Can I help you?' said the assistant.

'Yes, I want to try on those suede shoes in the window, please.'

Poor Ada nearly had a fit, 'Your Dad'll not like those,' she said.

But when I tried them on they fit perfectly - 'I'll take them, and a pair of silk stockings as well, please.'

Ada's face was a mixture of fear and consternation. 'Woe betide you when you get home. One thing's certain - *I'm* not coming in with you!'

As we got off the bus and parted company she turned round, 'I wouldn't like to be in your shoes tonight!' Then, realising what she had said, she went off down the street in gales of laughter.

As I approached the front door the enormity of what I had done began to dawn on me. My knees started knocking and my hands were shaking as I opened the door. Dad was in the greenhouse out the back.

'Did you get what you wanted then?' he shouted.

'Oh yes,' I replied.

'Let's have a look then.'

'I'll get tea first,' I said, pushing the offending parcel behind the armchair.

Tea was eaten in silence as usual, every bite seemed to stick in my throat. I rushed to clear away and was putting the dishes in the sink when I heard the rustle of the carrier bag - and then an ominous silence. It had to be faced so I walked slowly back into the room. Dad was holding my purchases at arm's length with a look of disgust and incredulity on his face.

'What d'you call these?' he roared. 'Rubbish! Cardboard - won't last a week. And as for these things—' holding up the stockings, 'they're indecent. You can see right through them. No daughter of mine is wearing things like that! Showing off her legs. This lot's going straight back first thing in the morning, d'you hear me?'

I didn't utter a word but rushed straight past him up to my room. I could still hear him shouting, 'Lisle stockings were good enough for your mother and they're good enough for you, my lady.'

He got ready to go out to the club. As he went to the front door he shouted up, 'They're going back first thing in the morning, d'you hear. And I'll be coming with you.' The front door slammed.

Next morning when I went downstairs he was waiting. 'Look sharp. We've got an errand to do. Get your breakfast.'

'I don't want any.'

'You'll eat some breakfast before we go out.'

I forced myself to nibble a bit of bread and sipped a mouthful of tea then off we went, me walking behind him down to the bus stop.

We arrived at the shop and Dad stalked in like a little Napoleon, me skulking behind him.

'Good morning, sir. What can I show you?'

'You can show me nothing. I'm returning these,' handing the bag over to the girl.

'What's the problem. Are they too small?' asked the assistant.

'Rubbish! Sheer rubbish!' he barked. 'And as for those things – you can see right through them.' I could hear the girls giggling in the back shop and wished I was dead.

'Don't you like them?' the girl asked me.

'She does but I don't.' said Dad. 'I want something more serviceable.'

The girl disappeared into the back shop to get the manageress.

'I understand you are not satisfied with your purchase, sir?'

'No, I want something more serviceable for my daughter.'

'I think you might be in luck, sir. We had a new delivery of clogs only yesterday.'

She went into the back room and came out carrying the most hideous shoes I had ever seen in my life – they had orangey tan uppers and bright yellow soles, topped off with bright yellow laces. 'These are the latest fashion.'

'Try them on,' he said. 'What are they like?'

'Fine. Just fine,' I said, keeping my head down, not daring to look at the assistant. I would have bought a pair of wellies just to get out of that shop.

'We'll take them – and a good pair of lisle stockings as well. Don't bother wrapping them. She'll wear them now.'

We left the shop and crossed the road to catch the bus – clip clop, clip clop. I was like a horse cantering down the road.

I clattered into the café and I can still see the faces of Lily, the manageress and the other girls as I clip clopped round to the back of the counter. All eyes were drawn like magnets to my feet, there was silence and then roars of laughter. I kicked the monstrosities off and thankfully put on my old shoes.

I never wore those clogs again. A cobbler made them into wedge heels and then they were sold. I vowed that I would never be made such a fool of again – well, I tried. There *was* the day I went and had a perm – but that's another story.

Mary V. Murray
Sunderland

Schooldays in South Hylton

The headmistress of Diamond Hall School rejoiced under the name of Miss Mudd. She was a fearsome woman. Her grey hair was scraped up high on to the top of her head and secured with numerous wire hair pins. She always wore black, a high collared blouse with long sleeves, a long skirt and black shoes. Her permanent expression was one of grim authority – I likened her to the witch in *Sleeping Beauty*. She wore rimless spectacles, had a pallid complexion and always smelled of carbolic and disinfectant. Never – not once – can I remember her smiling!

On Empire Day, May 24th, the school would be assembled for the 'ceremony' which was held in the school yard if the weather was clement, indoors if not. We were warned not to forget our daisies and our Union Jacks, which in those days cost about a penny. The daisies were pinned on our chests to symbolise St. Andrew, St. Patrick and St. George.

A teacher, seated at the piano which was pushed out into the yard for the occasion, would then strike up with the opening bars to 'Our Flag' and we would all, teachers included, join in with:

> Some flags are red, or white or blue
> And some are yellow too
> But that dear dear flag that we love best
> Is red and white and blue
> Then HAIL the flag

(at this juncture we raised and waved our flags)

> The bonny flag, of red and white and blue!

194

I noticed at school that many girls wore red braid armbands at the top of their arms over their sleeves. They, I learned in later years, had been vaccinated against smallpox. People were terrified of catching this disease - always lingering and always fatal. My mother had me vaccinated as an infant. The red armband was a warning that the scab should not be knocked.

When I started school my mother bought me a pair of 'sensible' high buttoned boots. To fasten the buttons a button hook had to be used. The procedure of poking a button hook through the hole and then drawing the button through to fasten it was torturous! My leg was always liberally marked with bruises where the flesh had been nipped.

Sunday School was a must for children in those days. Every Sunday, after the traditional roast beef dinner my cousins would call for me and we would set off from Franklin Street to walk to Park Road Church in Grangetown. It was at least an hour's walk and we would arrive at Park Road exhausted. This, after a morning walk in Barnes Park with my father - and in the summer we would finish off with another walk after tea to listen to the band in the park! My father used to compliment me on being a good walker - I'm not surprised - I used to walk miles on a Sunday!

Sunday School took place in a large room with rows of little white wooden chairs which made a terrible clatter on the floor every time we stood up. Older children sat at the back, younger ones at the front.

A child with a birthday was allowed the privilege of taking the glass sugar basin around for pennies. As this ceremony was being performed the others would all sing:

> Dropping, dropping, dropping,
> Hear the pennies fall,
> Every one for Jesus,
> He shall have them all.

I could never understand why Jesus received the pennies - and if he did, what did He do with them? Were there shops in Heaven? Whenever it was my turn to take the collection I used to shake with fear.

At the end of Sunday School we each received a small biblical text on pretty, brightly coloured shiny cards, usually decorated with flowers. I still have some in my Bible today.

Sometimes on Sunday evenings we would all congregate in the 'parlour' with aunts, uncles and cousins and have a family 'harmony' evening. Mother played the piano whilst the uncles accompanied on cello and violin. There were always some hymns from Old Sankey's Hymn Book and old favourites like 'Jesus wants me for a Sunbeam' and 'Roses of Picardy'.

I can remember as many as thirty members of our family congregating for our annual outing to the riverside at South Hylton for the Hylton Regatta. Hours of preparation went into ensuring that the family would enjoy the day; mountains of food were put into hampers, bottles of home made lemonade; sandwiches, seed cake, plate pies of meat, apple, rhubarb and bilberries and large custard pies. The food was always all consumed. We children were allowed on extension on boat race days and in the evening, after a game of 'hot rice' we would haul ourselves wearily up the river bank and back home.

Family relationships were deep rooted in those days and the home unit was secure, no matter what the circumstances of the family. Discipline was strong but there was great affection and values were learnt in the home from example: good citizenship, housewifery and the like. (Unfortunately, we were taught all too little about the 'facts of life'.)

Being a parent was a full time job - more so then I think, than it is today.

Gertrude Parsons
South Shields

A Village, a School and a Lighthouse

There is nothing left now of Marsden, the old pit village where I spent so much of my childhood. It owed its existence to the colliery - and now, incredibly, the colliery has vanished. Where it stood the landscape stretches emptily eastward to the distant gleam of the sea. It is somehow surprising to discover that there, behind the great sprawl of grimy buildings and railways, the belching steam, the bustle and the clamour, and the all-dominating pulley-wheels, the sea had been lying in wait all the time.

The death of the village came about gradually. Long ago some of the old rows of pit cottages had to be raised because the sea's steady encroachment had brought them too near the edge of the cliffs. The people moved out to a new housing estate a mile or two away. In time a new red brick school was built there, and the grey stone schoolhouse beside the lighthouse at Souter Point was forsaken.

When the life of the colliery came to an end the village took on the aspect of a Gold Rush ghost town. The church, the Miners' Institute, the Co-op and the Post Office were boarded up, the grass grew waist-high in the Colliery Welfare recreation grounds. One by one the derelict buildings were demolished, until only the abandoned schoolhouse and the lighthouse remained; the lighthouse, huge, sturdy and indestructible in its spanking red and white livery, contrasting sharply with the surrounding desolation.

A day came when I noticed as I drove by that the boards were down from the broken schoolhouse windows, and that light was showing here and there through chinks in the roof. I knew then that its days were numbered, and decided to make a last pilgrimage before it was too late.

From the road it seemed the grey stones had weathered well the salt winds of over a century. A rusting padlock still secured the iron front gates, so I walked round the side, to make my approach from the cliffs. The boundary wall had broken down and the once vanquished grass had burst triumphantly through the asphalt of the playground. Sadly I looked upon the silent deserted ruin beyond, then picked my way across the litter, coming first to what used to be known as the 'Little School'. Once it had been partitioned into three – now it was one large room, the wooden floor still sound.

I did not remember this place kindly. Coming here from a town school at the age of eight had been like stepping back into the days of Dickens, with gas lamps and no central heating, and the rows of little earth closets, the Geordie 'netties', at the bottom of the yard. We wrote on slates with squeaking pencils – a practice discontinued a generation before my time in South Shields County Borough schools – and I had to be initiated into the ancient mysteries of 'long division'.

A great deal of time seemed to be taken up by dreaded needlework; with clumsy fingers pricked and sore, many long panic-stricken sessions would be spent just trying to thread a needle. The autocratic schoolmistress with the gold pince-nez had long passed from authority, but the fear she inspired lingered uneasily here amid the sour atmosphere of decay.

Continuing over the lost playground, across another broken wall, I came to what had been the girls' entrance to the 'Big School' – a place of infinitely pleasanter associations, where a young and enlightened headmaster had increased the number of scholarship successes every year.

Forty years on, and my aging feet were mounting again the three worn steps into the ruins of the dim passage where we had crowded during break times on stormy days, our strident voices vying with the thunder of the waves which battered the foot of the cliffs. There were two doors in the passage – the one on the left had led to standard Five, the other to the rest of the school. I looked first into the large room on the right which had also been used for morning prayers, seeming to smell again the long ago pot-pourri of carbolic and camphor, of damp wool and aniseed – the characteristic smell of poverty. It was a different world from that of today. Although barefoot children were no longer commonplace, sometimes children stayed away from school because their only pair of shoes was being mended, and occasionally one of the bigger bolder lads would arrive with dirty bare feet. The Police ran a charity called the Shoeless Children Fund, and it would not be long before the enterprising lad would be squeaking to school in big black boots with the tabs sticking out at the back of the heels.

Certain girls were regularly absent on Monday mornings, to help with the weekly wash for huge families. Life was hard, and for the older children school was mostly irrelevant.

I turned back and went through the other door into Standard Five's room of happiest memory. I had not remembered that it was so small. The place where the fire once burned cheerfully behind the heavy iron guard was now only a blackened hole in the brickwork.

Sitting at our desks in this room, we were able to look from the left-hand windows beyond the playground to the sea, where the tough little colliers steamed constantly along the skyline, taking coal to London and returning. The windows on the right commanded a view of the colliery railway embankment. The chatter of trucks and the puffing of locomotives were part of the background to our lessons, and when the dense white haars closed in on us, the lighthouse foghorn, the voice of dear old Souter, blared out deafeningly at short intervals like some enraged wild animal, shaking the ground – a sound so familiar we never even noticed it.

To come from the autocratic old spinster with the pince-nez to the charm and understanding of the shingled young flapper who presided over this classroom was a wonderful transition. Her own huge enjoyment of life was infectious and we loved her. We loved her short pleated skirts and her strapped slippers, and the way she pushed the distracting flop of her black hair behind her ear when she wrote on the blackboard. She introduced us to poetry – the simple, haunting kind of verse which appeals to a child. Standing there in her derelict classroom, I thought of old Nod the shepherd and 'his blind old sheepdog Slumbersoon', and of the drowned steeples and turrets of 'a lost city in Semmerwater, deep asleep till Doom'. . .

This was the way to learn the intoxication of words, a joy once discovered, never lost.

Standard Five's classroom was used by the 'dinner children', those who travelled in from outlying farms and hamlets, for their midday meal. A huge black kettle sang on the fire throughout each morning, ready to make their cocoa. Each classroom was warmed only by a roaring coal fire, but I never remember feeling cold. We used to try with innocent glee to spot our young teacher's fancy garters as she reached over the fireguard to attend to the kettle. To remember the happy days of Standard Five was the most fitting tribute I could bring to the old village school as I said goodbye.

I went back over the ruined yard, skirting the corner where in summer we had danced 'Rufty Tufty' and 'Cochin China' to the tinny strains of the school gramophone. The breeze from the sea was good after the reek of filth and decay. I looked up at old Souter with affection as I passed, confident that he at least would endure to sweep the dark waters with his great lantern and to moo out his dismal warning long after we were dust.

But I was wrong. Perhaps nothing is forever. So far as Marsden was concerned the obliteration was to be complete – even the lighthouse was judged in the end to have outlived its usefulness.

When Trinity House announced the lighthouse was to 'go dark', to be replaced by an unmanned radio beacon, I grieved for the humiliation of Souter, who, it must be understood, in the way of sailors with their ships, was a person to us, always referred to in the village as 'he'. The splendid red and white tower still makes a proud landmark where the village used to be, and is a visitors' centre for the National Trust, but it is only an empty shell. I like to think that the departed soul of old Souter has gone to join those generations of sailors and fishermen he guided and comforted for 117 years through the rocky perils of the cruel North Sea.

Muriel Ryle
Low Fell, Gateshead.

Marsden - the Village that vanished

I was born in 1918 in a three roomed colliery house situated a few yards from the cliffs north of Souter Point Lighthouse. It was the home of my grandparents and their unmarried daughter, Aunt Lizzie. When father returned from war service he joined us for a short time until we obtained our own accommodation.

The house consisted of two rooms downstairs with a walk-in pantry off the living-room, and a bedroom which was approached by a narrow wooden staircase from the same room. These stairs were scrubbed every week. Before my arrival grandfather had created a 'Number 4 Room' in the space under the eaves, and this was entered through a low doorway situated in bedroom wall. As well as other articles, all the best clothes were kept there. These were always folded neatly and placed in a trunk every Sunday night. There were no wardrobes. Grandfather had also built a partition across the bedroom thereby creating privacy.

The living-room served as kitchen, dining-room, laundry, bathroom, activity room and guest room. Most of the visitors were relatives from west Durham villages and a desk bed in the living room came in handy when they arrived.

Auntie Lizzie was very industrious. Her three sisters had been sent to 'service', but she remained at home, and, after a short training in dressmaking, was given the task of making all the 'prints' for her sisters at work as well as many other garments. Her Singer sewing machine was in constant use.

Many winter evenings were spent in mat or quilt making. These were made on a frame which took up quite a lot of space in the living-room, but happy times were had by all who took part in this creative pastime. Neighbours dropped in to help, black bullets were sucked, gossip was exchanged, and hymns were sung. It was a social

201

activity.

Baths were taken in a small bath in front of the living room fire, and, until pithead baths were available, the water was always ready heated for grandfather's bath as soon as he came in from work. While he was enjoying this, Aunt Lizzie was brushing and shaking the dirt out of his pit clothes before hanging them up for next day. Ordinary hand and face washing was done in the pantry off the living-room. There was always a dish of water at waist height behind the door, with a soap and facecloth beside it as well as a towel hanging behind the door. With such scant accommodation there needed to be a 'place for everything and everything in its place'.

The other downstairs room could have been a sitting-room, but there was a double bed behind the door at one side, and an organ stood at the other side. This organ was very ornate, beautifully polished and trimmed with fretwork behind which was fixed some beautiful pink sateen material. On the whole this was an elegant piece of furniture as well as an effective musical instrument. Aunt Lizzie was the organist and many Sunday evenings were spent around it while voices were raised singing anything from the songs of the day like 'I do like to be beside the seaside' to lots of hymns from the Primitive Methodist Hymn Book. The front door led out of this room but it was rarely used; indeed it would have been difficult to cross the room owing to recently acquired furniture including a horse hair sofa with chairs to match – most uncomfortable to sit on if you were a small child with short dress or trousers and bare legs. Enlarged, heavily framed photographs hung on the walls. These depicted members of the older generation in sombre and unsmiling mood.

My great grandmother lived two streets away in a smaller dwelling with a wash-house in the yard, so Aunt Lizzie used to carry all the washing up to that house every Monday and carry it back to dry at home. When great grandmother left her home, the washing was done in the living-room of grandmother's house, and on wet days the poss tub was brought into the room out of the yard, and the attractively covered wringer in the corner was revealed for use. All water for washing in the tub and for boiling the whites was boiled on the fire in a large black pan, and it was impossible to boil a kettle for a cuppa until the washing was finished. I recall seeing grandmother filling her kettle with water from the only tap which was in the yard, and taking it to the next door neighbour's house where she had the water boiled on the fire for a pot of tea. Wet clothes festooned the living-room for some time, but there was plenty of coal for large fires.

The back door opened out of the living-room into the yard, but there was also a stable door fixed, and even in winter it was often warm enough to open the big door and let the air in and the steam from drying out.

There was a period during a strike when mother and Aunt Lizzie actually joined other members of the community to search for coal from the colliery tip because, without it, it would be impossible to wash, cook or keep warm.

Miners' allotments were situated about 250 yards from the house, but there was no standing pipe. I remember Aunt Lizzie carrying water in a pail down to the allotment on dry summer nights, because grandfather was very keen on growing his vegetables.

There were no water closets, and every week a man came round the village with a horse and cart and emptied the middens. The contents, including the ash from the fire were all piled on to the cart, and eventually tipped over the cliffs into the sea. It was a sad day when a horse and cart fell over with the rubbish. Fortunately the driver escaped.

Some people had a shop in the living-room, and their wares were displayed in the window. These could be sweets, home-made bread, home-made ginger beer, herb beer or newspapers. A customer entered the door of the living room from the yard, and a small counter was fixed round the corner where the goods were served. A Co-operative store flourished in the village, but grandmother chose to deal at Ryhope Co-op mainly, I believe, because they gave bigger dividends! Twice a year there was an outing to Ryhope to collect the divvy and indulge in a café dinner of pie and peas. The journey to Ryhope was quite an adventure because there was very little public transport in the area. Many travelling shops including Ryhope Co-op came round the village. There was a fishmonger, butcher, green grocer, ice cream man and rag man. The rag man gave balloons in exchange for rags.

Aunt Lizzie took a pride in brightening all the steel, brass and black-leaded gadgets every week and the fireplace area absolutely shone. We all need something to take a pride in and in those days when holidays were nil, outings few and pleasures limited, that fireplace was Aunt Lizzie's pride and joy.

In later years when grandmother lived alone in a pensioner's cottage, I recall visiting her one Friday morning. She was clad in a voluminous black overall and kneeling on a newspaper spread over the mat. She unwrapped a neat newspaper parcel which contained all the implements necessary for polishing her black-lead stove and fireplace surrounds. She was well over 70 years of age.

There was activity in abundance for those children who were old enough to play out of doors in that community. Of course there were the usual street games such as hide and seek, tag, skippies, marbles, buttony and bays (hopscotch). Seasonal activities took over from time to time such as tops and whips, bowling hoops and diabolo.

Nearby there was an ideal pebble beach at the foot of the cliff, and when the tide was low there were plenty of rocks to scamper over, deep pools to leap over and shallow pools to explore for crabs etc. There were attractive glass marbles found among the stone pebbles on the beach. These were formed from small pieces of broken bottles which had been battered about by the sea. As they were found in a variety of colours they were an asset when playing shops.

Walks or runs could be taken along the cliffs, south to Whitburn Bents Fishermen's Cottages, and north to South Shields. Half a mile to the north was the lovely sandy beach at Marsden Grotto where great fun could be had around Marsden Rock when the tide was out. Another popular bay was about half a mile south of the village. This bay was called the Wherry because fishing boats left the shore at this point. An outcrop of rock in the centre of the bay divided it into the boys' wherry and the girls' wherry. The children seldom moved out of their own territory.

Older children could walk half a mile up the Toll Bank to the High Road and find themselves in the middle of the country surrounded by fields. They played for hours in these fields, football, cricket, rounders and hot rice, but that was stopped when in about 1930 the fields became part of Whitburn Golf Course. Depending on the season, little girls would pick daisies, buttercups or cowslips and take them home for mother to place in a jam jar on the living room window sill.

More adventurous children would walk further to Farding Lake Farm where there was a pond which was ideal for fishing for tiddlers. These tiddlers would be taken home in a jam jar suspended by string.

The magic of childhood was truly captured and enjoyed. There was no time for boredom and the activities cost nothing. Without radio and television, the news of the day was very limited and many of the evils of today were unheard of.

Margaret Felce (née Archer)
Cleadon, Sunderland.

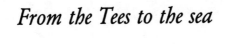

From the Tees to the sea

Myself when Young

I was born on March 6th 1914 and at the age of six months was taken to number 84 Yarm Lane, Stockton-on-Tees, the house where I lived until I left to get married.

It had been a fine gentleman's residence in its day but when we lived there the front part had been built out to make a shop. There were three floors and a cellar which in its day had been the basement kitchen and still had the cooking range and a horrible old sink. One could imagine the servants working in the semi-gloom and carrying food up the back stairs which were completely unlit. All the rooms were high and spacious with large sash windows, ornate plaster ceilings and handsome doors. We had no heating except coal fires and our bedrooms were icy. We filled stone ginger beer bottles, called Grey Hens, for hot water bottles. Better still was a baking sheet hot out of the oven and wrapped in flannel.

Although extremely hard work for poor Mum the house was heaven for children: the topmost floor was empty and we could play up there to our hearts' content. When last I saw it it had been divided into flats and appeared in a shocking condition.

Schooldays

After a brief spell at a private school I attended Holy Trinity Higher Grade School. When my older sisters went they first paid a small fee, but by my time it was free.

This school would appear very strange to present day children. There was no hall, no corridors. The classrooms led one from another. When we met all together partitions were pushed back between the two larger rooms. There was no staff room, no office;

the Headmistress simply had a desk in one room. She wore long skirts and high collars. Her grey hair was dragged back in a bun and she often carried a cane in her hand, which she was not afraid of using. She commanded respect and even affection. Two of her sayings I remember to this day. They were: 'Good manners come from the heart' and 'If you can't say anything good about a person, say nothing at all'. Wise words indeed!

She lived with her sister, Miss Dolly, in a schoolhouse on the premises. Sometimes I was called on to recite to their guests. I felt very privileged standing on a beaded footstool in their over-furnished sitting-room. I was, and still am, very bad at sewing and yet I amazed my Mother by taking home a pair of handsewn pillow cases, with perfect buttonholes. I never told her that Miss Thomas had done these while I did her shopping!

In my eleventh year a few of us were segregated to have extra lessons behind the blackboard and read the classics on our own. We were the chosen few 'scholarship girls'. With this system I believe our school got 100% passes! The rest of the girls stayed until they were fourteen.

We had several 'pupil teachers' learning school routine before they went to college. I still think that was a very good method of teacher training.

It was a church school and great emphasis was laid on learning the scriptures. We sang and prayed at the beginning and end of each day. Once a week the curate would come to talk to us and I remember him imitating the animals going into the Ark.

Great emphasis was laid on the 3 Rs. We had few books and no teaching aids, but no child left that school unable to read, write and calculate. Present day educationalists with their fancy ideas and huge budgets might well ponder the old ways.

We were a very close family. Every Sunday we walked out of the town and across the fields, our little terrier running up and down like a sheepdog keeping us altogether. On Monday nights Father would take us to the Hippodrome. I remember the smell of cigars and the thrill of seeing the curtain go up on a row of high-kicking chorus girls. Sometimes we would have the loan of a pony and trap and off we would go along the quiet country lanes – very few motor cars then. Later though, Dad did acquire a motor cycle with a large sidecar. It had to be large. It carried Mother, my baby brother, me, the dog, the picnic and other miscellaneous necessities for a family outing. On the pillion behind Father sat both my sisters. So laden it carried us to the seaside and over hill and dale on many a summer's day.

I was a Brownie and then a Girl Guide and found all their activities great fun. I only once went to Guide camp, though – I found I was homesick.

Two Red Letter Days stand out in my memory. The first was the Peace Celebration after the First World War. It was a Gala Day in our town. A platform was erected in front of the Town Hall and entertainments went on all day, including beautiful Tableaux Vivants. In the market place was all the fun of the fair with the hilarious spectacle of competitors climbing the greasy pole.

The other was the Centenary of the opening of the Stockton-Darlington Railway in 1925. First we went to the railway side to see Locomotion pulling the train from Darlington. Here she comes, her tall chimney stack belching steam. Behind her, coaches of all ages, with suitably dressed passengers waving and cheering. My two sisters were on that train. How I envied them, but I was too young to be chosen. My turn came in the afternoon when I was part of a Guard of Honour outside the first booking office. It was to be opened by the Duke and Duchess of York, he so tall and solemn, she petite in her favourite style of hat with its ostrich feather and the little fringe of hair peeping out. And oh that lovely smile that we still see on the face of our beloved Queen Mother.

My family were closely connected with Holy Trinity Church. As I have mentioned we all went to the Church School. We attended Church and Sunday School regularly. Later I went to Bible Class and for a few years was a Sunday School Teacher. There were many social activities connected with the church. I met my husband at a church dance. I also took a leading part in the operettas which were produced in Trinity Hall. My Mother was a keen member of the Mothers' Union and contributed generously by providing food for the various social meetings.

Our town

In my lifetime Stockton has completely changed, mostly for the

211

worse. Yarm Lane was in my day a busy shopping street. The Co-op had a whole block with butcher, grocer and greengrocer shops. There were two big grocery shops as well, three butchers, a mens' outfitters, confectioners and many many more. Now it is a ghost street with over half the shops closed and boarded up. The graceful spire of Holy Trinity Church dominated the skyline. It was pulled down as dangerous years ago, leaving an ugly stump. Fire has gutted the inside of the church and it is now due for demolition. The headstones have been removed from what is left of the churchyard. The schools have been pulled down and the vicarage turned into old peoples' flats. There was a popular dance hall called the *Maison de Danse* where I have spent many joyous nights dancing to Jack Marwood's band. That too is gone. When I was young there were still some fine old houses left. I used to visit the lodge of one of these and play in the garden. All have been given over to other purposes. It is a dreary and depressing road.

The High Street has fared even worse. At the corner of the east side was the Empire Cinema, built on the site of Stockton Castle. Imposing without, inside it was magnificent. A sweeping staircase, carpeted in red led up to the circle. Further along the street were two beautiful old inns, The Black Lion and The Vane Arms with arches where the coaches passed in the old days. Every building was different and the outline of the roofs full of interest. All this has gone to make way for a carbuncle of concrete called a shopping precinct. Further up, the graceful Victoria Buildings, built in that Queen's reign has been replaced by another monstrosity in dirty concrete.

Nevertheless there are parts of Stockton that have been improved. In my young days the most interesting parts, the oldest parts, were more or less derelict. The ancient Green Dragon Yard was a mess of decaying buildings, where once had been an old inn and even a Georgian theatre. This has now all been restored and is a charming and useful corner of the town.

The riverside was once busy with shipping. I can remember watching scrap iron being unloaded there. The wharf was a hive of activity and across the river the Head Wrightson Works were in full production and the Clevo Flour Mill was a landmark. All these are now gone and the whole riverside has been pleasantly landscaped.

Our chief amenity was the park donated by the ship-building

212

family, the Ropners. When I was at school, we marched in crocodile to play cricket and rounders on its fields. There were tennis courts, a putting green, an aviary, beautiful sub-tropical gardens by the lake, a secluded rose garden. On Sundays we stood beneath the trees, dressed in our best clothes to listen to the band who performed in an ornate bandstand. For a time there was an open-air theatre, but that could not withstand our inclement weather. Now, as an old man recently remarked to me, 'There is nothing here, missus, but fresh air'.

To give the council its due it has given us a new and better amenity at Preston Park and Museum. When I was young this was Preston Hall, owned and lived in by Sir Leonard Ropner, who made his fortune in the ship-building industry which then flourished by the Tees.

Stockton market and fairs

Stockton was given a charter by King John, and to this day there have been markets every Wednesday and Saturday. They are still there, but how quiet, orderly and dull! I can remember when every stallholder shouted his wares, joking with the crowds and offering all manner of bargains. The china man would range a dinner service along his arm and threaten to smash the lot if his audience did not accept his wonderful bargain. Sometimes he did, too. To visit the market was an entertainment in itself, listening to these Spiclers as they were called. To buy your Sunday joint you went to The Shambles, aptly called. The open stalls reminded one of medieval days. The Shambles was an old building near the Town House and the Market Cross, the real centre of the town. Now it houses stalls selling cheap clothes and other non-food articles and the meat market is now hygienically housed in the new shopping precinct.

If you were hungry after shopping, there were long tents with tables and benches, selling hot pies, faggots and peas. They smelt delicious.

Tram lines ran down the centre of our very wide High Street. The trams seemed to run incessantly, clanging their bells to warn careless pedestrians. When I was at Grammar School we went on the tram to Norton to play hockey. We thought it great fun, there on the top

213

deck.

The shops in the High Street are now a sorry sight, either cheap-jack stores or closed up altogether. We had lovely specialist shops as well as bigger stores. Woolworths still sold everything at 3d or 6d and if that was too much we had Piper's Penny Bazaar where everything cost only 1d. At the moment the High Street is being turned into a pedestrian area in the hope of bringing back the shoppers from the out-of-town supermarkets.

Twice a year the High Street was given over to the Hirings Fairs. They each lasted a full week and what fun they were. Roundabouts and rides galore, with all manner of stalls and entertainments. I remember being taken when I was very young to a Wild Beast Show. I was terrified. There were sword swallowers, fire eaters, acrobats – and all this went on late into the night. We were quite used to going down town at night, with no thought of danger. The markets stayed open late. Round about dusk you would see a man with a flat cart, laden with flaring acetylene lamps. These he distributed among the stalls and bargaining went on beneath their fitful glare.

The Good Old Days? I am not so sure but I do think Stockton was a more colourful and lively place to live in those days. There was poverty too. I remember the hopeless groups of men by the Market Cross during the 1930s, despair and even hunger showing in their faces. My first job when I started teaching was to take groups of children to be fitted with shoes under the Mayor's Boot Fund. We had to watch them afterwards, for their parents were not above pawning the shoes for drink or perhaps even for food. I also had to supervise the school dinners, which were free and only for the poor. The meal was invariably the same, a meat stew with plenty of vegetables, cooked in a sort of wash-copper and served with hunks of brown bread. No nonsense then of choosing between beefburgers and chips or pizza and salad. We are once again in a serious depression with massive unemployment, but families in the 30s suffered far more.

Nancy Bell
Stockton-on-Tees

The Way We Were

Teesport in 1993 is a sprawling industrial area with ships from all over the world bringing cargoes into the river Tees. Around 1920 the village of Teesport was a row of terraced houses with their kitchen windows looking out on to the flowing river. My grandfather lived with his wife and six children in one of those houses. In 1920 Herbert Hill was forty-six years old and a professional salmon fisherman.

It was a hard life for the Hill family. The two eldest sons, Herbert and Tommy, worked one of the family's three fishing cobles rowing on an early morning tide to cast long lines and salmon nets. Profits were small from the three boats, the *Mary Jane*, named after grandma; the *Ellen*, named after my mother, and the *Mary*, named after my auntie, the youngest daughter. The *Mary* was later to become – after fitting an engine – the first motor fishing coble on the Tees.

My auntie Betty, the eldest daughter, at sixteen, had 'gone into service' at a boarding house in Blackpool, whilst the three younger daughters, Elsie, Ellen and Mary were still attending Grangetown board school.

The mornings in Teesport started early with the three boats, crewed by Grandad, three 'part-timer's', Herbert and Tommy, off to the fishing. Grandma would make a start baking the daily ration of bread on a coal-fired range and the three girls would prepare fish boxes for the morning catch.

On their return the boats would moor alongside a narrow path which ran parallel to the rear of the houses. From the boats the catch would be passed through the window to the concrete paved floor of the kitchen. The fish, having already been gutted and cleaned aboard the boats, would be packed into fish boxes. After breakfast the girls would set off at seven-thirty for school with

215

satchels of home made 'doorsteps' of bread and butter over their shoulders, and carrying between them a trio of rope-handled fish boxes which they would take to Grangetown railway station to be put on the early train to Stockton. Over the footbridge and, screaming at the steam from the engine blowing up ankle-length gym slips, the girls would walk the remaining two miles to school.

My Grandfather would never put the boats to sea on Sunday. Not because he was particularly religious – he was often heard to remark that six days a week was enough work for any man. June 21 1924 then was a fairly memorable day for the Hill family in that it was the day of the charabanc trip to Redcar to see the opening of Zetland Park. More an excuse for Grandfather to talk fishing with Jack Thompson and Harry Picknet – a couple of friendly rivals. Grandma took the three girls to the pier to watch the Pierrots and my mother and her sister Mary were to enter and win the talent competition performing a Charleston dance routine.

Fishing was my Grandfather's life and, unfortunately, his death. Whilst setting lobster creels off Redcar's infamous Saltscar he was dragged into the sea by a creel hauling rope and was drowned.

The boats were sold and the family moved to Grangetown. The two eldest boys took jobs at Normanby Iron Works, and my mother and her sister Mary went into service.

I never knew my Grandfather, yet I know him intimately. Although he died before I was born, I was later told so much about him I almost believed he was immortal.

Fisherman, lifeboatman, gentle man.

Tony Ellison
Redcar.

Grangetown Revisited

Returning to one's hometown in Britain as opposed to, say Bosnia or some other troubled country, it might reasonably be expected that the house of your birth would be standing to bring back old memories.

I left Grangetown in the mid 1950s having lived in Bolckow Road for some twenty-five years. During my working life in Merseyside, Scotland and finally, the South Coast I have regularly returned with my family for visits to Teesside. Over this period of time I have witnessed the gradual dereliction of the community that I grew up in and its replacement by a maze of anonymous highways and industrial development.

Our most recent visit this summer took us to a Grangetown that we barely recognised, with the old part demolished and bisected by roads and a large proportion of the remaining houses boarded up. The side of Bolckow Road where I had lived was a green wasteland and the remaining houses in the road were largely abandoned.

My most vivid memories of Grangetown were the 40s and 50s, two decades which encompassed a world war and the advent of a new era in technology, During most of this period, Bolckow Road was at the heart of the community. Along its length could be found St. Mary's Catholic Church, St. Matthew's Church of England, the Wesleyan and Methodist Chapels, whilst close by in the adjoining streets there was a Mission house and a Spiritualist church. Leisure needs were met by the Lyric Cinema and a dance hall above Lanny's ice-cream parlour, whilst the police station, complete with cell and the doctor's house and surgery were at hand for more stressful events.

Bolckow Road was intersected by the main shopping area, Whitworth Road which led down towards the Steelworks and the station. On the four corners of this crossroads stood the police station, the surgery, the junior school and Brown's Emporium. Leading off Whitworth road on both sides along its length, like the spines from a fishbone, were the streets of small cottages. These were named after local worthies associated with the history of the town such as Cheetham, Vickers, Wood, Laing, Stapleton, Vaughan and Bessemer Streets, the latter adjoining the Steelworks founded by Bolckow and Vaughan and later acquired by Dorman Long.

Whitworth Road contained a full range of shops. There were two chemists, Vaux, in which I began my career in pharmacy, and Kingston, which was also an off-licence. Butchers' shops included Coates, the pork specialist, Caney and the Co-op. A selection of grocers ranged from the large stores of the Co-op, Duncans, Hintons, and Gallons to the smaller Walter Willson's 'smiling service' and the general stores of Sivills and O'Neils. Shoe shops were represented by Sims and the Co-op. Fruit and vegetables by both Allicks anbd Rogers and every possible sweet from luxury chocolates to 'gob-stoppers' by Ginny Jones. The large corner store of Lenny Brown catered for ladies' fashions and drapery, the ubiquitous Co-op for gentleman's clothing and McTighue's hardware shop stocked everything from nails to carpets. There were fresh and fried fish shops, two pawnbrokers and jewellers and two newsagents.

Midway along Whitworth Road was the market square, a wide space used for the market stalls, public gatherings, parades, funfairs, brass band concerts and 'hot gospel' prayer meetings. The square was, also, the terminus of the 'trackless tram' service which connected with Southbank and North Ormesby. The trams, mainly double deckers, would today have been hailed as the ideal form of 'green' transport. Powered by overhead wires they ran smoothly and silently producing no polluting exhaust fumes. Stepping off the tram in the market-square one was at the commercial heart of the town with Whitworth Road and all its shops, the busy central market and the Middlehouse Hotel which provided liquid refreshment for steelworkers coming off shift.

Apart from the trams and occasional delivery vans, Whitworth Road provided an environment for shoppers almost as peaceful as the modern pedestrian shopping precinct. This allowed for relaxed shopping such that 'going down the street' represented the opportunity for socialising and gossip. I particularly remember the bustle of Christmas shopping with the shops a blaze of light, the smells of fresh produce from the open shops and stalls, the Salvation Army band playing carols in the square and the throngs of shoppers. The sense of community was further evident on New Year's Eve when large congregations attended the 'watch night services' and then gathered in Bolckow Road outside the police station to sing 'Aulde lang Syne' and exchange greetings. Traffic was so sparse that I recall only an occasional motorist patiently waiting for the ceremony to end.

For young people in Grangetown life was happy. There was not, of course, the range of sophisticated entertainment now available. The cinema together with dancing represented the typical 'night out'. In the home radio ruled supreme although the record player was making rapid inroads as 'pop' music began to emerge. Television was a rarity and then only black and white with seventeen inch being the usual large screen. We knew nothing of video recorders or computer games but regularly walked or cycled along the 'new trunk road', as it was then, to visit the library.

A major contribution to our happy youth was the absence of the scourge of unemployment. Upon leaving school there was a job waiting in the steel works or local shops or the new ICI development at Wilton. By present day standards wages were low, maybe, two pounds a week for a school leaver but the cost of living was low. The countryside was within a stone's throw of Bolckow Road with leafy lanes leading to Greenwells Farm and the 'fifty acre field'. Cycling was a pleasure on the traffic free roads. The red buses of the United service gave cheap access to the coast or Middlesbrough allowing us to enjoy miles of golden sands, visit the cinemas, the parks and the museum or see the brilliant Wilf Mannion, 'Boro's' golden boy, mesmerise the opposing forwards at Ayresome Park.

Church and chapel attendance was high and I remember standing on the doorstep of our house to watch the seemingly endless stream of worshippers walking along Bolckow Road to Mass at St. Mary's. All were in their Sunday best and the high proportion of pretty girls ensured that I was not alone in my vigil. The regular attendance of the young people that I knew at the services owed much of its motivation to the social activities associated with the church and chapels. The genial and wise vicar Frank Travers of St. Matthews, formed a youth club named the 'plus-fourteens' which met in the

219

Church Hall after the evening service. Here we also had social events at weekends and it was a place were many budding romances began. We knew nothing of 'rave parties' or drugs other than alcohol and nicotine, our personal transport was a bicycle, or for the opulent, a motor bike, and yet I am sure that courtship in our unspoiled environment had a unique quality. The 40s and early 50s were a time when car ownership was a relative novelty. In Grangetown private cars were few enough to be known by sight with the owners being the doctors, the Catholic priest, the chemist and some other shopkeepers and one or two wealthier townsfolk. For the population at large public transport was so cheap and regular that the need for a car, even if it could have been afforded, was minimal. The possible exception to this might have been in high summer when, despite duplicate buses, the service to Redcar and Saltburn could barely cope with demand. A common device to avoid the queues at Grangetown was to take the tram to Southbank or even North Ormesby and catch the United bus there for the coast.

Walking and cycling were popular leisure activities and for this we were well placed with Church Lane leading to Eston, being a winding country road over which the branches of the trees met. Eston was truly a country village and the roads leading out such as Flatts Lane were rustic and devoid of traffic. Eston Hills were particularly in demand for rambling, brambling and courting. A pleasant evening walk was to take the track via the deserted 'pit top' hamlet to the Cross Keys pub.

Revisiting Grangetown, and in particular Bolckow Road, now it seems hardly credible that the heart of a thriving community has gone. The people, their churches and houses lost beneath grass and concrete and with them a way of life lost forever.

Malcolm Parker
Hawes
N. Yorks.

Summer Saturdays

Thomas Moore's 'Oft in the stilly night' contains the words 'Fond memory brings the light of other days around me' and goes on: 'The smiles, the tears of boyhood's years'

I've no idea what age Moore was when he wrote those words. But I know what he was feeling.

I was born in nineteen twenty-eight so I'm sixty-five years old this year, 1993. Looking back is easy and I try not to do it but it's difficult when I don't seem to have many years to look forward to. I have the feeling that I don't belong in this present age of, to me, endless violence, greed, vanity, lies, conceit, treachery. Is this another sign of my fading future? Am I missing compassion, patience, tolerance, understanding, virtue, and generosity which in moments of nostalgia I remember so much more of?

I remember how we lived amongst much poverty, dirt, bad health and poor sanitation, unemployment, neglect and all sorts of abuse, prejudice, suspicion and drunkenness. The most vivid memories of all are of the hard physical labour amongst men when there was work to be had, and amongst women all of the time. This aspect of my life as a child formed my character, warped my judgement and left marks on my mind which I'll carry to the grave.

On Teesside, where I lived, it was all hand leathers, clogs with irons on, aprons, moleskin trousers, knee pads, shoulder pads and sweat towels. Imagine that – towels to wipe or soak the sweat from your body! And lots and lots of noise: foundries, shipyards, blast furnaces, steel plants, rolling mills and docks were places of noise, heat, sweat, dirt, and sheer physical effort and hard labour. Until the Second World War started this was the domain of man and his brute strength. Those who aspired to office or service jobs were deemed to be a bit soft. They had what were termed soft jobs no matter how bright or ambitious a person might be. Women wore shawls, had kids, fed them at the breast, made dinners, washed clothes with poss sticks then ironed them. They scrubbed floors, sanded steps and went to the pawnshop. They were there to cry, to fight with or fornicate with, whether you were child or adult.

Yet, I want it all back. Why? Because I envy the innocence of childhood. These are my childhood memories. If I had my childhood back I could shed all of my responsibilities for the rest of my life's misdemeanours and also have so much time left in front of me. It cannot be: once lost, innocence is gone forever.

In 1938 I was nine years old, my brother Peter seven years, my sisters Norah, Margaret, and Ollywne five years, two years and three months respectively. It was summer. It's strange that whilst I can remember many stormy, rainy and wintry days, my usual memories are of bright summer weather and smiling faces. As I sit writing this memoir, it is Saturday night on the 6th March 1993 and my rose coloured spectacles have just dropped down on to my nose as I drift back over fifty-seven years to the summer of 1938. The year before the Second World War.

So it's Saturday morning, the flat racing season well under way and the summer holidays soon to start. I feel a pleasurable anticipation of four weeks off school and an endless list of things to do and places to go. Dad would get a week off work with pay – a new novelty this – being paid for being off. He would sub his pay at the start of his week off and it would take until Christmas to pay it back. Then he would get another one and take until April to pay that one back. We were at that moment solvent. That is, apart from the tallymen, ticket men, furniture men, insurance men, diddleum club and other Saturday callers! It seemed a fine day.

Dad worked for Dorman and Long at Ayrton Sheet works. He was a Bar Dragger. That's a man who filled a furnace with steel bars, heated them until red hot, then dragged them across the mill to the 'Breaker down' who then fed the hot bars to the rolls. He then walked back to the furnace and repeated the operation on a continual basis. He once told me that he walked about twenty-seven miles a shift, including walking to and from work, and all in iron shod clogs which he swore were the most healthy and comfortable for the job. He was now sleeping like a log after coming in from night shift at about a quarter past six that morning.

He slept up in the front bedroom of our grimy, black brick, slate roofed two up and two down terraced house at one hundred and ten Milbank Street, Middlesbrough. His black greasy clogs stood under the kitchen table, the cold sodden sweat towel over a chair back, his tea bottle and bait box on a board beside the sink.

This was Saturday, the sun shone, no school today. It was a fine morning and breakfast was over. Porridge, fried bread and two eggs mashed between four of us. Then Mam said,

'Come to the cobblers with me, Joe.'

She always called it the 'Cobblers', it was quite some time before I discovered its real title, the 'Pawnshop'.

It was a twenty minute job to slip out of the back door, walk up the narrow alley and along Cannon Street to Ushers pawnshop on the corner of Rockliffe Street to redeem Dad's suit. On the way home we called at Graster's fruit and veg., then Walter Willsons for broken biscuits then to Moore's Stores for the general groceries, crossed over to Crowe's Butchers and back home loaded with bags and parcels. Four kids aged seven and under waiting for us.

About eleven o'clock, three small boys come to the door.

'Is Joe coming to the baths?'

'Can I go, Mam?' and a smaller voice, 'Can I?' said brother Peter.

'All right. I'll just take your Dad his breakfast. Then I'll get your things.'

On Saturdays, off nights, Dad had his full fried breakfast taken up to bed. We didn't even own a tray and I used to follow Mam who carried the plate of eggs, bacon, tomatoes, bread, salt, pepper, knife and fork, the bottle of sauce, ten Woodbines and a morning paper. This miracle of transport was carried out with me following close behind with a cup of tea wobbling about on a saucer.

How she unpacked the suit and groceries, fed and changed baby Olly, fried Dad's meal, took it up to him and cadged the money for the baths from him, gave us towels and swimsuits and sent us off with our pals, not forgetting washing, dressing and amusing Norah and Margaret, all before twelve o'clock, beats me to this day!

The old baths in Gilkes Street was a noisy experience. The shared cubicles with half doors on the pool side meant that your clothes could get very wet indeed, but at least you could see them or any body near them. A couple of patches of grey scum would be floating at the deep end and the small corner foot bath would be a heaving mass of small boys, (mixed bathing not having arrived yet) all trying to sit in it as the water was rather warmer in there. Then some imp would pull the cold shower chain causing a wild scramble of near naked young bodies to plunge into the shallow end and the delight of utter silence as your head went under. Hold your breath for as long as you could, then with lungs bursting jump upward and surface to the sheer pandemonium of children's shouting voices and Blackie, the lifeguard, shouting at them.

A group of children with clean faces, damp hair and wet towels straggle along down Gilkes Street and wander on to Newport Road - all of them ravishingly hungry. A lucky few will call at Jim's snackbar for a savoury bun and share it with the less wealthy. Peter and I can't wait to get home, and yes, Mam's been baking bread. Large round flat cakes on the back kitchen windowsill in the yard, Fadges and fattie cakes on the table and a salad swimming in vinegar. Chopped lettuce, tomatoes, scallions, cucumber, and onions in preparation for our Saturday tea. For now, we get warm new bread and best butter. Dad has been cobbling shoes. His last and toolbox are on the floor in the kitchen. A stick of heelball and a blue stained rag on the wooden stool he sometimes used as a bench. 'Don't touch that knife. It's me cobbling knife. Sharp as a razor that knife,' he warned. Baby Olly is asleep.

From out in the back alley comes a low rumble of voices. I don't wonder what it is. It's quite a natural sound. People talking. Occasionally there will be a shout, something about the favourite, or what won the two o'clock?

Just opposite our back door, on Granny Tully's wall is a board with a big sheet of newspaper on it. A rather heavy man with a red face and wearing a blue overcoat and flat cap is standing beside the board. I know his name is Fat Davis because I've heard our Mam call him that. He talks to people who walk up or down the alley and give him money. Sometimes he gives them money back. Now and then, he shouts to the men at each end of the alley. They're the runners. The other runners that I know about, are the horses in the races.

Dad has been for a couple of pints with my uncles Steve and Morry and now he's smiling and talking to Mam who is setting the table for tea in the front room.

Peter and I stand at the table for our meals. Dad sits down with

Margaret on his knee. Mam has baby Olly on hers. Norah is too small to stand so sits for her meal.

Our new Philco radio plays softly in the corner. We sit down to eat. Suddenly there is a loud shout. 'Hey op, police,' followed by the explosive bang of the faded red back door flinging open into the yard. With Fat Davis in the lead, they're trying to get through the door two at a time. Maybe twenty-five people. All jostling and pushing and running up the yard. They run through our kitchen, through the door into the front room and through the front room door and lobby out into the street. Across the street and into Smith's front door to do the same thing again. There seemed so many that it was possible that they were still coming through the back door as the leaders were disappearing through the door opposite ours. This quiet, frantic procession of rather calm but running people said, 'Sorry, Joe,' or 'Sorry, Winnie,' to Mam and Dad as they passed through. The last one bolted the back door and left. Peace reigned. The sun shone. The wireless played and all was well.

I learned years later that the price for this frequent disturbance, was a free threepenny bet for Mam or Dad whenever they chose to take it. Mam liked a little flutter. I never heard her complain once of losing, but if she had a win, then we all shared. Or as she put it, We 'Got a beb'.

After tea all four of us kids go out to play street games with a large crowd of children of all ages, possibly fifty kids aged between three and thirteen years old. To this day I can remember almost seventy full names of children who played in that street. Games long since forgotten: T Mac, Foot and a Half, Monna Kitty, Kicky Tin Spyo, Dillys; and amongst the older ones: Span, Pitch and Toss; and the girls: Dolls and Prams, Fairybikes, Group skipping, Itchy Bay (Hop Scotch) and the inevitable Sonja Henie on roller skates.

Twilight comes and the numbers dwindle as parents call us in for the night. Some of us protesting and having to be chased up or down the street, caught and brought home cheerfully struggling. The next struggle is bathing them all and preparing them for bed, to the sounds of In Town Tonight on the wireless. As we had been to the baths, we could miss out on this Saturday night bath time and go straight up to get ready. If we hadn't been swimming then sometimes we would go over to the only house in the street with a bathroom. Mrs Leadbitter, a very large lady with a very large family, an ex World War One nurse who could and did, lend money without interest, help with births and lay out the dead, had a handy son George who had built a bathroom in the backyard. What luxury now and then to use a proper bath then be carried home over the street and put to bed all warm and clean. Next day all the older boys would ask if we had seen the daughters with no clothes on and, 'What did it look like?'

So that was a summer Saturday in '38. I'll leave Sunday with its best clothes, boredom, Mass or Chapel, the smell of Sunday dinner cooking, the union meetings, the walks in the park or trips on the river until another pink tinted time.

C.J. Bradley
Stockton.

The Birth of ICI

My father was a miner in Selby, Yorkshire, until like many others in 1926 he was made redundant and was left with a wife and three children to bring up and no money coming in. Things were desperate.

My grandfather was a farmer and managed to give my dad a few days work snagging a field of turnips. This brought in £25, a lot of money in those days. He left my mother enough to feed the family for a while and set off to look for work.

He hitched lifts on lorries and heard on the grapevine of a firm by the name of ICI which was under construction. The building was being done by a German firm and they were looking for workers. When he arrived there was nothing on the site but two wooden huts and a farmhouse.

He got the job and eventually was able to send for his family. After a while we got an ICI house and we settled down.

My father never had to look for work again. He stayed there for 34 years.

Vera Graham
Billingham

Teesside

M y earliest memory was when I was about four years old in 1933 – I was playing in the street. A Council cleansing cart went past, spraying water at the front, with a white coloured liquid flowing from the rear. 'Fantastic,' I thought, 'they are giving free milk away,' so I laid on the kerb and drank some of this 'milk' which tasted horrible, as though it was bad. I didn't know it was disinfectant.

However, I ended up in the isolation hospital with scarlet fever afterwards, possibly because of this, and from that day on, was always suspicious of 'something for nothing'.

This was in Billingham, and we lived in an ICI house as my father worked there, and houses were provided via the council for any employee wishing to have one.

There were playing fields at Synthonia, where the annual party and sports event took place for the employees' children. It was great, jelly, ice cream, sack races, egg and spoon races etc., and it was here that I made another discovery, early in life, at the age of 5 or 6.

At that time, even though some people did have baths, showers were almost unknown. I stepped into one, and being curious, turned on a tap, but instead of turning it off, or leaping immediately out of the shower, stood yelling. As no assistance appeared to be forthcoming, I clambered out looking like a drowned rat.

A trip to the seaside was always fun and usually it was Seaton Carew, mainly because our relations lived nearby. Gran lived not far from the beach and the locomotive sheds, and Grandad used to take me to see those majestic leviathans that seemed to pulsate life, with steam hissing everywhere, unlike the inanimate diesel, or diesel electric locomotives that we have today. These sheds have now gone, just like the 'engines'!

228

Just across the road from the beach was a steelworks, and a huge storage area for pit-props, used in the coal mines nearby. There must have been whole forests stored at any one time, and once there was a great fire that could be seen for miles around, and huge palls of smoke. It took days for the fire brigade to finally quell the smouldering embers.

One day, when Grandad was taking me for a walk round the docks, a ship was approaching the coal staithes to tie up. A small rowing boat (foyboat) had positioned itself under the bow waiting to take a mooring rope when someone dropped the anchor. It crashed straight through the opposite end of this little boat to where the boatman was standing. He must have been the luckiest person alive, but his boat was wrecked.

The long, smooth, golden sands of Seaton Carew beach, one of the finest in the country, also had other attractions, driftwood, but most especially seacoal. This was deposited free twice daily by the action of the tides, and was a boon to people on the dole as a source of heat.

The essential items for this venture were, a rake, a shovel, some empty sacks and a bicycle. Wheelbarrows were not all that popular as you could not ride them to the beach, and were awkward to handle when loaded. The seacoal was scraped into a pile, trying not to get too much sand mixed with it, then shovelled into the empty sacks. Usually, one sack was poked through the crossbar, then another sack placed on top of the crossbar, or one suspended from either side.

When coal was rationed - in the days before we had gas central heating - in the big freeze of 1947, seacoal came in very useful. After this, some entrepreneurs - my cousin was one of them - started to collect seacoal on a commercial basis, selling it mainly to industry. As long as it was mixed with coal, (it is only a kind of coal dust) it did eke out existing coal stocks, and burned all right in boilers.

All you needed was a 3 ton lorry - being able to drive this on an existing car licence - rakes, shovels, sacks, a weighing machine, and plenty of 'muscle'! This was usually obtained by hiring labour, either part-time, or full time. However, as more and more lorries kept coming on the beach, and the internecine squabbles escalated, Hartlepool Council banned the number, and size of lorries.

The war came in September 1939 and I was evacuated to a farm in

Slingsby, and by a strange coincidence – although I wasn't to know it for many years to come – the farmer had the same name as my wife's maiden name. Plenty of good food, but too quiet for a 'towny'.

Having moved from North Ormesby to a shop in Middlesbrough, I was used to living on a main road, with a bus stop outside the door, and traffic passing my bedroom window at all hours. The docks were not more than 500 yards away from the back door, and the locomotive sheds, with all the noises associated with them.

To 'hear' silence all day long, apart from the 'dawn chorus' of the birds –'and their twittering during the day – the lowing of cattle, and the 'oinking of pigs' (not far removed from 'Today in Parliament', come to think of it) was just too much to bear. I stayed until Christmas, came home for the holidays, but did not return, preferring the noise.

There wasn't a lot to do anyway, and it seemed that the only 'excitement' was watching the grass grow, and waiting for the paint to dry, except for a brief period at harvest time. Most of the farmers hired steam traction engines to do the reaping and threshing, and ah! what bliss. To be allowed to stand on the footplate, and even stoke the boiler, I can – nostalgically – smell the steam, smoke and hot oil.

Things were going on after I returned home, air-raid shelters being built in the streets – and other things like signposts taken down, and huge water tanks with ample supplies of water in case of fire – which were supposed to be accessible to members of the public but were locked. However, the key was always available from one of the unofficial, unpaid street wardens/firewatchers.

These people volunteered to do a night's 'watching' on a rota system, in case an air raid warning came, when they would ensure everyone left their homes and took to the shelters. The main reason for keeping the shelters locked was that the interiors were lavishly equipped with beds, bunks, blankets, food, lighting, heating etc. which would have been temptation to 'light-fingered Larry's' – even though crime hadn't reached today's proportions – and even illicit lovers. Today, the shelter would probably have been stolen as well!!!

There were a few underground shelters, one of them opposite where I lived, in the basement of the Co-op store (later bought by BINNS after their store caught fire and burned down) which was lovely and warm on account of the central heating boiler, and hot water pipes. Many times our family went there about 10 p.m. and slept the night as it saved the hassle of being woken up and having to dash for shelter. They did a similar thing in London, sleeping in the underground stations, but they must have been cold and draughty in comparison.

One night a bomb scored a direct hit on the gents underground toilet outside the town hall in Corporation Road, Middlesbrough (fortunately, at that time of the night - early morning - nobody was in it, it would have been a sure-fire cure for constipation!!!). Pandemonium broke out in the shelter with people fighting to *get out.*

As sound travels quicker through water and solids than it does through the air (for some strange reason) the noise in the basement shelter seemed much louder, and nearer than it was, causing panic, scaring everyone except me. I slept right through it, and knew nothing about it until I awoke hours later!!! I'm still able to do this, sleep through storm and tempest, even a nagging wife!!!

Living in a sweet and tobacco shop had its advantages during the war, giving you a good bargaining position. Of course, there were the usual 'sunshine friends' as my mother was to discover later. Someone she had never seen for years appeared, and after the usual gossip, the subject came round to cigarettes. She secured a 'weekly ration' for years until cigarettes became plentiful, then we never saw her any more. This isn't surprising when she travelled some 20 odd miles round trip.

Very little went 'under the counter', and probably 95% were sold on a 'first come, first served basis', with a maximum of 5 packets (100) cigarettes per person. When the ration arrived from the manufacturers, we put a notice in the window 'Cigarettes on sale here, 4 p.m. tomorrow' and the inevitable British queue would start to form about 1 p.m.

Once, without thinking, I had gone home to the front door, and was told, in no uncertain terms to 'get to the back of the queue', ever after that, I made sure than I came home via the back door.

J.M.S. Lethbridge
Middlesbrough.

231

Early Memories of Darlington

The year was 1916 and it was my first day at school. I waved goodbye to my mother at the school gates and mingled with girls of all ages. I looked around with interest. The newcomers looked tearful and apprehensive, while others were skipping or playing in groups. Suddenly the sound of a whistle startled me and the noise from the children stopped abruptly as teachers formed the girls into their respective rows. At the second whistle we younger girls were ushered into a corrugated building marked 'Infants' while the older pupils disappeared into the Big School, as it was called. I vividly remember these early days in Darlington especially the slates and pencils which squeaked as we copied words from the blackboard. I remember chanting the multiplication tables with the rest of the class in sing-song voices and the smell of chalk and plasticine from which we modelled animals.

I was soon promoted to the 'Big School' where I would stay until I was eleven years of age. Exercise books, pen and ink took the place of the horrid slates and lessons were much more interesting. We were an odd assortment of girls whose parents ranged from middle to working class. Many of the girls were known as 'Home Girls'. They all lived in a large building some distance from the school. I was told their parents were in the workhouse. Some of the girls had their hair cropped short. Pinafores covered their thick dresses. They wore boots and stockings on even the warmest days and their faces glistened with perspiration. They had to help with their home's housework before and after school, so their hands were rough and they smelt of carbolic soap. Most of them would become servants when they left school. The more fortunate of us could wear pretty dresses and shoes and socks and we wore our hair in curls or plaits.

At the far end of the playground was another building with a balcony. This was an open-air school for the many girls who had T.B., or consumption as it was called. We were told not to play with them because of possible infection.

The day that we heard war was over we celebrated Armistice Day with a holiday, but first we had to march in formation from the school to Eastbourne Park where we were each presented with a bag of buns. There were flags and streamers across every street and there was great excitement everywhere. We sat on the grass to eat our buns and listened to a brass band playing 'Land of Hope and Glory', and other popular songs of that time.

During weekends a popular picnic spot was on the banks of the Tees, occasionally a day by the sea at Redcar. We had to make our own amusements with concerts in each other's back yards charging a penny admittance, or sales of work after spending weeks on making pin-cushions, lavender cases or dolls' clothes. The proceeds went to buy gob stoppers, which changed colour as we sucked, sherbet suckers, dolly mixtures or liquorice bootlaces.

Eventually it was time to sit for the scholarship exam which was in two parts, the result determining whether the pupils would attend the High School or the Commercial School. I passed the first half but couldn't take the second part because of illness. There was only the one chance so I had to attend the Secondary school. This was a much larger school than the Elementary one with more teachers, many of whom were harsh and sarcastic and used the cane for the most trivial mistakes. As well as the usual lessons of the three R's, we had to attend a cookery class as well as laundry and housewifery. These classes were held in a nearby building called 'Domestic Science'. Learning to cook was a nice change as we could take the results home after we had taken the ingredients to school. However the laundry class was in a hot steamy room and we had to wash a soiled garment by scrubbing it with hard yellow soap on a scrubbing board. The clothes were then hung in a drying room before ironing them with a heavy iron heated on a gas ring. I hated this school and was glad to leave at thirteen, using the visit to relatives as an excuse to get away.

Darlington market every Monday was a popular shopping place with St. Cuthbert's Church in the background. I well remember the Public Library close to Pease's Mill, the *Northern Echo* office and many other buildings. The names and locations of many shops come to mind, as I stroll down Memory Lane. There was Fox's Café, with its aromatic odour of freshly ground coffee, in Bondgate; Hill's Bazaar, later Marks & Spencers, in Northgate; Carrick's Cake Shop in Skinnergate where we could buy the most delicious cakes; Thwaite's Shoe Shop in Parkgate - these are only a few shops which stand out.

There were quite a few cinemas where we had to queue to see black and white films especially when 'talkies' arrived.

A special treat was an evening at the Hippodrome where we saw a troupe called the Ridgeway Parade.

Later still, as the cinemas were transformed into ballrooms, I spent many hours dancing the modern waltz, slow foxtrot and quickstep.

I marvel at all the changes that have taken place, but I'll always remember how it was in those days of long ago.

Dorothy Appleton
Tasmania

The First Atlantic Crossing

I am sitting on my mother's knee in a white washed cellar which is packed with women and children. There are no men. Someone has a kitten in her arms; there is an old fashioned gramophone and opposite me an old wringer, all the wrought iron painted green and the handle bright red; there is a galvanised poss tub and a dolly stick. The cellar is in Todd Street, Hartlepool, just a 'good spit' from the New Fish Quay. We are sheltering from the bombs.

When I first looked back on this event I thought it must have been when the German warships shelled Hartlepool but that was in 1914 and I can't remember that far back! I now realise it was the third Zeppelin raid, March 18th, 1918, when eleven bombs fell on the town and one Zeppelin was shot down in flames. I was 4 years old but the memory is breathtakingly clear.

My dad had his skipper's ticket and we kids were trawler mad. I remember the day my elder brother, Bob, decided that we would sail to America! We were going to steal a coble, our destination Cocus Island and Captain Kidd's treasure.

Early one morning when it was still dark we went down to the sands. We had our eye on the *Gideon* but it was high and dry so we settled for one of Bondie's hire boats. The four of us climbed in, Bob and his best friend, John Horsley (both ten years old), young Walt and myself (I was eight). We wouldn't go hungry because Bob had been to the family butcher – 'Four pies, please, and put it on the bill.'

We got well south of the Tees buoy before we were spotted. Our plan had been to hug the coastline right down to Land's End and then go straight across! We must have been the youngest crew ever to attempt the Atlantic crossing.

Funnily enough both Bob and I did eventually get our skipper's tickets, as did our younger brother, Rodney, ten years younger than us. We had four skippers in the family at one time.

When I left school I was still too young to go to sea so I took the first job that came along, in the Excelsior Pawnshop on Durham Street, belonging to Mr Levy. I saw a new side of life there. The boss was a great character, always telling jokes to the customers. Times were hard but he certainly brightened their lives up.

Shortly before I was fifteen I got my wish and went to sea with my dad as a trainee cook, unpaid. I suffered agonies of sea sickness and conditions were terrible. I got no preferential treatment because my dad was skipper, quite the opposite in fact. There were no toilets, you used salt water for washing and there were no beds – you either slept on a wooden shelf or bought your own palliasse (called a Donkey's Breakfast) for 2/6d. There were ten in the crew and I was classed as the lowest form of life. Anyway I stuck it out and eventually ended up working from Hull on the Arctic trawlers until the war broke out.

Before I finish these memories of Hartlepool I must mention the great fire when the timber yards, containing miles and miles of creosoted pit props, caught fire. I was only eight at the time but it seemed as if the whole world was on fire. The Central was bounded on two sides with timber stacked high. Almost every family had to evacuate their home, furniture, such as it was, was piled on to prams, handcarts, whatever and wheeled away to be stored in the yard at Hart Road School. Many of the houses were either destroyed or left uninhabitable. The tram lines were twisted into grotesque shapes by the intense heat. A hurricane force wind from the south-east fanned the flames and it was said that if the wind had changed all of Hartlepool would have burned down.

Many years later I learnt that the trawler fleet had actually seen the flames from sixty miles out and had sailed through mountainous waves to get home and save their families.

It was also told that dozens of local men spent hours in the cellar of the Klondyke in a valiant attempt to consume all the beer before it was destroyed by the heat! For this story I am indebted to my late father-in-law, Pop Meadley, a great character who lived with us until he died. He it was who compiled for me a list of 98 pubs in Old Hartlepool (as distinct from West) with their nicknames, locations and landlords!

I would like to conclude these memories with the words from one of the songs I remember singing with the Galleys Field Boys School Choir which won the North of England Challenge Shield two years running:

When you look back and forgetfully wonder
What you were like in your work and your play
Then it may be it will often come o'er you
Glimpses of note like the catch of a song
Visions of boyhood will float them before you
Echoes of dreamland will bear them along.

W.S. Sheader
Hartlepool

Hartlepool through the eyes of our young'n.

The surface under my feet was cold and wet to my toes as I ran towards the sea; the sand was saturated and compacted, rippled and almost horizontal as it lost itself beneath the ebbing tide.

The wave that smashed itself to pieces and rolled up the beach towards me held no fears for me for I knew it would reach only just over my ankles. It hissed rather than roared as it broke upon the sand and served only to egg on my determination to be the first of our party to plunge into the inviting coolness of the North Sea.

Suddenly I became aware of two ladies walking close to the water's edge and I realised that their amused chuckles could only be directed at me. The source of their amusement was perhaps the fact that I was nude, wearing no 'cozzie'. I never found out for, confidence shattered, I turned and, with a shriek, ran back towards the picnickers sprawled on the dry sand higher up the beach.

I needed comfort. At three years old who would not?

I am over seventy now but this memory stays with me, the first of many recollections of Hartlepool. My growing up takes in the different methods of transport as we were overtaken by progress.

We moved house from Howard Street to Montague Street aboard a four wheeled flat dray powered by a real live horse. Most short removals were carried out this way. Coal was delivered on carts similar to this. Heavy jute sacks full to almost overflowing, held exactly one hundredweight and were stacked aboard two tiers high, sometimes three on the back half. A team of two was required, one man on the cart itself lifted each sack on to the leather protected back and shoulders of his mate on the ground who carried it through the back-yard and tipped the contents into the coal-house. Some houses had a square door let into the outside wall giving access for coal delivery direct into the coal house from the back lane.

There was always a degree of consternation on wash days when clothes lines hung from one side to the other, back and forth across the lane, draped with row upon row of newly washed clothes and bed linen stretched out to dry. Normally, good natured banter was traded between coalman and housewife as a path was arranged for the cart to go through. Not always though, sometimes voices were decidedly raised.

The rhythmic thump-thump-thump as poss-sticks were wielded heartily in the wash tub, announced to the world that today was wash day, the bane of the coalman's life.

The high sided horse-drawn corporation carts removed household ashes and rubbish to be dumped on the tip at Spion Kop on the north side of town. The Destructor there, with its tall chimney, consumed the combustibles but the ashes were tipped over the great man-made cliff facing towards the sea. Dozens of souls picked over the trash in case there was anything of value to be salvaged.

A three wheeled petrol engined 'Mechanical Horse' owned by the L.N.E.R. was replacing their immaculately turned out heavy horses and we still saw quite frequently the steam driven beer delivery vehicle belonging to Newcastle Breweries at Castle Eden, its days as numbered as the teams of Shire horses it was helping to oust. We did not know this of course, we simply thrilled to have it rattle past us with smoke pouring from its short neat stack. The brew was in barrels which were rolled or slid down chutes in the pavements leading directly into the cellar under the pub. To prevent you from falling into the hole, two wooden doors like trap doors were folded into place and bolted from the underside forming a walking surface, which never felt very safe, at pavement level.

The rattle of the electric trams is hard to forget, but they were soon to be swopped for the trolley buses which whined and click-clacked with their much superior acceleration. They had smooth, shining, soft padded seats instead of slatted benches and fixed brass bell pushes for communication between conductor and driver, instead of the leather thong hanging loosely from the ceiling.

The conductor was obliged, perhaps three times during the journey from West to Hartlepool, to record on his sheet the numbers of the tickets still held in his ticket holder and to punch a hole in your ticket, using a chromium ticket punch strapped to his shining leather belt. It let out a beautiful 'TING' at each operation. This was very necessary and most important as very often the Inspector would come aboard to carry out a spot check, not only on the conductor but each passenger had also to show his ticket to see it was valid and punched according to where you had got on and where you wanted to get off. I think I might have liked to be a bus conductor save for the fear of that Inspector. We did not like him but could not help admiring the way he expertly leaned backwards and stepped off the bus as it slowed down at the Cement Works or Trinity Church. He never ever stumbled and pulled up within a step or two.

It was a halfpenny from the Station in Northgate to the Cement Works and we often walked so that we could spend the money on sweets. The rails upon which the trams had run were either lifted and removed or buried in the relaying of the road surface. They remained visible in Cleveland Road outside the Tram Sheds for years afterwards. (Twenty years later on a frosty morning the front wheel of my bike failed to negotiate a rail standing a little proud of the road surface and I went a purler there.)

Steam traction engines used to transform the 'Moor' into a Fairground for August Bank Holiday as they hauled behind them a train of four great trailers and living waggons. These were heavy wooden constructions on wooden spoked wheels with solid rubber tyres. One sometimes got the chance later on of a quick glance inside and they were certainly luxuriously fitted out. They were based on the conventional gypsy caravan but more like houses on wheels.

As kids we thrilled with anticipation as we saw trailers laden high with 'Drive your own cars' or the swing boats, 'Lusitania and Mauretania', or the 'Murphies Jumping Horses' and 'Penny on the Mat'. The self drive cars were electrically powered, the shape of things to come, but the swing boats and the jumping horses were steam driven. The 'Penny on the Mat' was gravity controlled as you clambered up dark rickety stairs and at the top sat upon a coir mat and slid down the smooth chute spiralling round the outside of the tower towards the ground. One or two of the stalls were electrically lighted and some of the 'barkers' spoke into microphones. Many were illuminated with flares and just used their voices or had small megaphones.

One could write a whole chapter on the Hartlepool Carnival and the Fancy Dress Parades.

Wirelesses were not too common then and wars were announced – I had been told – by a Special Edition of the newspaper, the news boys running through the streets shouting at the top of their voices 'SPESHALE' to make you stop whatever you were doing to rush out and buy the paper. On one Sunday afternoon when this happened, I was terror stricken, being only five or six years old, but was soon to be consoled as it was explained that the R101 had crashed on a trip to France.

Some years later we were treated to the sight of the Graf Zeppelin as it did a fly-past down the coast of Britain. It was only a few hundred feet up and nobody really trusted the Germans after the First World War, many said it was an excuse for a photographic mission.

Memories of Hartlepool have roots in the personalities of the time. PC Greenlee's name was never mentioned without fear and dread in the hearts of us kids. As fearsome as his name and appearance were, he always gave a comedy performance at the yearly Swimming Gala, when he appeared in full but ill-fitting uniform, red nose and riding a bicycle – the only form of transport for bobbies in those days – round the edge of the bathing pool. Inevitably by the time he got to the chute he had gone over the side into the water.

There was the 'fisherwoman'. She was a small lady round like a barrel and she sold her wares from a specially adapted perambulator, her fingers gnarled and chapped from years at the trade, chopping and cleaning fresh fish; the pikelet boy – he used a barrow, home-made from a condensed milk tin box on two wheels; the rag and bone man, who lived in Hermit Street – he gave us a windmill for jars or old clothes and that is the name we knew him by – Windmill.

John Ward was the lamp-lighter, who used to walk around the streets at dusk, with his long pole with a hook, to turn on the street lamps, then go round at dawn and switch them off again. He fell off his ladder one day cleaning the glasses in the lamps and broke his neck. He wore a plaster of Paris collar for many months, recovered and started a taxi service. I remember a Terraplane, an American luxury car which he went down to London to buy; it really was the last word.

Dickie Bird was another personality, small, tubby and weather beaten faced, who plied his wares with the call 'Skimmed milk, penny a pint.' The milk was fresh from Best's farm, not far from the Cross Roads, conveyed in a special milk cart with large diameter wheels. He pushed this himself. The measures, a gill or a pint, hung inside the big conical churn on long handles formed into a hook at the end. He dipped these into the churn and expertly tipped the exact amount into your own jug or container.

If you got sick you would probably be visited by Dr Gibb, whose surgery was in Friar Street. No matter what was wrong with you his first question was always related to the movement of the bowels. If the answer was negative there was but one treatment, Gregory powder. Yuk! As children we considered ourselves lucky if he could not come and sent his daughter, Dr Margaret, instead.

Probably the least educated of the personalities we knew, was the foy-runner. The word is a corruption of fore-runner. A fishing port of such repute as Hartlepool would not have worked so successfully without the foy-runner. His beat was the promenade and up along the Moor towards the Battery. As fishing boats came over the horizon and ploughed towards the harbour, he recognised every individual boat. Before most of us could tell whether it was a drifter or a trawler he knew the name of the vessel and off he would run to warn the wives of the boat crew that their man would be home in an hour or two.

And who could forget Sylvester, the ice-cream man? He himself baked the cones which for a penny were piled high with his delicious home-made concoction, liberally spread with 'bull's blood' and guaranteed never to go soggy at any time in the duration of the eating process.

Maybe our young'n has grown old now but he still loves to talk about Hartlepool.

Cecil Holmes
Pietermaritzburg
South Africa

242

Impressions of Hartlepool

My grandfather was a 'knocker-upper' in Hartlepool. He used to tap on the upstairs windows with his long lighter cane which he also used to light the gas lamps.

My grandmother, Margaret Ann Spence, was the first young lady to ride the hansom cab from Smith's Funeral Parlour to the Railway Station.

The day the Zeppelin came down we all hid under the kitchen table until my dad shouted for us to go outside and watch. It broke in half in flames and fell into the sea.

During World War One women and children fled from the houses down in the town thinking they would be safer in the country. Many of them came past our house in Cundall Road and we took some of them in.

I remember the Victoria Docks fire when I had to run and get my father from the football ground to evacuate my aunt from Stephenson Street. The fire burned for a week.

In the Second World War we lived in Campion Street which has since been knocked down. A bomb fell on Lister Street School and the blast blew our windows in. I took the children into the little bedroom and threw myself on top of them saying, 'If this is it we'll all go together!'

After that we got an Anderson Shelter, a steel plated frame with a top on and our mattresses underneath. We used to tap dance on top of it.

My mother was an air raid warden. She would go around the streets making sure no lights were showing and warning people to have their gasmasks ready.

Eveline Balderson (née McBean)
Hartlepool

Proud to be a Pitman

Born in Hartlepool I always loved the docks and seeing the ships come in.

The streets were cobbled and lit by gas lamps. For lighting in the houses we had Kelly lamps and candles until the advent of electricity. I can remember the excitement when we 'went electric', running up and down the stairs switching the lights on and off.

I never liked school and was glad to leave and work in the shipyards. I worked for Greys, Central Marine and Graythorpe, as a rivet catcher and also cleaned out the bilges of the ships.

During the war I joined the Merchant Navy as a gunner and travelled to Algiers and Sicily among other places. I was demobbed in 1947 and came out and married a colliery girl and settled in Easington Colliery where I eventually became a miner. I am proud to be able to call myself a pitman, I found the people of Easington to be the most warm hearted and friendly in all the world.

My worst memory is of the explosion in 1951. I had been on shift and as we came up in the cage we never thought that the men who passed on their way down to start work were going to their deaths. I learnt about the explosion at 4:30 in the morning. I went straight down to the pit head and the Salvation Army Van was already there giving out tea and comfort to the waiting crowds. Myself and many more went down the pit to help with the rescue. I can remember the smell was terrible, it stayed with you for days after, you couldn't get rid of it. We all worked to get the bodies out on stretchers, praying each time that we would find some alive. We retrieved them all eventually but it was a terrible disaster which none of us will ever forget.

B.S. Smith
Easington Colliery

244

Teaching Paul Daniels in Redcar

I was born on a farm in Cumberland in 1896. I had to walk one and a half miles every morning across the fields to school. There were only twenty-two at that school and six of us won scholarships to the Grammar School, which was five miles away from home. We all had ponies and we used to meet at the corner and ride to school, then let the ponies off in the fields for the day and ride home again at night.

At Leeds University I studied maths, physics and, curiously, geology, a subject which was no use to me at all although I rather enjoyed it. My chief subject, however, was mathematics. This was in wartime and there were not as many students there as there would be nowadays. I was rejected for the army as I had TB and weighed only seven stone.

After university I applied for a teaching post, at a school in Redcar. I came over for an interview and had lunch with the head, a very old man, who put his hand on my shoulder and said: 'I hope you'll have a happy time here and I hope you will stay a very long time.' I never thought I would stay for forty-five years but I enjoyed every minute of that time. Coatham Grammar School, it was, and it became very famous for turning out many pupils to the Universities. But of course we had to work, hard - six days a week, with forty-two periods a week and only one free period. I started on £175 a year and in 1922, when I got married, my salary was £225 a year, paid in three instalments: Christmas, Easter and July. £75 a term to live on: imagine that now! You certainly had to watch the housekeeping money and could not go on holiday as they do now.

We turned out a few famous names from that school. Lord Bancroft, the head of the Civil Service, in London; Sir Rex Hunt, Governor of the Falklands, and, above all, Paul Daniels, whom I

245

could never get to work - he just used to play cards at the back of the class! I am afraid that some of us just used to watch him - he was a marvellous boy! I should think he is far happier now than many of those who gained academic success, and he has always maintained his links with the school. He came to the present Sixth Form College very recently and asked me to go along. A blackboard was laid out for me to write on and he stood behind it and we joked with each other, and when the photograph appeared in The Gazette I was contacted by former pupils from all over the world. After so many years it is quite difficult to remember those boys who are all now grown men. I still hear from boys all over the world. At our diamond wedding celebration in 1982 we had letters from all over the place, and people with all sorts of jobs. I taught my doctor, my solicitor, my dentist, my hairdresser, my chiropodist - and they all still come and visit to see how we are getting on. Many also are now farmers on the moors roundabouts and they often seem more content than those who were academically successful.

When I first came to Redcar I was in digs in Station Road. I had all my meals there, and it cost me 15/- a week. One weekend I was unable to get out of the house because of a flood. The sea came right up to the house, past the town clock and up to the station steps. I don't think many people here ever realise that happened. I was very lonely that weekend!

One story I remember from my time at the school during the war concerns our headmaster, a Mr Littler. One night, during a raid, the head appeared before the All Clear had sounded. He was challenged by a guard across the way, and in response to the question 'Who goes there?' he replied, 'I am Littler'.

The guard mistakenly thought he heard 'I am Hitler' and he fired. The head panicked, I'm afraid. Unfortunately the papers got hold of the story, and he had to resign shortly after.

From an interview with
Jean Brittain
for Langbaurgh Talking Newspaper
Redcar

When the Lights Went Out

World War II brought many changes to our lives in Hartlepool and by the time hostilities were over both my father and one of my brothers was dead.

My eldest brother, Roy, was only 16 when war broke out but he volunteered as an ARP warden and as soon as he was seventeen and a half he joined up with the RAF and trained as wireless operator/ gunner. He came home on leave occasionally but somehow he looked different, he didn't even talk the same. He and his friends communicated in some strange jargon which I couldn't understand. The day when he was posted abroad was a sad one, my mother and father had tears in their eyes when they saw him off. We younger ones couldn't understand what all the fuss was about but sadly that was the last time we saw him. He was shot down over the Adriatic in 1944.

My father was in a reserved occupation in Richardson and Westgarth Shipbuilders down at the docks. He was a pattern maker, making warships for the Navy. He had seen action in the First War in the Army as had many of the men. He died suddenly of angina in 1944, only three months before Roy was killed.

When rationing was introduced there was quite a bit of juggling to be done trying to feed and clothe the family using the coupons to the best advantage. It didn't matter how much money you had, you needed coupons to buy everything. Not that there was much in the shops to buy.

Every family had an air raid shelter at the bottom of the garden and we spent many nights in them at the beginning of the war. I can remember being permanently tired from nights disturbed by bombs, planes and anti-aircraft guns. Schooling was very disrupted, after an all night raid we had the day off so it was all a bit 'hit and miss' for us. Part of our school was turned into a First Aid post and another part was given over to homeless families so our classes were sent to anywhere suitable. I remember being taught in a Baptist Chapel.

There was great excitement when we heard that some Italian prisoners of war were to be camped on the Rec. near our street. We used to go and look through the wire fence at the men and try to communicate with them. They used to point at parts of their bodies and faces and ask the names. When they pointed at the eyes we would say 'Peepers' and then run away giggling. They did eventually manage to pick up some English and were allowed out to work on the farm at the top of the street for a shilling a day and their food.

The bombing continued and several people were killed in the streets near us. The whole of the town centre was literally a bomb site with bricks and rubble. At night the blackout was in force and everyone had to carry a torch. All the bus windows were painted blue and car headlights were covered. Windows had gummed paper on them to stop the glass shattering - life was very dull and gloomy.

My mother, like many of the other women, was one of the unsung heroes of the war, carrying on as usual despite losing both her husband and her son within a few months of each other. Life had to go on.

When V.E. day came in May 1945 everyone was overjoyed. The lights came on, the blue paint disappeared and the paper came off the windows. We celebrated in the streets and the whole atmosphere changed. It was lovely - but things would never be the same again.

Marcia Warnes
Hartlepool

After the War

The Christmas of 1949 is not one that my family remembered with much joy as my Father had been ill with boils, quite a common ailment in those days, and had been off sick for some weeks. It had been distressing to watch him struggling to work not wanting to lay off and as one of those disgusting abscesses cleared up another would break out somewhere else to take its place. It was when one developed about an inch below his right eye that he was forced to admit he was beaten. How he never lost that eye is a mystery to me and it left him with a terrible scar that he was to take to the grave with him.

It was a hard life that my Dad and many of his generation had led. He left school at the age of thirteen during World War One as there was a shortage of workmen at the local steelworks in the rolling mills. During the 30s like may others he was for some time unemployed until he got work at ICI which he left at the end of the Second World War saying he was sick of travelling. He took a much poorer job as a plumber's mate in the shipyard which paid only seven pounds a week and was barely enough to live on unless he worked a great deal of overtime. Sick pay was only three pounds so how my Mother managed to keep us going on it I have no idea.

Apart from myself there were my younger bother aged three and my older brother aged eighteen who, although working, did not earn too good a wage as apprentices did not get paid much. So taking into account the family allowance, and what my brother brought in Mam had about six pounds a week to manage on which left little (if any) to celebrate the festive season with.

Poverty was something that people felt ashamed to admit in those days so to save face Mam sent me to our local Co-op butchers to tell them some cock and bull story about Dad's brother living in

249

Hereford sending us a turkey and we would not now be wanting one from them after all.

I don't think that they believed me as everyone knew that Dad hadn't worked for some time and we would be rather hard up. I myself had left school but would not be able to work until I reached my fifteenth birthday a few weeks later, but I was allowed to work part time so I was overjoyed when Mr West the manager of that same butcher's shop asked me if I would help out delivering the Christmas poultry as they were up to their eyes in work.

Although the war had been over for some years rationing was still in force and was to be for some years to come so people had been given extra coupons for the festive season and were literally making a meal of it.

Also, as no one owned a fridge or a freezer in those days, they all wanted their meat delivered as near as possible to the time they would cook it. I worked for a day and a half and received six shillings wages but the money I got from tips came to just over two pounds.

The following week being New Year I was asked to help out again and I did so and earned roughly the same amount. That helped out a great deal as I shared it out with Mam, leaving myself with more than I had expected to have.

Like I said, Mam's little white lie fooled no one, particularly Mr West who then asked me if I wanted to work there full time a week later when I would be old enough. I accepted and so got my first job.

Anyone aged fifteen in those times found themselves very much in demand by employers, most of who would use them for a year and then pay them off and recruit fresh school-leavers to take their places rather than increase the wages. I found it quite the usual thing to be approached by the bosses at some of the places I called at and being asked if I would like to work for him instead. Once when I went to the sawmill to collect a bag of sawdust that we put on the shop floor each day the foreman came up and asked me if I wanted a job working there filling sacks with sawdust. I told him no thanks, the job that I had may not have been perfect but it was a lot better than that.

One girl that I knew told me the amusing story of how she landed her first job before she knew that the place existed. Her friend got an interview and after being told to start next day was asked if she knew of anyone else who might like a job there. She told them that her friend might be interested, so they took her particulars and told her to bring her friend with her. Next day they were both surprised to find that they each had a clocking in card with their names on waiting for them.

Although the war had been over for something like five years food rationing was still in force and judging by the meagre portions of meat I delivered I wondered how anyone could be bothered to waste the gas or electric or mess up the kitchen with so little to eat at the end.

The usual thing was for people to eat sausage during the week so saving their coupons for the weekend joint, that would be the highlight of the week for them and if it had not turned out to be a good joint then come Monday morning the boss and the staff would suffer all kinds of verbal abuse. In fact on one particular occasion after a woman had come in and gave them 'what for' her husband came in after he'd been to the pub, screaming and shouting at everyone and only departed when the boss picked up the phone and threatened him with the police.

Another thing hard to come by were decent cigarettes, although not on ration they were in short supply and dealers would only receive limited stocks which would go straight under the counter and only people who did regular business could expect to get an unofficial ration.

For instance, if someone had a daily paper delivered then he or she would know that they should be in a privileged position with that shop for a certain amount of cigarettes and would soon change newsagents if not.

No one ever asked for cigarettes by amounts or what brand, after making a purchase the shopkeeper would enquire 'Anything else, sir?' to which would come the reply, 'Oh yes, have you any cigarettes, please?' and the reply would be 'I can let you have-' and would name the amount and brand that he was in his opinion entitled to.

It was noticeable however that the boss and the staff of the butchers delivered the meat to the surrounding shops in person and the delivery boys (there were three of us) never got to see what was in the bags that they took in or what they brought back with them. I don't suppose that they themselves went short of life's little luxuries such as milk chocolate, toilet soap, and, of course, cigarettes.

Recently I watched a play on T.V. set in that period and found it amusing to see a man walk into a shop which had well stocked shelves and ask for and receive a twenty packet of a well known brand of cigarettes. If there had been such a shop it would soon have enough men queuing up outside to have filled Wembley Stadium.

It was a way of life that everyone could in some way get what they wanted. However the tricks that others stooped to were to say the least despicable as well as criminal.

I remember one day when there was a small queue of about six women in the shop when one of them found to her horror that her entire family's ration books had been stolen from her basket.

The poor woman was quite hysterical and no wonder, my Mother had lost a book of clothing coupons once and when she went to claim a replacement she told me that she had really had a bad time of it, being passed from one person to another, each one interrogating her in a manner that would have put the Gestapo to shame. It took her nearly a whole day before they were satisfied that her claim was for real and warned her that she would be summoned for negligence if it happened again.

The unfortunate woman's books (or what was left of them) were found a few days later, someone had slipped them under a pile of wrapping papers that were kept next to the scales on a counter that was not in use when the theft took place. All four were found to have had their pages neatly removed, the covers were all that remained.

The staff suspected some woman who they knew had a bit of a shifty reputation who had been in the queue, but as they say, suspicion is not proof. For months afterwards that woman would be able to draw her own family's food and then remove the pages from her books and replace them with the stolen ones and then go back for a second helping.

What she and her family did not eat themselves could be sold on the black market as plenty of people were only too eager to pay sometimes double the price for stuff like tea and sugar and other food stuffs.

I enjoyed working for the Co-op but I knew that I would be paid off at the end of the year and my parents like many others wanted me to learn a trade. However, although jobs might be easy to come by apprenticeships were not. To get taken on by one of the top

252

companies the same rule applied then as it does to-day, 'it's not what you know, it's who you know.'

To get what we would call a 'Plum Job' it was necessary to have some relation who had worked there for some years, who would speak up for you and 'Get you in' as the practice was referred to.

Sometimes a family friend who had no sons of his own would be asked to use his influence and it was quite common for some men to find out where such a person went for a drink and go looking for him. A man would find himself having drinks forced on him by a complete stranger who would inevitably swing the conversation to work and then enquire quite casually 'Any chance of you getting my lad a job in there?' It meant that anyone who managed to get an apprenticeship or a decent job had to be beholden to someone. That I could not tolerate and years later when I went and got myself a job with ICI my Mother told me a few women had asked her 'Who got him in there?'

I kept working happily at my job with the Co-op until September and then on my Dad's advice went and applied for an apprenticeship at the shipyard where I was taken on serving my time as a blacksmith which I did not much care for but Dad was adamant that I grabbed at the chances that he had missed out on. So I wasted nearly six years before I could leave and take a job that I wanted.

I disliked the place from the start and would have left the very first day but my parents would not hear of it.

The pay was a meagre twenty-five shillings a week and was to rise very slowly after each birthday. I was only earning four pounds a week when I packed it in at the age of twenty.

Even if I had gone there as a labourer the pay would not have been much better as the company paid juveniles what was known as 'Boys' Money' and even though the job they would be doing was no different than a man's they would have to suffer the indignity of having the word 'Boy' stamped at the top of their clocking cards and would be paid less than half what a man got. This meant that teenagers would still be dependant on their parents to keep them and so parents had much more control over their offspring in those days.

The work that I would find myself doing most of the time I spent there was not on the tools as I expected and although there were only five blacksmiths working in the place there were seven of us

253

apprentices and there was not always enough work to keep us all going.

My parents, like all working class people at that time, had endured a great deal of hardship during the depression and if their sons could learn a trade thought that they would be made for life.

Some employers like that firm exploited this and took on far too many youngsters most of whom would be used as cheap labour.

If anyone turned up late for work he would have to ask the foreman for a chit before the timekeeper could give him his card to clock on, and on days before a statutory holiday, no foreman would issue such a chit so as well as that person losing that days pay he would not receive the holiday pay either. Shipbuilding as well as most other industries was enjoying a post-war boom and the company was always reassuring everyone that they had enough orders on their books for years to come.

Within ten years shipbuilding in the Hartlepools came to an end and most of the lads I had worked with found that their particular talents were of little or no use to them unless they happened to be joiners, fitters, plumbers and such. To have got an apprenticeship at any of those trades that time old system applied. My friend for instance served his time to be a joiner and his Dad happened to be the foreman painter in the works.

Men I worked with told me that before the war when the government passed a law that anyone with a year's unbroken service had to be given three days' holiday with pay the company made sure to lay men off now and then to ensure that hardly anyone qualified for it.

About five years later it saddened me to see men, real hard-working men, proud men, paid off with only their two weeks wages some after many years of service. Their standard of living in the 50's despite their hard graft was not as high as people living on Social Security to-day.

One man a few years older than me said he felt a proper failure because his children were getting free school dinners. Like I have said earlier, people in those days thought that poverty was something of their own making and something to be ashamed of.

Peter Nunn
Billingham